PEOPLE
AND OTHERS
ANIMALS:

PEOPLE
AND OTHERS
ANIMALS:
Story of a Neighborhood

Indrani Sircar

CITI OF
BOOKS

CITIOFBOOKS, INC.
3736 Eubank NE Suite A1
Albuquerque, NM 87111-3579
www.citiofbooks.com

Hotline: 1 (877) 389-2759
Fax: 1 (505) 930-7244

Ordering Information:
Quantity sales. Special discounts are available on quantity purchases by corporations, associations, and others. For details, contact the publisher at the address above.

Printed in the United States of America.

ISBN-13:   Paperback   978-1-963209-96-9
           eBook   978-1-963209-97-6

Library of Congress Control Number: 2024904619

Contents

Characters

Mark
Sam
Charlie
Valerie
Tom
Don
Vera
Laura
Toby
Mel
Bumper, Kim, Speck, and Snow
Inky (a.k.a. Sumo)
Flyer
Tippy (a.k.a. Tipper)
Janie
Talia
Patricia
Sally
Beth
Frank
Tuxedo
Tortie
Tiger
White Tuxedo
Colleen
Sean

D'Marcus
Pallavi
Eric
Ed
Dr. Frank
Dr. Gyulassy
Dr. Hovde
Dr. Wolf
Dr. Aki
Dr. Schmidt
Dr. Marker
Dr. Quarterman
Dr. Bell
Dr. McCoy
Phil
Cayla
David
Michelle
Shreen
Ardene
Johnny
Kay
Rev. Penny Nixon
Anjali
Theresa
Jeffrey Holec
Susan Dosso

This book is dedicated to Dr. Marilyn Frank, DVM, longstanding veterinarian of Camino Real Pet Clinic, Burlingame, California.

Inspiration for this book came from a feral cat whom I named Toby. While with me and far away, she connected me to her wild self with a golden cord of animal love. Toby may be the only known feral who carried a veterinary health plan in her life.

I make special mention of Susan Dosso and Jeffrey Holec of Orillia, Ontario, Canada. In a friendship that lasted two decades, Sue and Jeff bridged two countries with their affection, advice, letters, and conversations on animal love.

My deep appreciation goes to Ben Yount, who helped me edit my drafts and choose my photographs. This work would not have been possible without his encouragement. Dr. Yount is a dentist who spent his youth with cats.

What was once enjoyed and deeply loved, we can never lose. For all that we love deeply becomes part of us.

— **Helen Keller**

Preface

Distance, I believed, is a state of mind. When I left Ontario, Canada, in the year 2000, I realized that 4,500 kilometers was a physical timescape to be traversed in seven days. My partner and I were headed for California, and as we drove away from Toronto, a sense of the unknown escalated. My mind locked the doors on a place we had called home.

I called the journey an adventure. We were to rebuild a life with the jigsaw of the past and the present and make a relationship out of the bonds that had frayed. There was expectation, newness, and disquiet. The season was midsummer—blazing sun, highways, and open fields with furrowed land and scattered cotton wool clouds.

The roadmap near the dashboard was crisp. This was our compass across the Canadian border into Michigan.

Behind us, the U-Haul carrier contained the belongings of a spartan Toronto household. Although they had been efficiently packed, the nature of our possessions was not quite harmonious. They were an amalgam of two personalities trying to merge home and hearth. The six boxes of books were our prize collection of favorite fiction. We did not let the books scatter and lose themselves in the course of packing. The rest was furniture that makes a human habitat comfortable.

I was not driving. Being a passenger was a luxury. The driver gets to count the navigate traffic, count truck stops, and maneuver exits to motels. The passenger gets to see the big sky, grasslands, and standing crops and feel awe at human endeavors for building highways across a continent.

After Michigan came Illinois, Iowa, Nebraska, Wyoming, Utah, Nevada, and finally the destination, California. I soaked up the roads not to write a travelogue but to remember the exhilaration of mobility and the sense of the outdoors. The big city faded away from me, and whatever urban angst had remained within me was lost in the sweep of breeze through the open car window.

Open spaces have abundant power. I, a tiny human, was a moving speck day into night, watching the color of the horizon change as noon blended into evening. The sky turned into a canvas of red, pink, and purple. Strands of clouds converged into the pinpoints of perspective, and the road seemed to go on forever. Nightfall brought out the stars as bright as Christmas ornaments.

We were alone on the road. It felt good. There was a feeling of peace, although the terrain was unknown.

Should anyone have asked me what I would remember many years later after having taken this road, I would say the spirit of the land and the little bends where we stopped to rest.

At Kalamazoo, Michigan, we ate our first American meal.

Entering Chicago, Illinois, we saw our first humorous billboard:

I do not question your existence. (signed) GOD

Then we counted skyscrapers just to make ourselves look heavenward.

Des Moines, Iowa, brought a thousand flowers within sight. A botanical garden is not a drive-through. We could not stop to smell all the roses.

Omaha, Nebraska, stood on the banks of the Missouri River. The riverfront was etched with history as Lewis and Clark's landing place. I bought my first postcard in Omaha with a picture of the meadowlark, Nebraska's state bird.

A sleepover at Denver, Colorado, was notable for the first good mattress for tired bones. The motel was a random pick. Larimer Square's restaurants beckoned, but I recall eating in. It was not fast food and not in a paper bag.

The Old West came right afterward. Cheyenne, Wyoming, seemed like an urban oasis after vast fields of standing wheat and corn. Someone had said, "When you see God's country, you will know." Where the sky and fields meet is where God lives. Wyoming was a close encounter with earth's bounty.

Salt Lake City, Utah—the only "wagon" on the road was ours. We drove through Salt Lake with some reverence, remembering Brigham Young and ignoring the conspicuous Budweiser billboard. Temple Square called for a detour, and we made it. Something irresistible had beckoned.

Reno, Nevada, was a playground. We played slot machines and had a buffet lunch. We let our hair down. I bought my second postcard showing a deck of cards on a green baize table.

We passed through San Francisco's Cesar Chavez Street but did not stop in the big city. Farther south on the road was Palo Alto, California. We were in the elbow of Silicon Valley.

Mark was a technical writer. He had accepted a transfer to the United States from the Canadian counterpart of his company. His career in the world of IT had started in the late 1990s when he made a transition from copywriting to the realm of technology. We had known each other since our days in graduate school. Both of us had degrees in communication and had been buffeted in the competitive turf of freelance writing.

I was now footloose in the United States. Mark had a job that would consume an enormous part of his life. He seemed to like the prospect.

Finding a Place Called Home

I found myself alone in Palo Alto for the first two weeks in California. Mark reported to work and was absorbed instantly by his IT team. I explored downtown Palo Alto in shorts and a T-shirt, seeking out grocery stores, a movie theater, and a coffee house with a patio. The days were all mine, and when I did not want to go back to the motel room, I would browse a bookstore and look for art supplies.

Eating out was expensive, but we managed our budget—pizza, Indian, and Mexican cuisine. The evening meal was a time I could hear Mark talk about his work. It was the only time I would see him unwind and cleanse his mind of projects.

On the weekend, we drove to Stanford Shopping Center with its array of everything desirable—clothing, shoes, electronics, kitchenware, home décor, and science toys. I needed nothing for a life still in motion. We were hunting for a place to live.

Rent was a recurring motif in the days that followed. Sustaining ourselves on one income in affluent Palo Alto was not feasible. Mark looked grim after each phone call to the property manager. I looked apologetic for not being able to pitch into the piggy bank. We started looking farther away in adjoining cities still untouched by the rent bubble of Palo Alto.

Fifteen miles north was San Mateo. On a postcard, San Mateo displayed a Japanese garden, a glimpse of a small shopping district, and a landmark railway station. Its history came from a brochure I found at a gas station.

Before the Spanish settlers came to San Mateo in 1776, the land was the home of Ohlone Indians. Among the explorers were mission padres and soldiers. Among them were Juan Bautista de Anza and Jose Joaquin Moraga, both lieutenant colonels in rank. Padre Pedro Font, who founded a mission outpost to oversee his new Christian converts, named the area San Mateo. In 1894, San Mateo was incorporated as a town.

San Mateo, as we found it, felt like a suburb. After all, we were Torontonian. Rents were lower than in the surrounding cities. Homeowners and renters had no stark demarcations of territory. The city had one newspaper, no movie theater, a public library, and a large park with bleachers and tennis courts. We saw dogs, toddlers, and joggers.

Our first application for an apartment got a response. The place was a stucco low-rise with a backyard. We hitched the U-Haul carrier back onto the car and headed to make another home.

Mark would commute to work, and I would unpack to create another human habitat out of familiar objects. I would have long hours to myself.

Snooping Around the Block

In a placid corner of San Mateo, Seven Oaks, home of banker Amadeo Giannini, stood empty. It was a slumbering edifice with overgrown shrubbery and high wrought-iron gates with padlocks—entirely out of place in its urban nook.

Giannini, founder of the Bank of America, lived in this mansion until 1949, and after his passing, his wife, Clorinda, kept the cherished home until 1997. This family home, eligible for the National Register of Historical Places, was now in the shadow of possible demolition.

The apartment we chose was two blocks from Seven Oaks. One morning, walking in Northern California fall in Gore-Tex and sneakers, I saw a silver-haired woman with a platter of dry food—cat kibbles. She parted the thick hedge on the west side of Seven Oaks and set the platter down.

"Meow . . ." she called, and she waited. As she saw me approach, she smiled tentatively. "It is for my outside pet," she said.

I had never seen a feral cat before. Neither did I know I would meet many—nor little did I suspect the forgotten menagerie of Seven Oaks was home to a colony of hidden ferals.

Hospitality seemed to be in the temperament of San Mateo. Two well-fed domestic cats visited my narrow backyard for midday treats—curious prowlers, not "outside pets." They were neighborhood celebrities, Sam and Charlie, who often had a friendly meal on a welcoming porch.

The days brought squirrels and hummingbirds. Night brought raccoons and grazing deer from the hillside. Across the fence were cat owners, among them a couple who owned nine cats. I, who had never had a pet in a lifetime, learned that they rescued ferals from an urban habitat behind a midtown office building. The cats they fell in love with stayed in the household, which brimmed with ferals of all ages.

Mark was curious about my days spent exploring. The furniture had begun to configure in the new space. I had gotten myself a library card, and the stack of new reading grew on the coffee table. The afternoons in the backyard, with the mild September sun, were made for a book lover's pleasure.

While watching his favorite news channel one evening, Mark asked, "Have you written anything lately?"

"No."

"Maybe you should. You could find something to do before you get bored."

For the Love of Sam

Sam, the next-door neighbor's orange tabby, visited every day. He appeared on the ledge of the fence that divided two properties in the late mornings. He sat like a chunky Buddha on the fence until I sighted him. This was his cue to leap into my side of the yard and peer through the back door.

He loved my kitchen, and he was not looking to be fed. In the corner of the kitchen was a built-in bench where he made his perch. Sam would sit and watch me prepare lunch or the evening meal. He then followed me around the apartment, brimming with curiosity, nosing into boxes of books, and batting crumbled balls of newspaper he dislodged from cardboard boxes.

I did not know what he ate at home, but I got Sam some Whiskas treats on my next trip to the grocery store. I quite forgot to look for the calorie count. My visitor relished Whisker Lickin's.

On occasion, Charlie, the brown-and-white sleek prowler from across the street, caught up with Sam. The nose rub greeting was a signal for backyard play, and I watched the two in mock chase and tumble. They watched the squirrels dart on the fence and sent the sparrows flying into the trees above.

I was not surprised to hear that Sam was close friends with the previous occupant of our apartment. He had been a solitary man and enjoyed the presence of a cat without being a cat owner. Sam may have seen a similarity in me, although there was a significant difference in my feelings for this endearing cat. Had it not been for the collar and tag of ownership around Sam's neck, I would have taken him in as my own.

As a child, I grew up with a yard full of stray cats. My father nurtured strays of the neighborhood, and the free roaming visitors made themselves at home in a habitable garage. The pregnant queens and prowling toms were never spayed or neutered because there was not a veterinarian within miles. The cats were aloof but responded to affection and touch. What then makes a feral cat different? A simple fact: the lack of "socialization" with humans.

A feral cat is not homeless. The outdoors, great or small, is its home. Feral cats have very little or no contact with humans. Humans terrify them. Often ferals live in colonies, in wooded areas, barns, or farms, and a group may include males, mothers, and kittens. They endure the hardship of terrain and weather and hunt for their own food. A stray cat may turn feral after being away from human presence for a long time.

As my fascination with the local animal life grew, I decided to volunteer at the local SPCA. In 2001, I was accepted as a vet clinic volunteer at the shelter.

My work did not resemble a veterinary tech's labors. I wore jeans and sweatshirts and a denim apron. I cleaned kennels and changed cardboard litter boxes. I refilled water bowls and replenished food. When the essential chores were done, I had a chance to brush the cats and administer oral medication. When it was a good day at work, I sang acapella as I worked. The kennel-bound kitties tended to perk up at the sound of my voice—or so I wished would happen. There were special kitten days when I tended only to young ones, and I had tiny paws and claws clamoring up my chest and nesting at my neck, my lap a jigsaw of gray, orange, brown, and white balls of fur.

Every animal entering the portals of a shelter has a story. Some have happy endings from the ramp of adoptions. My early days as a volunteer were tinged by rose-colored spectacles. I had never been acquainted with the problems of pet overpopulation and overcrowded shelters. The politics of space and measures of adoptability were a lurch to my notions of humane care.

Untold stories of shelter animals outnumbered the ones the scribes recorded for popular consumption. One day, after a while with domestic cat care, I entered the feral cat holding. The sight of captive, stressed, crouching, disoriented felines in kennels shook me to the core.

For the time I spent at the shelter, I never saw a feral cat released into its natural habitat. I just knew when a kennel in the windowless holding was empty, a cat had been euthanized. Trap–neuter–release (TNR) was not in our vocabulary.

I left the shelter feeling despondent and spent the year that followed with backyard visitors, furry and feathered.

Work of a Different Kind

I needed an antidote to the experience. I wanted to find work that had a creative pulse, a workplace that would not sap the emotional energy out of me. I started applying to local bookstores, and a small privately owned store on Third Avenue dedicated to crime mystery caught my attention. M Is for Mystery had a devoted clientele. A steady stream of mystery writers was invited as guest speakers. Ed, the owner—a retired lawyer and a passionate mystery reader—had started the specialty store to make his dream a reality.

My first meeting with the store manager was dismaying. There was no budget for a new bookseller. Here I was, an avid fiction reader at the threshold of a dream job. The obstacle was not insurmountable. Time was on my side.

Mark was enthusiastic about my application to M Is for Mystery. He came up with a suggestion.

"Why don't you ask for an internship?"

"An unpaid one?"

"Why not? It might lead to something."

I liked the idea. I also knew this would be my entry into a different profession. I had never visited the realm of book retailing.

"You could write when you are not selling books," Mark added dryly.

I had made a few attempts at writing fiction. Displeased with my own efforts, I tossed the pages away. I liked writing on paper and sometimes longed for a fountain pen, which seemed to make my thoughts flow better. As a child, I was given a fountain pen at age ten. I had learned to fill the old-fashioned barrel with a dropper from the inkwell. The ink was traditionally blue, and if I held the pen too close to the nib, I got ink stains on my middle and forefingers. I graduated to black ink when I was older. Pens changed. So did the texture of the paper on which I wrote.

A short story I wrote by hand was called "The Lama's Cat," set in a monastery in Tibet. The main character is a cat who belonged to a Buddhist monk, Lama Rinpoche. Joiyo, the cat, is the observer of life in the monastery and the bonds of villagers in the hills. Goatherds and farmers send gifts of milk and produce to the lamas as gestures of amity. A young village girl, Chunni, who brings goat milk every day to the llamas, befriends Joiyo. The cat–human bond explores the mysteries of reincarnation and the secrets of Chunni and Joiyo in the lives they lead, together and apart.

Mark had a manual typewriter that I liked to use. He had placed it in his closet next to his cherished backgammon set and houndstooth beret. If I felt like a break from pen and paper, I would get the typewriter out. The sound of striking keys was comforting.

The clacking of typewriter keys was once a ritual lullaby. My mother, a magazine editor in her youth, worked late into the night on her writing. As a child, I often fell asleep to the sound of a busy manual typewriter. I never asked for a bedtime story or a song.

Mark stayed long hours at work. He took a break by working out at the gym at the office. I cooked for two but often ate alone. Cafeteria food took the place of a real meal. Neither of us spoke of our shrinking time together.

My proposal for an internship at M Is for Mystery received a warm response. I started work alongside two managers who doubled as booksellers. I felt excited to go to work. I immersed myself in the learning experience—shipments of inventory, merchandising (which involved shelving and creative display), and planning events with authors. The store had a special mail order section for readers outside San Mateo.

The advance reading copies (ARCs) of books arrived from publishers. An ARC had less visual allure than a book with a dust cover, ready for release. I got a taste of authors poised for the bestseller shelves. When a new release arrived, I sometimes got to write brief reviews on cards to go on book displays. I read voraciously and put serious effort into "taking work home."

When Michael Connelly came to speak at M Is for Mystery, he was mobbed by his fans. *A Darkness More Than Night* had been released. *City of Bones* was in the works. While I helped set up the event, I knew the closest I could get to him was to have a T-shirt signed. *Void Moon* was a book without Connelly's mascot detective, Harry Bosch. The T-shirt was stark with a moon in eclipse for graphics. Connelly's signature was in black marker. It did not wash off for half a decade.

I never quite acquired the taste for true crime. Agatha Christie, Arthur Conan Doyle, and Edgar Allan Poe were my authors of choice when I ventured into this genre. Over the years, I had lightened my taste to Sue Grafton, John Grisham, Janet Evanovich, and Sara Paretsky. At M Is for Mystery, I read Alexander McCall Smith for the first time. His No. 1 Ladies' Detective Agency, with its female private eye Precious Ramotswe, took me to Botswana. I finished *Tears of a Giraffe* in one long read.

When travel writer Pico Iyer was invited as an off-beat guest, I did not seek an autograph. It was my day off, and I sat in the audience and had a moment to converse with the author of *The Global Soul*. Pico Iyer was not all about jet lag, shopping malls, and a search for home. There is a spirituality to his cosmopolitan exterior.

I next discovered Rita Mae Brown whose books I did not read in chronological order. Her feline coauthor, Sneaky Pie Brown, brought a talking cat onto my list of sleuths. I tend to get their plots jumbled for having read too many too fast. *Pawing through the Past* was a groundbreaker.

When the September 11, 2001, attacks happened in New York City, I was about to leave home to run a few errands around San Mateo. I had a midweek day off. Sam had already paid his visit to say a prolonged furry hello. The radio was playing in the kitchen.

When the first American Airlines Boeing 767 crashed into the north tower of the World Trade Center, radio broadcasters were speculating in urgent tones about a freak accident. The plane had struck the 80th floor of the 110-story tower. There were no live images for me, just words on the airwaves.

I was not counting eighteen minutes between the two attacks. The south tower was struck on the sixtieth floor by a second aircraft, a United Airlines Boeing 767. The south tower collapsed in smoke and dust. Both airplanes hijacked were scheduled to land in California. The pictures of the devastating inferno were not seen until later in the evening.

In the heart of San Mateo downtown was a historic landmark, the Ellesworth Post Office. Inside were early nineteenth-century murals of bear fights and cattle hustlers. When I reached the post office on Ellesworth Avenue shortly before 1:00 p.m., there was a short line of people. Everyone stood in eerie silence. When I reached the window, the familiar face of John, the veteran postal worker, looked up at me solemnly.

Without preface, he asked, "Who do you think did it?"

"Osama Bin Laden," I replied. I did not need to ponder.

"Terrorists?"

"Yes."

"We have not been attacked since Pearl Harbor."

"True."

"You want to send this first class?" John continued, indicating the flat envelope in my hand.

"Yes. To Canada." I handed the envelope to John.

The envelope was addressed to Jeffrey Holec and Sue Dosso, my two most enduring friends whom I had left behind. The letter was yesterday's news.

Today's event, which came to be known as 9/11 in history, eclipsed all else that had seemed important before. I stepped out to buy the evening edition of every newspaper I could find in San Mateo. The destruction of the World Trade Center became as vivid and horrifying as the death toll.

Mark came home late. We had dinner in silence. The nightly news on television reported casualties from the attack on the Pentagon and the crash of a fourth hijacked plane in Shanksville, Pennsylvania.

The emotional impact of 9/11 on spectators was measured three years later. The American psyche, severely wounded, had been further battered by media exposure. Hostility against all people of Islamic heritage was the backlash of the tragedy. Those too young to remember would be the most fortunate.

When the new year rolled along, Mark and I made a decision to live apart. A company merger put a curve in Mark's work in the IT industry. Worn out by the long hours and commutes, he now wanted his dream city and a dream career. The latter would take a few years to take shape. Neither of us labeled the change as a midlife crisis. Nonetheless, we were facing midlife. His move to San Francisco divided our belongings but anomalously strengthened our friendship. The day he drove away, I remembered we had made plans to visit Anaheim to spend a day in Disneyland. I let the thought fade.

I continued to live in San Mateo. I sharply felt Mark's absence in the evenings. Little else changed around me.

A Visitor on the Fence

One spring morning a little gray cat, tabby-striped and timid, appeared on the ledge of my fence. Underweight and hungry, the cat eyed the bowl of dry food by my back door. I made myself invisible. From behind the closed door, I heard the rapid crunching of a cat devouring a meal.

I named the cat Toby. The name was gender-fluid. It would be weeks before I discovered Toby's gender. She was a female, perhaps two years old, and very pregnant. *Toby, my little visitor, was feral.*

Toby adopted me. She returned every morning to eat but vanished after the meal. My feral-friendly neighbors advised me she would soon seek a birthing place, but my backyard had no place to hide. I prepared a large box lined with blankets ready to use in case I found Toby in labor and sat at my back door and fretted when my little feral did not appear for a few days. *She is a wild one*, I consoled myself.

The year was 2005. I was now working at a larger bookstore, which was proudly a "brick and mortar" Fortune 1000 company. I chose to work a late evening shift. Homebound one night, I wondered if I would ever see Toby again. As I walked past my front gate and into the driveway, I saw a shadow emerge from under a parked car. It was a little gray cat—Toby on the wrong side of my home. I slowed. She followed me until I reached my front door. She hesitated, and as I opened the door, she entered my apartment unasked, ahead of me.

Toby seemed happy indoors. Clueless on litter box etiquette, she scratched with curious energy before she stepped in. My very ordinary camera, loaded with black-and-white film, captured her unfamiliar domestic movements.

Nine days after her grand entry, Toby gave birth in my bedroom in the birthing box I had made for her. Her kindle of four kittens were uncannily unmatched—snow white, orange, white with black speckles, and gray with white speckles. *Not one was tabby-striped like the mother.* The fifth was a tiny stillborn fetus with distinct facial features. Perhaps Toby's womb could not make room for this one.

Toby licked her little ones clean as they lay huddled, eyes closed in newborn blindness. Then she ate her own afterbirth. I had naively sterilized my first aid scissors in case I needed to cut the umbilical cord. Only one newborn had the birth thread attached to the belly, and I gently snipped the cord to place the kitten back with Toby.

I named Toby's kittens Bumper, Speck, Kim, and Snow.

Feral Flight: A Sooty Path

Toby was an edgy mother, skittish and suspicious of every sound and movement around her. She had started feeding her kittens, and I believed all would go well until the day after the birth when my doorbell rang. It was Mark. Toby, hearing heavy footsteps, reacted with a lightning bolt out of the birthing box.

Poised for flight at the bedroom door, Toby eyed the open wood fireplace in the living room. Above the grate was an open flue which appeared to be an escape route. Toby was a blur in motion. She leaped and vanished into the flue before I could stop her. Panic set in. What would happen now?

I peered into the birthing box. Nestling together were three kittens. Who was missing? Bumper, a male, gray with white speckles. Toby had scruffed him up the flue when she bolted.

The phone rang early next morning.

"I heard you were having cat problems," my landlady asked in understatement.

I had spent a sleepless night sitting cross-legged in front of the fireplace, calling Toby with every platitude and song, asking her to come down the chimney flue. Through the cinder block hindwall of the fireplace, I could hear the tiniest "meows" of a kitten in distress. Toby had dropped Bumper in the hollow before vanishing up the flue. Behind me, in the bedroom, were three motherless newborns.

The front of my fleece pullover was stained with Esbilac. My attempt to bottle-feed the three kittens with canned kitten milk was a success. What did not go into tiny mouths dribbled onto my clothing.

My living room felt crowded. My landlady's emissary, the building manager, his handyman, and animal control's humane officer had gathered for the rescue. A trap to fit a bear cub sat in the middle of the floor with a can of cat food in it—a lure for Toby. The sound of the handyman's hammer resonated in the room. The man was on his knees by the fireplace, dislodging the cinder block bricks with a chisel. Bumper's feeble meows were drowned as he worked.

I had a good Samaritan friend, Laura, a veterinary technician who worked at San Mateo's emergency clinic. She made a startling entrance to join the crisis crew.

"I am going to feed the kitties for you, and they are coming with me," she said, holding up a padded shoebox for kitten transport. She had come prepared with a homespun kitty carrier. "Where are they?"

Three kittens lay huddled in the birthing box, oblivious to the chaos a few yards away. Their bellies were full. Bumper, behind the fireplace wall, had had nothing to eat for a day.

The sound of the hammering stopped. I was afraid of what I might see when one brick came loose and then another. The handyman's arm stretched into the inner darkness and seemed to sweep the cavern. Still on his haunches, he brought out a tiny furry body. It was untouched by the soot and motionless in the gentle grip of the man's hand. Then I heard a beautiful sound—"meow" and, again, "meow." Bumper was alive. Toby was nowhere in sight.

The animal control officer was a burly fellow in navy blue. All eyes turned on him, with everyone anticipating the next move.

"Leave the bricks for now" he said. "I know exactly where she is."

Toby had wedged herself on a ledge at the base of the chimney and sat there, motionless. The officer stuck his head into the fireplace and then straightened himself.

"I can reach her with my arm, but I don't want to scare her. She could bite me."

What is in a bite from a little feral cat? I muted my query. My indignation was not visible. I was no authority on cat bites.

"She will come down when she is hungry," the officer declared in finality.

The living room suddenly felt empty. My vet tech friend had scooped up Bumper, given him a wipe-down, placed him in her shoebox with his siblings, and departed. The handyman insisted on replacing the cinder block bricks because they would not hinder Toby's downward climb when she chose to come down. The trap remained in the center of the floor, ominously huge, lying in wait for Toby.

Two days went by. On the third night, I was sitting on a step by my back door when I saw a silent shadow walk across the living room. Cautiously avoiding the open trap, Toby walked down the hallway toward the bedroom. In a soundless sprint, I followed her. She was black, covered in soot. I shut the bedroom door, locking Toby in. It took me all my strength to push the large sectional couch to barricade the fireplace. Toby must be hungry.

She hid herself under the bed. She climbed into a rollaway drawer containing my clean socks and lingerie—soot and all—and refused to move. Food did not lure her out. Toby did not look for her kittens. I prepared a bath with soap and water to wash to soot off her short fur. She would never have been able to feed her kittens even if they were with her. Her breasts were smeared with soot and grease.

I waited for Toby's milk to dry. She had sniffed around the birthing box a few times and around odd corners of the bedroom as if she remembered someone who was once there. Her kittens had stayed with their vet tech "wet nurse" and, at six weeks, had been adopted in pairs by San Mateo neighbors.

I made plans to have Toby spayed and zealously kept her indoors. I hoped my devoted care would tame the wild girl, but she still yearned for the outdoors. She sat at the back door, peering through the lower glass pane, watching shuffling raccoons and darting squirrels. At night, a hefty male tabby, Mel, my neighbor's "outside pet," came to prowl. Mel was my old friend, and he showed a robust interest in Toby.

Unfamiliar with mating behavior, I was startled by Toby's rollicking rolls at the back door when she heard Mel's guttural meows. Apparently, I was never meant to be a good guard for a feral cat in heat. One evening Toby broke all the barriers of the couch and chairs and shot out through a crack in the back door.

I sat down, stunned. Then I wept.

For all the havoc my spartan household endured when Toby chose to step into it, I missed her terribly. This time, I never expected her to come back. Her hunting instincts were still alive despite the time she spent indoors. Now that she was free of kittens, my anxiety was not about her survival in the neighborhood but the reality that she might get pregnant again. She missed her spay appointment and was vulnerable with the feral toms that prowled her ground. Mel—the hefty, unaltered feral—was likely to woo her.

Days passed. I placed food in the backyard with fresh water in case Toby remembered her way back. In the afternoons, I kept vigil on both sides of the fence. Toby's forays for food were usually around noontime. Every feline visitor crossing my backyard raised my heartbeat. A feline voice had me rushing out to greet the visitor. Late spring weather set in. Life returned to normal with work and my solitary hobbies. I sketched cats and squirrels while sitting at the backyard table and mused about Toby's whereabouts over morning coffee. She knew where to find me if she needed me, so I consoled myself.

Early in April 2005, Toby reappeared at the back door. She was a slightly scruffy version of herself. She leaped onto a ledge by the door and helped herself to the cat food in the bowl, no warm hello or a look in askance—"Are you happy to see me?" I hid my happiness well. In my excitement, I forgot to berate her about the missed spay appointment, but I did lock the door with every intention of keeping her inside until she saw the vet.

Just as well, I was delayed getting Toby to the vet clinic. After a brief wrestle, I got her into her carrier, a gift from a cat-owning neighbor. Toby got her physical exam, shots, and deworming medication—and I got the proud news that Toby was pregnant.

My job at the bookstore had me on an evening shift, coming home on the night bus. I gave Toby all my attention during the day so she may feel like a pampered mother-to-be. She turned plumb, with a shine to her gray fur. I imagined she smiled at times, breaking her sullen expression like sunshine on a stormy day. The grocery store yielded what she liked best, Meow Mix for starters, and when this brand paled, she chose Friskies. Toby had uncomplicated tastes. Food that tasted good was good food. My budget did not stretch to gourmet diets, and I heard no complaints from my feral friend.

Cats gestate for sixty-seven days at the longest. I anticipated her giving birth in mid-June and, this time, prepared a cardboard box lined with towels from the local thrift store. I gave her a feel of the birthing space so she might make herself comfortable in case she went into labor when I was at work.

In the wee hours of June 10, 2005, still wrapped in sleep, I felt Toby by my pillow. She started licking my forehead through my tousled hair, and I woke up to this gesture of affection. Toby moved away, and I must have fallen back into slumber, only to be awakened by the sound of a tiny "meow," a kitten's meow. Toby had given birth to her first kitten on the bed, very close to me.

I rose carefully. At the crook of my knee was a kitten, still slick with amniotic fluid. In semi-darkness, I discovered Toby's firstborn was male. The only light in the room was the dull hue of streetlamps through the window. I first moved the sturdy brown-hued kitten to the birthing box and then gently lifted Toby next to him.

The next to be born was a gray kitten, a miniature tabby-striped version of Toby. Toby lay on her side in an aura of patience. Her third kitten emerged, distinctly colored calico with white paws. Finally, the smallest of the kindle emerged, another gray tabby-striped clone of the mother cat.

The time was past 3:00 a.m. I do not know how long Toby had been in labor, but the delivery lasted three hours. The birthing box was close to my bed this time. I peered in to see Toby's head move in measured rhythm as she licked her kittens clean. They gathered around her belly, their hungry mouths seeking her milk.

I forgot to set the alarm. I had a day off ahead of me. I slept as if a world of joy had descended on me and did not wake until late morning. The first move after I sat up in bed was to get Toby's bowl into her birthing box. She seemed sublimely content with her offspring nestling around her. She was hungry.

In daylight, I looked closely at the four kittens. The firstborn with woodsy brown hues was male. The brother with gray tabby stripes came after him. The slender calico kitten with white paws was the only female in the kindle. The smallest of them was a male and looked as if he had a tough battle for leg room among his siblings for his mother's breasts.

I would name them another day. I had an errand to run, and I walked downtown to See's Candies and bought a box of chocolate cigars. The sunshine seemed brighter and skies bluer as I walked to Toby's vet clinic. There, I presented the vets and staff with celebratory cigars—edible cigars. Life was beautiful!

My photography was an unpracticed skill. I had bought color film only for the occasion of the birth with the full intent of returning to black-and-white photography later. Of course, this did not happen. My capturing kittens in every step and motion and recording Toby's maternal pursuits made for a difficult subject. Most of the photographs were spontaneous, awkwardly framed, and blurred. A dozen or so that may be grouped under "well taken" were proudly shared with the neighbors and vet.

At my workplace, I worked the occasional shift in the children's section. Here, I discovered Ursula Le Guin's book Catwings. Her series included four titles with stories of four cats born with wings. Their mother was an ordinary stray tabby.

Mrs. Tabby could not explain why all four of her children had wings.

"I suppose their father was a fly-by-night," a neighbor said and laughed unpleasantly, sneaking around the dumpster.

"Maybe they have wings because I dreamed, before they were born, that I could fly away from this neighborhood," said Mrs. Tabby.

They were beautiful children, well brought up, but Mrs. Tabby worried about them secretly. It really was a terrible neighborhood and getting worse—car wheels and truck wheels rolling past all day, rubbish and litter, hungry dogs, endless shoes and boots walking, running, stamping, kicking, nowhere safe and quiet and less and less to eat. Most of the sparrows had moved away. The rats were fierce and dangerous; the mice were shy and scrawny.

So the children's wings were the least of Mrs. Tabby's worries. She washed those silky wings every day, along with chins and paws and tails, and wondered about them now and then, but she worked too hard finding food and bringing up the family to think much about things she didn't understand.

— An excerpt from *Catwings*

Toby Catwings and Her Second Family

I gave my feral companion Toby a surname. She was now *Toby Catwings.*

Toby's eldest was nicknamed Sumo for his size and demeanor. He had the promise of an alpha in him. Her next was Flyer, gray tabby striped. Tipper, the youngest, was a gentler version of him. Between Flyer and Tipper was Toby's girl, a startling beauty—so different from her mother and three male siblings. She was named Mary Jane. Her markings of white, brown, orange, and shades of ochre were like the brush marks of an artist.

Toby's presence in my home was registered with the county. San Mateo County had well-worded laws preventing residents from capturing and restraining wildlife. Was a feral cat a member of local wildlife? If yes, then I had violated San Mateo's animal welfare laws. If I ever had to answer for Toby's conversion from feral to domestic, I would have no champion to provide an account of Toby's willingness to enter a human habitat.

My delving into animal health care unearthed insurance plans for pets. I would not offend Toby by calling her a "pet," but I could describe her as a whimsical companion. I got a health plan for her and hoped she would stay in her human habitat long enough to enjoy its benefits. If she decided to make a run after weaning her kittens, Toby would be the only feral cat in the world with a portable health plan.

In the meantime, the kittens enjoyed their young mother's presence. I said to Toby's vet that my whimsical companion had a sense of humor. For the time her bosom is full and crowded with hungry kittens, Toby answers to the name of "Mae West." For the first time, I heard Toby say "meow" in a voice of contentment.

We never mentioned her first kindle of four who were now four months old with forever homes. I was told that cats forget their young once separated. Such was nature's way to ensure the survival of the species.

Mary Jane was the first to open her eyes. The kittens' blue eyes turned color to hues of green with dark irises. I got closer to Toby while watching her kittens grow. I noticed that her left eye had a distinct brown spot. The pigment was an unusual identifying mark. If Toby ever was lost in a forest full of gray tabbies, that eye would set her apart.

Touching Toby's kittens was a privilege. She gave me tacit permission to hold and cuddle them. Anyone else would have met Toby's feral snarl. I could lift the young ones out of the box onto my bed and watch their movements. I felt an overwhelming tenderness when I was near them, a sensation new and enduring as I watched them grow.

I could touch Toby too. Her body was small and muscled even after childbirth and even after her life indoors. Her fur was not as silky as her kittens' soft hair. Her feet and nails had traces of her walks in scrubland. I noticed the brown patches that interspersed her gray stripes on her lower back. The backs of her feet were a solid black. Her teeth were a primal carnivore's dream. She probably had been a mouser in the backyards of my neighbors. When she picked up her kittens to bring them back for their feed, she used her maternal jaw on the scruff of their neck. There was no sign of a primal carnivore in the grasp.

Kittens feed eight to ten times a day. Toby lay on her side, four kittens feeding off her breasts. I continued to place her bowl of wet food close to her head, and she ate between her feedings.

A month after the birth, I built a cardboard tunnel in the corner of my bedroom with tiny toys to amuse the little ones. Part of the tunnel had an open roof. The kittens had started walking, their wobbly crawl turning steady and coordinated. I often sat cross-legged on the edge of my bed, watching Toby play with her brood.

My attire at that time was far from glamorous, chinos for work and jeans for casual wear. The navy sweatpants I donned at home had seen many washes, yet no fabric I wore protected my legs from the tiny needle-like nails of rambunctious kittens. Soon, I had turned into a favorite cat tree to Toby's exploring brood. The kittens climbed every surface that lent a grip, my legs included.

The warm water of the shower nipped at the scratched skin. I looked at my bare legs to see a map of little red marks from ankle to thigh and winced. *How do I love thee?* I thought as I rinsed off the soap. *Let me count the ways . . .*

The reality of four growing kittens and a mother cat in my home was, at times, intimidating. Laura, my vet tech friend, did not participate in this birth. I was all alone with the prospect of finding good homes for Toby's kindle. I woke up to one truth in the morning: I did not want to part with them. However, I started conversations with friends and informed Toby's veterinarian that I had kittens for adoption. To me, they were the most beautiful kittens in the world.

Flyer and Tipper appeared identical to me. The facial features that made them separate beings emerged much later. In their infancy, I resorted to my own devices. I used a tiny dot of red nail polish on Flyer's tail, and the mark stayed for weeks until I got my first social visitor since their birth.

My landlady, Patti, dropped in amiably. She had adopted two cats at home from the local humane society. She was not about to take in another, but she nudged me wisely.

"Remember the window of time. Feral kitties can be domesticated if you raise them indoors like a housecat."

I was blind to what might be feral behavior in a kitten.

Toby was not headed anywhere until she was spayed. The longer she stayed with the kittens, the better for them. She was still nursing at nine weeks, and her robust brood still hovered over her breasts as if they knew no other food.

My laundry basket was divided between humans and cat. I could not see kitten pee, but tiny strands of poop were visible on the towels as Toby massaged the kittens' bellies on her own to stimulate the bowels.

I would have to lift them onto litter box granules someday soon—but not until Toby gave me a cue. I looked to Toby, a sudden mother, for guidance now.

The bookstore where I worked had generous employees "perks," and I got 30 percent off whenever I made a purchase. Mostly, I bought crime fiction from the bargain section. The cat is an icon for mystery, and I felt the feline psyche blend with every fictional sleuth the publishing world offered.

When I stole time for myself, I read voraciously—Sue Grafton, Lillian Jackson Braun, Michael Connelly, John Grisham, James Patterson, Rita Mae Brown, Sara Paretsky, Carl Hiaasen, and Janet Evanovich. Of course, I placed Sneaky Pie Brown and Macavity on separate sides of the fence of fictional cat icons. One was a sleuth and protagonist of Rita Mae Brown's bestsellers, the other T. S. Eliot's infamous character in *The Old Possum Book of Practical Cats*.

Browsing new releases in the bookstore's sprawling "Pets" section, I found a book on cat practicum written by Dr. David Brunner and Sam Stall. *The Cat Owner's Manual* hinted at knowledge flavored with humor. The subhead said, "Operating Instructions, Troubleshooting, Tips, and Advice on Lifetime Maintenance." The format was exactly the same as that of a *car* owner's manual.

Page 27

Top-Selling Models

Most of the world's cats are the products of random genetic combinations. These are called "mixed breeds." There are also selectively bred models that reliably reproduce a particular suite of aesthetic traits. Felines created this way are called "pure breeds."

Page 38

Non-Standard Off-Brand Models

The vast majority of America's 96 million cats* are mixed breeds. Available primarily through such informal distribution channels as private owners and animal shelters, they usually make excellent pets. However, there are some vital points to consider before adopting. Since most cat behavior is learned, it is important to uncover as much as possible about a kitten's upbringing. For instance, a kitten that was not raised among humans . . .

I skipped the rest of the chapter. Toby's kindle would be human friendly.

The little alpha, still nicknamed Sumo the Wrestler, broke his feeding routine unexpectedly. I walked into the bedroom and peered into Toby's corner to a surprise. Sumo had left his siblings on Toby's belly and had tipped his mother's feeding bowl on its side. The Meow Mix pâté in the bowl was being devoured with delight and vigor. Sumo was barely a month old, and what he was relishing was not kitten fare. I picked up the phone and poured my shock on the first listening vet tech.

No harm done, I was told. I just needed to stock up on kitten food to be prepared for the new menu. Sumo's snack was a foreshadow of his eating habits and his size in the years to come.

I was not a gourmet cat food purchaser. Purina had entered my kitchen, and I sought Meow Mix and Friskies kitten food out of familiarity. I could not tell if Toby consciously pushed her kittens toward eating kitten fare. What I did see was an increase in her mobility when her milk was not popular anymore.

My calendar lit up with a spay date for Toby. Other days penciled in were visits from people who wanted kittens. One adopter was a woman referred through Toby's vet. Another was my neighbor who had a grown cat of her own and wanted a young companion for him.

The days seemed ominous to me because I did not want to part with the little ones. Could I raise the brood on my own?

When Talia walked in through the door with her ten-year-old boy, I thought I had met a kindred soul. She exuded animal love and wanted a kitten for her son. She was self-employed and lived in a condominium. Toby vanished into the bedroom with the sound of visitors. I gently brought the brood out, one by one, and let them run free on the couch.

Sumo made an impression. Fearless and nosy, he was unfazed by strangers. Tippy fell between the cushions and decided to hide. Flyer snarled, his little face entirely hostile to being approached. Janie trotted back into the bedroom, not to be seen again. They were eleven weeks old.

In a few days, I would stand by the door after having Sumo say goodbye to his mother and siblings. As Talia's beaming self moved down the driveway, I could still see Sumo's face in the mesh of the cat carrier. He seemed to be asking a heart-rending question—do I have to leave? He knew he was leaving home.

Toby showed no resentment at Sumo departing, but she did look at me in a way that said, "So be it. You know I fed him well." I had an empty feeling deep inside me.

Sumo got a new name in his new home. Talia's boy chose his kitten's name, Inky. So his life began all over again with the pampering an only child can get—a new bed, toys, and feeding bowl and the same vet that had first seen his mother.

Every week I got an update on Inky, and I gave Toby the news I culled with eagerness. I am told cats can understand human language if they hear it spoken often. I spoke with deliberation in the hope of building Toby's vocabulary. I tended to forget her feral origins.

My neighbor Patricia came by for coffee. Coffee and kittens were on the cards. I knew Patricia well from the dance class we attended together. Our lives had intertwined with mid-east dance and our personal stories. Patricia's adolescent daughter was an ardent cat lover, and we had often met on our walks in the neighborhood. The visit had a tone of informality despite the ritual of kitten viewing.

Flyer was spared the stress. He stayed in the bedroom with Toby. Tipper was wide-eyed and placid in Patricia's presence. Janie, true to herself, scampered back to the bedroom—but not before being told by Patricia she was a very pretty girl.

Tipper was Toby's youngest and the one I had given my constant attention, making sure he had his share of mother's milk. Small as he was, he tended to be jostled but had grown into a resilient little fellow. Patricia decided to take Tipper home the same day with her. I tried to imagine what his life would be without the family he had known. The stab in my heart became tangible. I held him to my chest and then gave him to Patricia. I could not face Toby afterward.

I now knew for a fact that Flyer would stay with me. Janie, temperamental and naughty, still had a chance to find a home. My colleague Sally at the workplace was definitely interested.

A few animal welfare organizations caught my attention that year. The Humane Society of the United States deserved a piece of my modest paycheck for donations. PETA and Ingrid Newkirk were making headlines. I discovered Alley Cat Allies and avidly followed the organization's activities. Whether or not I would ever be able to make a dent in the national statistics of animal rescue was not a question that mattered at the wake of any day. I just knew that one little feral cat in my backyard had changed the way I viewed the bond between animals and humans.

Outside the home front, my silver-haired neighbor who fed the Seven Oaks ferals often ran headlong into me while she walked to her feeding spot and I was finishing errands around the neighborhood. Her name was Valerie, and she was quite the icon, tray in hand, sharing stories with all who might listen about cats she had met on the edge of the mansion. I had only seen two: a tortoise-shell female with a slight limp who had the demeanor of an abandoned domestic cat and a strapping gray-striped tom who resembled my backyard Mel. Gray stripes were an indication of a feral clan in Seven Oaks, and it was likely Mel had siblings roaming the area. Mel's sibling got a name from me. He was Tiger. Valerie had already named the tortie cat "Meow."

Beyond the feeding grounds, I rarely saw Valerie. There was an occasion when I saw her at a small grocery store that had a fresh food deli and bakery.

"My son does all my groceries," Valerie said in the checkout line. "I just come by for a few odd things."

Whenever I saw Valerie, I felt a rush of kinship, as if I had known her for decades. She was sprightly, in her seventies, and dressed in flat heels, tan pants, and shirts. Those tailored shirts with floral patterns or embroidery gave her a distinct old-world aura. Her face had classic European features that made an impression at first glance.

Standing with my care packages to Toronto under my arm at Ellesworth Post Office, I once saw Valerie ahead of me. She was lost in thought. Before it was her turn to go up to the counter, I caught her eye. Valerie did not seem to recognize me, and her gaze across the short aisle was confused. We went to separate windows, and I lost her before I finished my business.

Much to my delight, I was invited to Valerie's apartment on our next encounter.

"You must meet Ben," she said. "I call him Ben-Ben." She was not talking of her son but her cat.

On my midweek day off, I walked over to Valerie's place, which was a short way from my home. The condominium complex was well manicured, and flowering shrubs were everywhere. I sprinted up the stairs to her second-floor apartment.

There she was at the door, beaming in recognition, and was in full view of her living room couch with a large tan-and-white cat lounging on it. Ben had plenty of Maine Coon in him and was handsome enough to make the front page of Cat Fancy. The large screen television had a game show playing, and neither Valerie nor I had much interest in the contestants. Ben acknowledged my pat and continued watching television.

I smoked in those days. With my cigarettes of choice being Benson & Hedges Deluxe menthol lights, I carried with me a book of matches. I had never owned a lighter.

"My son smokes," Valerie said, serving coffee in a mug. "I know you might like one with the coffee."

In 2005, it was entirely acceptable to smoke inside, and there was no ban on cigarette smoking in apartment buildings. So I lit one. It was a small breath of paradise.

Toby and the kittens were at home, and I kept an eye on the clock. Ben was aloof but curious about me. He sat close to Valerie, who played with the long strands of hair around his shoulders and neck.

She untangled stray knots with her fingers, saying, "I do this without a brush."

Valerie's living room had a collection of oils and framed big cat portraits, a cheetah and a lone Siamese. The centerpiece was a painting of racehorses from the local Bay Meadows track.

"My son still goes there, though I doubt he will ever get rich . . ." Valerie said wryly.

I had never met Tom, Valerie's son, but he often entered the conversation as if he were part of our everyday encounters.

When I did meet Tom, Valerie's son, he seemed like a long-lost relative, not a stranger. He was a taller version of Valerie—softspoken, spectacles and all. A retired mailman, Tom had a route that brought him to my neighborhood for a decade. In quiet retirement, he walked two cockapoos in the morning and drove from his home in Belmont to visit his mother in San Mateo. Tom had been a young man when Valerie and her husband Woody had come to live here.

"Where were you before you came to California?" I asked Valerie when we were alone.

"Chicago, I think," she replied. "You have to ask Tom. He will be here to take me to the doctor's soon."

"Something wrong, Valerie?" I asked.

"Nothing. I am fine. I just have something I have to live with." Back at home, I got news about Tipper. Patricia was worried. Maverick, her male cat, was bullying the little one just to put the pecking order in place. Tipper was scared of his housemate and had spent a day under the couch when Patricia was at work. He would possibly do this every day. Patricia's household had seen a mismatch.

Tipper came back after a week of hiding under the couch in his new home. Patricia was tearful when she left him with me. Maverick did not take to a rival to Patricia's affections. I held Tipper close to me and felt his relief as he nestled at my chest. I knew immediately that Tipper would not leave me again.

"Kindle" Becomes "Clowder"

I was familiar with the expression "herding" cats. It alludes to an impossible task. However, a group of cats do not make a "herd." They are a "clowder" of cats. A "litter" of kittens is appropriately a "kindle." My kindle at home was growing before my eyes.

On his return, Tipper became Tippy and joined his siblings as if he had never left. I could now tell Flyer apart as his face had emerged with a pointed chin and, in expression, become more bold. His voice had a higher pitch than his siblings' meows. Tippy, with his benevolent eyes and gentle ways, could have a passport as a domestic gray-striped tabby.

Mary Jane was called Janie. She grew up looking like the *Mona Lisa* of kittens. Small and serene, she epitomized Da Vinci's words: "Even the smallest feline is a masterpiece." The artist had several cats. The one he sketched most often has lost her name in history.

When Sally, my colleague, came to look at Janie the first time, Janie came out of her hiding place to the living room. Quite fearlessly, she parked her little self in front of Sally, wrapping her tail around her feet. Her gaze was steady, eye to eye with the visitor. When she stood up, the orange stripes on her white flanks looked like custom brush strokes.

Sally looked as if she had fallen in love. Her own cat Princesa lived in the family home and had bonded with the household "gang." Sally's studio would be a good home for Janie, but she had to have a convincing conversation with her landlord to make her habitat pet-friendly.

Janie's relationship with her mother, Toby, grew stronger as her adoption was delayed. I worried about the separation as the days went by.

I took Toby to her appointment at the local SPCA's spay-neuter clinic. My neighbor gave us a ride that morning to the same facility where I had been a volunteer in my early years in San Mateo. At check-in, I made certain the staff knew Toby was a feral twicemother. Toby sat silent and still in her hard-shell carrier, but I could see the tension in her eyes.

I had seen spay surgeries before. Toby would feel nothing under anesthesia, but she would lose her vital organs that made her female. The procedure is an ovariohysterectomy. A small incision is made in the midline of the abdomen, just below the umbilicus. The entire uterus and both ovaries are removed. The incision is then closed with several sutures.

Toby was under supervision at the clinic until late evening. She came home with an e-collar, looking as sullen as Queen Elizabeth Tudor. Her litter box was free of granules because sand could get into the surgical wound. I had filled the box with shredded newspaper. For the next two weeks, she would have to wear the e-collar to keep her from licking her sutures.

Toby still had three growing kittens for company: her own Flyer, Tippy, recently returned, and Janie, a lady waiting to hear about her future.

Inky was happy with his adoptive family, pampered and full of antics. All news was good news. He had been neutered by the family veterinarian. He was overweight and was being fed only dry food. When I made a visit to Talia's, holding him in my arms felt as if he still belonged to me. He was the same robust, bouncing Inky.

One small worry nagged me. Inky was not taking to potty habits well. He averted the litter box and pooped on ceramic in the bathtub. Small acts of discipline, chiding, and even changing the brand of litter had no effect. The ceramic was a magnet. I could not explain this quirk. He had used a normal litter box as a kitten. Smooth ceramic surfaces were not known to Inky while he had been with me.

Feral cats instinctively scratch loose earth to cover tracks. So do domestic cats. I saw this behavior in the litter box and often had to sweep up scattered grains of litter from all around the bathroom floor. Toby scratched with the vigor of a horse's kick.

Little Flyer was also the most mobile and nosy of the kindle and often investigated corners the others would not explore. The chimney flue was securely shut. The back door was double locked, and I opened the front door with my foot wedged in the doorway. I could never presume no one was behind me, ready to run into the grassy patch outside. Chasing a feral kitten around the block would be résumé material for humane employment.

I was still working as a bookseller. Dan Brown's *The Da Vinci Code* had made the bestseller list and was inching up the *New York Times* nationwide fiction ladder. Barack Obama's *The Audacity of Hope* followed as the printed word. E-books had not yet eclipsed the physical paper book. I worked at the information desk, with a bevy of customers that ranged from schoolteachers to new parents, sophomore and senior students, and casual readers. Then there were professionals and aspiring professionals—medics, nurses, and techies from the outskirts of Silicon Valley. My colleagues were an eclectic group of people with one common thread: a passion for books. We had not yet been overpowered by digital technology, and the brickand-mortar bookstore still stood tall.

Among colleagues, I had my favorites, and Frank, the children's bookseller, had the biggest share of my affection. He was a retired auditor and had crunched numbers all his life. For years, he moonlighted as a bookseller and then embraced the bookstore as his second-wind career. His own children were young adults. He had an amazing affinity with children of all ages and made a riveting storyteller. I was invited on some occasions to sit in for story time to read the "book of the week." Sitting on the floor of the low stage, I read out from Margret and H. A. Rey's *Curious George* collection, and the world-famous monkey who held so many young minds in his grip came to life through my voice.

Then there was Beth, who had worked for the vice president of the local SPCA, and she captured my attention with her animal love. However, I stayed guarded about my own experiences as a volunteer in my early days in San Mateo. I did not wish to mar our relationship with debates on humane administration. The SPCA where we had a shared experience had not yet evolved to a no-kill facility. I stood starkly no-kill and could not subscribe to any shelter euthanizing healthy "surplus" animals.

Sally, another close colleague who had set eyes on my Janie, was moonlighting to bring a new spark into her life. She worked for law enforcement and kept her day job shrouded for the sake of professional conduct. I never saw Sally in uniform, and only once did she say in sotto voce, "I work for PD." I was certain she knew the underbelly of San Mateo County, from parking tickets to forensics.

By the time Sally told me that her landlord would not relent on pets in her building, Janie had blossomed into a beauty. The orange and shades of brown on her back stood in startling contrast to the pristine white of her belly and legs. An arrowhead of three colors marked her forehead. Her lower face and chin were white, and two symmetrical teardrop marks were imprinted under her green eyes.

Perhaps it was Janie's destiny to stay with me. At six months, she was smaller than her mother, Toby. Compared to her hefty brothers, she was miniature, sleek, and only weighing five pounds. Janie had fully bonded with me. With visitors, she was wary and scurried out of sight in haste, revealing true feral nature. Sally did not visit my home again but frequently asked about my "clowder of cats." Toby's maturing kittens were no longer a "kindle" of newborns.

Flyer, Tippy, and Janie made a trip together to the SPCA's spayneuter clinic and were altered by a veterinarian I knew well from my volunteer days. I again made sure the crew knew the kittens' feral heritage but did not receive the stamp that feral cats do at alteration. A clipped ear marks an altered feral in an outdoor colony feline. Toby had been spared the ear clipping too.

I spent a day alone with a fretting Toby at home while her three offspring were at the vet's. Flyer, Tippy, and Janie were almost six months old. Calming Toby was not easy. I talked aloud to her as I often did, but my voice did not appease her.

She endlessly circled my feet until I sat down on the kitchen floor and held her, saying, "They will be back. Three o'clock . . ." I pointed to the kitchen clock. "I will bring them back!"

Her fretful gait ceased. She must have understood.

There were no e-collars for the three little ones. Just like Toby, they had had their lower abdominal area shaved in the surgery. The boys did not express discomfort. Janie's movements were visibly slow, and her pink belly was bared to my scrutiny. The litter box once again had the *Wall Street Journal* cut to strips for their use. I usually stacked old issues of the newspaper near a favorite play area because Flyer and Tippy liked climbing the piles, indulging in scratch antics. I still find a cat's attraction to newspapers inexplicable. For that matter, why do they like cardboard boxes?

Being an "accidental" pet owner, I lacked wisdom on nutrition and changes in behavior after the three kittens had been neutered and spayed. If they ate more than their usual share, I did not notice. I had dry cat food around for an all-day buffet. Wet food was served once a day, and I usually saw clean bowls at the end of a meal. I did not know that this freestyle eating would lead to three plump cats because Toby, Flyer, and Tippy began to look like striped tea cozies. Janie remained svelte and more active than all of her family. Perhaps fat genes ran in the clan. Inky seemed to have a heavy waistline too. News of him always had stories about his kitchen forays and erratic bathroom habits.

I loved my cat family. I wished Toby would stay this time. I lost track of the world when I was with them and watched the kittens grow as if in a slow-motion film. They brought the eagerness of living and the adventure of discovery into the stillness of my own existence. My daylight hours were spent caring for them. I was part of the closing crew at the bookstore, and I got home on the bus a little before midnight. My first-floor apartment had a back driveway with eucalyptus trees and a row of carports. Before entering home, I usually smoked one of my Benson & Hedges by the dimly lit area. Toby sensed my presence. I would see her silhouette appear in the bedroom window.

Toby was my welcoming committee—a ritual that had started when she was pregnant with her very first kindle. I greeted her in the early days with the words "Toby, are your puddies here yet?" Now her appearance at the front door was followed by the patter of tiny paws as her group of near-year-old kittens made their appearance.

My living room curtains were drawn at night. My family had all the privacy they needed, and there were no curious neighbors asking about my expanding family. Another call from my landlady asking, "Cat problems?" would have a whole different scenario for an explanation. Toby was still with me. Her kittens were different. The cat population was a little high for my living space. I had not missed the "window of time" for taming feral newborns. They were not fearfully aggressive and hostile to humans. Their adopters just did not have the patience.

Flyer had stopped his lion-like snarls. Tippy was angelic to look at and spent his time sitting on my glass desktop and watching birds. Janie was still skittish but lay on her back in contentment whenever she found a soft nook—on my bed, in the padded cat box (which was Toby's), the couch, or between the cushions.

Toby played mock-hunt with her offspring in the darkness of the living room when I slept at night. I would hear vocal signals not typical of normal interaction as I dozed. "All meows are not equal," I had heard somewhere. The purpose of the meow must be understood. Cats make dozens of sounds that vary in pitch to express emotion. A cat meows to interact with humans. Cats seldom meow to one another. However, kittens meow to attract their mother's attention.

Felis silvestris lybica is the Latin name for Toby's genus of cat. They are supreme hunters. With flexible spines and claws for traction, cats have speed but only for short distances. They can run up to thirty miles per hour. Feral cats are more impressive and can run fifty to seventy-five miles per hour. Certainly, they can outrun the fastest humans. Taming the feline has been a ten-thousand-year journey, beginning in Egypt. In this small neighborhood in Northern California, a cat named Toby was still not tame. She had come to me in need and, in her wild heart, had grown to care for me and adapted to a human abode. All the time, I was aware that she had the ability to live without me.

"Do you have a boyfriend?" Valerie asked me one day as I sat on her couch, brushing her cat Ben.

I had bought a pin-and-bristle brush for him at the downtown pet supply store. I sprayed his tan and white hair lightly with a detangler before brushing him. I felt good about my grooming skills.

Now I had to answer Valerie. "I don't have a boyfriend," I said quietly. I hoped the subject would drop, but it did not.

"So you are sitting at home feeling sorry for yourself? Go do something. Get a job in a pet store."

I remembered telling Valerie about my work at the bookstore and my growing cat family. I felt a surge of surprise that she had forgotten. I had also told her about my divorce, a human relations mishap from which I had not quite recovered. I was not looking for a mate. Fortunately, I did not have to work too hard to change the stream of Valerie's thoughts. She found another subject swiftly enough.

"I get my hair done tomorrow," she said, relishing the prospect. She touched her silver mane and continued, "My son Tom's first wife was a hairdresser. I never had to worry about my hair. She did my hair all the time. He is married to a schoolteacher now. He is henpecked."

All this rushed out in a stream, and I realized we had come a long way in our friendship.

Valerie's cat Ben was a cherished pet. Ben's age was a mystery. He was six, maybe seven years old. I was no expert at telling a cat's age, and I later learned that the teeth are a good clue. Ben had been a rescue at the SPCA and adopted as a Christmas gift for Valerie. She had been without a pet for a long while after Bo, her Siamese, had been killed in a hit-and-run while crossing the street. I saw photographs of the blue-eyed beauty and wondered how he had slipped out of an upper-story apartment door and gone prowling.

Ben's self-contained nature was a contrast to the tumult I saw at home. Toby was a little more than three years old. Flyer, Tippy, and Janie were brimming with adolescent energy and ran amok over every surface they could find. The mantel above the fireplace was the only place on which they could not stand—too narrow but not too high.

I felt like paparazzi seeking fan photos as I chased them through their capers. The kitchen was a favored playground—on the counters, in the sink, from the unlit stovetop to the top of the fridge. Tippy, the littlest brother, now matched Flyer's size and showed full athletic prowess. Gone was the kitten who used to struggle for a place in the squeeze for his mother's milk. I wondered how Inky was progressing, but I kept my curiosity within bounds to phone calls, not home visits.

My "clowder" of cats was now covered by pet health insurance plans. Rabies shots were imperative in the county, although there had been no trace of rabies for fifty years. I had a family of raccoons visiting at night, and I enjoyed their presence. The babies were delightful, and they helped themselves to squirrel nuts and the outdoor bowl of cat munchies.

Across the fence were neighbors Don and Vera, who were used to the mother raccoon bringing a new "gaze" of pups every year. When I looked out of the window at night, I would see the family walking along the ledge of the fence in silhouette. I was allowed a peek into the nursery, and the quicker I adapted to them, the better. My backyard was their turf, and I was the new human on the block.

Mel, my male feral visitor, kept cordial relations with the raccoons. I once went into my backyard at midnight and was surprised by Mel and a large male raccoon sitting on the fence at a comfortable distance. They seemed unfazed by each other's presence. I suspected Mel had been Toby's mate for her second kindle of kittens. Janie's amazing coloring possibly came from a suppressed gene in Toby. The boys would likely resemble their father in their adulthood.

Mel had been my night visitor even before Toby came into my life. He knew my favorite poetry songs, and he had often sat near my feet, unafraid, as I shared my voice with him. I sometimes lit a candle on the backyard table and smoked a cigarette before going to sleep. Mel sat by me in a pool of candlelight or in the scattered glow of the moon through the tall trees. I did not try to touch him. I loved his company and memorized his large muscled gray presence, the wide forehead, and bright eyes—and never took his friendship for granted.

On a bright, sunny day, Vera, my cat-loving neighbor, and I stood on tiptoe on either side of the fence and had a serious conversation. Mel had been one of Vera and Don's "outside pets" for many years. After visiting me, Mel usually headed to Vera's patio for a meal and sometimes curled up and slept there. No one had tried to neuter Mel, and he had fathered many kittens in the backwoods.

Vera gave one of her chuckles and said, "He is untrappable!"

As we spoke, the nosy young cats came to the back windows. Vera was in full sight of Flyer, Tipper, and Janie.

"Do you think they are Mel's children?" I asked.

"Maybe," Vera said, and she did not speculate on paternity.

In the year 2006, I started reading *Warriors,* Erin Hunter's fantasy series on feral cats. I was as eager as a fourth-grader would be for *Harry Potter* to read the new release of *Warriors.* I had to keep up with the cat characters as if I belonged in the forest with the cat clans. In my enthusiasm, I missed the fact that "Erin Hunter" was a "collective artist," and the mantle of Erin Hunter hid six authors who contributed to the creation of the series.

Clan Names

Mel reminded me of the character Greystripe of the Thunderclan in *Warriors*. The feral cats of the forest had lyrical names: Tigerstar, Ravenpaw, Cinderpelt, Brambleclaw, Silverstream, Whitestorm, Feathertail, Lionheart, Nightcloud . . .

I decided to give "clan" names to Toby's three young ones at home. Had they been born outdoors and raised on the hillside, they would have had names resembling their true nature. Flyer became *Flyer Windheart,* Janie was *Mary Jane Morningstar,* and Tippy was *Tipper Tenderheart.* They still bore Toby's last name, *Catwings.* I created a world of my own, enmeshing fact and fiction with my furry housemates. There were occasions when I read aloud to them as if in story time.

In the midst of literary pursuits with my family, I did try to memorize the expansion of the vaccine FVRCP when I took them in for a booster—feline viral rhinotracheitis, calicivirus, and panleukopenia, all three highly contagious diseases. The young cats were beginning to venture into the backyard during the day. The fence was high enough to protect them. I thought they deserved a taste of the outdoors.

I slept with the cats scattered on my bed, wherever they wished to be. A real cat bed with a cushion was Toby's, but she sat in it at whim. There was a blue-and-black plaid wool blanket on the bed, which the cats loved for its rough texture. They gravitated to the bed at night without much ado, and I awoke to curled-up croissant shapes of my cat family. The bird calls in the backyard were heard before any human wakeup call. Nature worked very close to us. Just like sleep, I learned to rest like cats.

Rest is not idleness, and to lie sometimes on the grass under trees on a summer's day, listening to the murmur of the water or watching the clouds float across the sky, is by no means a waste of time. — Sir John Lubbock

I had a Moleskine sketchbook that fit in my jacket pocket. I drew with a mechanical pencil. Sometimes I colored my sketches with felt-tipped pens. I liked my pencil drawings the best. I drew Toby, her nestling the kittens, faces of raccoon pups, squirrels in the feeder shelling sunflower seeds. I occasionally captured a human face, and Wade, my bookstore manager, an Arkansas native, was a happy model. The watercolors I did in my backyard were forgotten. Watercolors were now a mussy effort.

My life at home was shared with a few friends. Don and Vera had grown closer, and their visits to my home were full of anecdotes about the cats they had rescued and adopted. Don's cat adventures included a bobcat that they could not keep. I lost count of how many ferals stayed in their apartment at a time. The numbers changed, and the faces at the window had different colors every time I looked. The cats had a vet who had stopped asking questions on the origins of his patients.

Don was a retired graphic artist. When Erin Hunter's *Warriors* series was developed into graphic novels, I brought them *Graystripe's Adventures* to give them a glimpse into Mel's secret life. The fact that the *Warriors* collective creators had an adult fan following will never make book club news.

Don and Vera had never been members of Alley Cat Allies. They were not "joiners" and kept their rescue efforts low-key. They were a twosome with their own feeding colonies. The trunk of Don's car was always filled with food, bowls, drinking water, tarps, and planks for setting up makeshift shelters. The Seven Oaks ferals were known to them, but they did not go into this territory. Coyote Point had a larger colony of free-roaming feral cats with corporate benefactors. Volunteers fed nearly a hundred cats, but Don and Vera did not venture into the waterfront neighborhood.

Both Don and Vera knew Valerie well. I was never certain as to whether Valerie had chosen to be a loner on the feral route or got left out because of her reclusive lifestyle.

I invited her to my home once, and she accepted, saying, "You might have to come get me. I don't remember the streets on your side."

Before Valerie came over to spend an evening with me and my cat family, Tom took me aside and said, "Will you make sure you walk Val back home? Sometimes she forgets familiar routes."

I got a strong clue of what had been puzzling me about Valerie all this while. "She has Alzheimer's."

This news did not change our relationship. When Valerie visited, she sat in my backyard at the glass-topped patio table. We had tea and fruit salad and talked about her days in Illinois. She had actually held the position of acting postmaster before moving to California. Woody, her late husband, was a skilled tradesperson, and Valerie, in her mosaic of memories, did not remember what he did for a living.

"I worked, you know," she said. "I have worked ever since I was sixteen."

Her own memories of childhood were blurred except for the vivid dislike of her stepmother. She had married Woody at seventeen, and Tom, her only child, was born within the next two years.

One afternoon, when I had a day off, Tom and I sat in Valerie's living room. I had the day off, and Valerie was fixing us coffee.

"Val was offered a full scholarship to go to Radcliffe when she was young," Tom said. "She had met my dad and got married instead."

I could imagine Valerie being a straight-A student in her time, and the realization that she was in the middle stage of Alzheimer's rankled. The irony hit me hard. Ben was sitting by Tom, being pampered, and we sipped our coffee in silence.

Valerie's visit lifted a curtain on my life with cats. Toby had shown perfunctory interest in the visitor. Valerie had gently reached out to touch her, and the interaction ended here. The curious faces of the young cats had framed the doorway. None had ventured too far into the living room, but their presence brought a thought out of Valerie: "You want to give them away? It will break your heart!" The parting with Inky and the efforts with Tippy and Janie went untold on the occasion.

The Cat Owner's Manual did not prepare me for life with four cats. My vital realization was that I did not "own" these cats. I was merely participating in life alongside them.

I learned cat anatomy from this lightweight encyclopedia. Afterward, I bought *The Nine Emotional Lives of Cats* from the bookstore. Author Jeffrey Moussaieff Masson owned five felines, whom he observed in writing this popular animal treatise. Masson diligently tracks the evolution of the "solitary jungle creation to a human companion." Curiosity, humor, jealousy, and love were spontaneous expressions in my feral family. Tension, anger, and anxiety, I had witnessed singularly in Toby's early days in my home. The feline heart is mysterious. So is a human's, and the depth of feelings can only be measured when sharing living space.

Feline emotions aside, I had learned how to trim cats' nails and clean ears as a volunteer at the SPCA. I still did not dare brush Toby's teeth. Having been bitten several times, I took it for granted that all thirty of her teeth were in good shape. The tooth fairy must have visited when I was asleep and left no presents under the pillows because Flyer, Tippy, and Janie had permanent teeth emerging, and I had yet to find a loose tooth around the house for a keepsake. Three growing cats and not a tooth for my collection!

The morning ritual of brushing Toby after her breakfast stretched to her offspring. They gathered on the bed, waiting their turn. I treasured the time I spent grooming them. Toby's fur, which had a coarse texture, had softened over time. Janie felt like a swath of velvet, and the boys, with gray and charcoal markings and white bellies, were pictures of health. I always thought of Inky between the brush strokes. He took pleasure in the morning ritual.

In my yard, the bird calls had stopped, and the squirrels hurried away at the sound of the fence gate swinging open. Our handyman made an entrance with a barrow full of wood chips, which he proceeded to scatter over strips of barren earth at the far ends of the space. The cats, sending a stranger's presence, dived under the bed. The yard was on the slope of the San Mateo mounds, and the soil was rocky. My attempts to grow flowers had met with resistance as the roots struck rock within inches. The chips lent a "Zen garden" look to the space that I hoped would be a hangout for the young ones when I was home to keep an eye on them.

Feral cats jump higher than an average domestic cat. The jump is "an explosive extension" of their back legs. The back limbs' strength and their muscle mass are greater in ferals than in domestic cats.

Talking about fence construction with neighbor Don, I figured that Toby and the young ones could never be left unsupervised in the backyard. I had a wooden vertical slat fence, seven feet high—an easy jump for a feral cat. Running, Toby could clear eight feet. There was a narrow gap at the base of the fence where the sloping ground met the slats. A lithe feral could easily wriggle out to explore and get a taste of wilderness. Flyer was destined to be a prowler.

A phone call from Inky's household broke my cat care routine. Talia had been offered a little rescue poodle for adoption, and she was enchanted with the dog. She wanted a cat-and-dog household, and Inky, a mellow year-old, was a few days away from having a fourlegged companion. I hid my consternation, and I wished her luck. I was certain that Inky would freak out with a dog. I thought it would be better for Talia to find out on her own.

Inky did not take well to his new housemate. I could have predicted this situation. As an alpha and the "senior" household member, he acted huffy. He did not respond to any overtures at play. Inky increased his protests—his toilet habits became more erratic. Ultimately, he stopped using the litter box. I called Talia frequently to find solutions, but just as in a film played backward, I found Talia at my door with a carrier in hand. Looking out of the front mesh was a familiar and adorable brown furry face. Inky was being given a break to be retrained. He came home to me.

The break was a long one. Inky never went back to his adoptive household. Somewhere along the way, Inky had lost his affection for them. Talia's boy would probably miss him, but I could never put Inky through an emotional wringer again.

Inky's return was a milestone in 2006. I had to reintegrate him with his birth family, and I had five cats to look after. My love for them was immense, and this was the feeling that eclipsed all other concerns—space, neighbors, and landlord.

Having stepped out of his carrier on that fateful day, Inky ran headlong into his mother, Toby. Toby, taken aback, reacted to this impressively large male with a snarl. Inky barreled into the bedroom as if he had never left. Flyer and Tipper quietly stared without making a move. Janie hid under the bed. It was hours before she would reappear like the household prima donna.

Cat siblings are identified by smells, I learned. Kittens forget their mothers after a long separation. Cats are not pack animals, and unless raised together for a definite time span, they are most likely to forget their birth family. Perhaps I was the only member of the cat–human household that Inky knew—I the human, while his own species looked upon him as a stranger. I was determined to make him feel that he had come home and that whatever love he had left behind, he would find it again with me.

I knew one thing that would remind Inky of his childhood—wet food. I served him what was now the menu of the day, Fancy Feast pâté, and he easily devoured a three-ounce can by himself. Inky loved his food, and the overwhelming emotion I felt as I saw him eat blinded me to his girth and character. Inky was destined to be a chunky alpha and, without doubt, a bully.

Curiosity drew Flyer close to Inky. He sniffed Inky, making an overture. Did he recognize Inky? I could not tell. They sauntered around the apartment amiably, their paws making tiny pitter-patter noises on the hardwood floors. The couch was a "peace bridge" of sorts. Inky's brown tabby stripes stood out against the blue-gray cushions, while Flyer looked camouflaged in comfort. They were sitting together. Toby had stopped snarling. Tippy drew close and rubbed noses with Inky. Something was going right. Inky had made a few "friends."

Girlfriend at Home!

There is always a textbook description for feline dynamics and a controlled environment that has led to a thesis on cat behavior. However, when two generations of cats have bonded in a household, the connection among the members displays an intimacy to which an outsider may not be entitled. Janie, now more than a year old, was slender and athletic, strong-willed in every way but entirely reclusive with people. Her displays of affection toward Flyer and Tipper were profuse, and she often curled up to nap between her two brothers and groomed them ritually.

When she sat next to Toby, the contrast between the two females was startling. My "cinder-pelted" Toby had produced a ramp model for a Parisienne cat show. Of course, one should not be deceived by appearances. Deep down, Janie was as feral as her mother.

To Janie, Inky was a stranger. By late evening, Janie decided on an appearance from her hiding spot, and her little nose and white chin emerged from under the bed. It was mealtime, but I do recall her appearance was not without anxiety. Within seconds, Inky sensed her presence and clamored off the couch. A girl cat—Inky came alive! His eyes brightened, and his pace increased to approach Janie. Janie's reaction was explosive. She planted her haunches to the floor, her ears flattened on her head, and she hissed with terrifying intensity.

Inky backed off but remained fixated on Janie. This was a very haughty girl facing him. He did not remember his one pretty little sister at all. This is how it would always be between the two of them— admiration, impatience, affection, and many chases with Inky in hot pursuit. They would never be siblings again.

I liked watching the cats. I watched them in repose, at play, as they ate their meals and drank from the bowl, when they groomed themselves or sat at the window in long moments of daydreaming. They knew exactly what they wanted to do, and every move had a defined grace.

They touched and groomed one another as a social ritual. Inky, amazingly, fell into the heart of the small tribe with eagerness, albeit no longer a member of the family.

The role of a feral cat advocate seemed an onerous one. I did not have the means of transport to join caregivers of a cat colony. I had a wellspring of compassion within me to care for the cats within reach, but getting a hands-on community role seemed unattainable. At best, I could put a poster up on my glass windowpane that had a cat resembling Toby. The caption said, "She is not homeless. This is her home. She has lived outdoors for eight years." Such is the life of feral cats. Toby was an exception and had mysteriously conceded to becoming an indoor companion.

Unlike Valerie, who relied on instinct to care for the Seven Oaks ferals, I put myself through self-study to familiarize myself with cats. Facts from the web and know-your-cat books startled me. I knew kittens were born blind. They are born deaf. The first milk teeth they sprout at two weeks are the incisors. I used to hold the miniature paws of Toby's newborns, which were the size of a flower bud. I counted the paw pads and felt the pinpoints of the claws. Newborns cannot retract their claws and carry these weapons from the moment they enter the world.

My cat family perceived me to be one of them. I just happened to be taller and biped. If they noticed inadequacies in my humanness, they were not critical. The cats had a keener sense of smell. Their ears swiveled. My ears were just stuck to the side of my head. They heard two octaves higher than me, but this did not include sirens and car horns.

Holding Janie's face in my palm, I saw she had two whiskers above her eyes. On the right side of her nose was a thumbprintshaped brown patch—a splash of random pigmentation that did not occur anywhere else on her body. This little face was loaded with scent receptors, perhaps fifty million of them around the nose. There were more on the roof of her mouth.

Seeing the World

There was an impish innocence in the eyes of the young cats. It came through when I photographed them. I did not succeed with portraits, but I did catch them sitting still by the windowpanes or curled up on the rug. On a good day, I would photograph them with their gaze on the camera lens.

Toby had wicked eyes full of mischief. Her pupils were vertical slits. With her having no need for nocturnal hunting and no unannounced visitors, Toby's wicked orbs always showed comfortable slits. Toby's world had become predictable.

Cat Facts on the web said felines saw ultraviolet light, and the rest of the world was seen through lenses of blues and grays. They saw exactly what I, the human, saw except the scene would be slightly blurry, with no hint of reds or pinks. It is all a matter of rods and cones in the retina, the mathematics of which I had yet to discover. The boys had inherited the gray-green eyes from Toby. Janie's were a pale green.

Even when I was around my own cats, Ben was on my mind. I had time to spare. I visited Ben, brush in hand, and both he and Valerie seemed pleased to see me. Ben was visibly more affectionate, and his silky length of hair was a contrast to my tribe at home. Valerie was walking around the apartment, chatting about the week past, when I noticed a bruise on the side of her forehead. Strands of her hair hid part of it.

"I fell," she explained when I asked.

"How?"

"Just fell as I was getting out of bed. I hit my head on the floor."

I was dismayed. This elder—so proud of making it through life alone, so possessive of space and lifestyle—had just admitted to a frailty. So far, she had not mentioned her Alzheimer's and the toll the disease had taken on her independence. The bruise looked worse than a bump on the floor.

"Tom took me to the doctor's. I'll be okay."

Ben lay on his side on the couch as I brushed through a few difficult tangles on his belly. I cleaned his ears on some days but never trimmed his nails. Ben kept his claws out of sight. Afterward, I went into the bedroom with Valerie, and she pointed to the place where she had fallen. Valerie had struck her head on the side of the low bedside credenza, which explained the sharpness of the bruise.

Valerie hugged me on my way out, and it was tighter than her usual embrace. She reached the chair by the door and handed me a bag of groceries.

"Here, take this home with you. Tom got me more than I need."

I looked inside. There were cookies and a specialty coffee mix. The fruit cups were Valerie's favorite. Nothing that needed a can opener or too much dexterity could be bought for her. She was losing strength in her hands, but mostly, she was losing patience.

Refusing would hurt her feelings, so I took the bag home. Perhaps Tom had over-shopped. The essentials, the microwaveable meals, were likely in Valerie's freezer. I had no reason for concern. I made a note to myself to remind Tom to buy kitchen scrubbers. The one on Valerie's sink looked worn.

At home, with my evening off, I idled with my family. Five cats padded around the room, and I, the sole human, was on the couch. It was a most normal evening. I had no television set, so I watched my cats. My neighbor Frank's saxophone could be heard from his balcony, and the neighborhood was still. The traffic on El Camino Real was muffled. We forgot we lived in a city not very well-known on a map.

From between the cushions, faces with perky ears peeked at me in a feline hide-and-seek that only cats do so well. I felt their lithe bodies brush against my torso and nuzzle my shoulder. Even little Janie had joined in the scamper. Toby, like a contented matriarch, pulled away to sit on the rug. I watched Inky's broad frame burrow past his brothers toward me. Close up, he brimmed with mischief. Inky was a year and a half old and growing bigger. The tiny kitten born at the crook of my knee had grown into an eleven-pound male in charge of his surroundings. Inky had staged his own reunion. He had only once pooped out of the litter box on the bathtub ceramic as a matter of free expression.

The evening on the couch had a déjà vu. Years ago, when I was unpacking my worldly possessions in this apartment, Sam, my neighbor's hefty orange cat, used to sit on the same cushions with me. A few cardboard boxes were still piled in the corner. Sam loved jumping in and out of them. When I sat down to take a breather, he would climb onto my lap, curl up like a giant croissant, and close his eyes as if he had found his secret heaven. Much of Inky's was reminiscent of Sam's warmth.

One of the first places I had sought out when I arrived in San Mateo was a hairdresser's. On Third Avenue was a salon with a name that did not spell or spout glamor. It was called Time. I liked the name. I was a hardy person without a grand budget. Streaks of silver had already appeared at the back of my head. Time, I thought, was a good place to be. I stepped inside late one morning to find two people at work. Eddie, the suave Vietnamese owner who had the manners of a Frenchman, and Eileen, a cheery blonde, exuding a spunky quality. I chose Eileen.

I grew very fond of Eileen. Hairdressers often become confidantes and confessionals simply because they do something so entirely intimate to a person. They style hair. We live with this hair, just the way we live with our face—every day until our next hair session. Jesus may have said, "Love thy hairdresser as thyself."

When I walked into Time Salon in 2001, my hair had grown long and a bit unkempt with the unpacking and huffing around the abode. I wanted to shear a lot of it off, and Eileen was encouraging. I bargained with the mirror and decided on a short bob, which would need very little styling.

Eileen talked while she cut hair, but she was also a great listener. She liked decorating and had tried her hand at interior decor. Time Salon had some of her touches.

I regaled her with stories of my move from Toronto and the adventures of setting up a home with Ikea furniture and mismatched kitchenware from cardboard boxes. I had not been sure how long I would stay in one place, so I clung to the packing boxes and bubble wrap in case I was uprooted again. It turned out that Eileen and I stayed friends for a decade, so all my cats and ferals at Seven Oaks became known to her. "How are the kitties?" was her first greeting whenever she saw me. My own hair was discussed afterward. She even gave me hairstyling razors with which to groom my cats.

Occasionally, after a haircut, I felt an odd pang when Eileen swept my hair off the floor with a soft broom.

"I wish I could do something with it," I once said.

"Try donating to Locks of Love," Eileen said solemnly.

I had never thought of shearing my head to give hair to cancer patients, and the prospect seemed rather intimidating. However, Eileen's suggestion brought a certain sensitivity to the cat hair that I culled in my home. It would make fine yarn someday.

There was pleasure in being groomed. I liked having my hair cut as much as the cats liked being brushed. I could see it with Toby, who would sit like a Buddha when I brushed her. In intense pleasure, she would turn on her side in a fetal crouch, grasp my arm with her forelegs, and scratch with her hind paws. It was a contortionist's "thank you." I had started using a metal comb on the young, cats and I realized I was gathering hair from their outer coats and occasionally swept up the soft undercoat hairs. I just did not feel like throwing the strands away.

Flyer sought me out to be groomed. His meow was slightly higher-pitched than his brothers, and I knew when he was fully relaxed. He lost all feral quirks, turned on his back, and placidly demanded a belly brushing.

Tippy was more reserved during grooming rituals. He stared at me with his large gray-green eyes as I worked on his back. Inky needed to be chased but melted into slackness under the brush. Janie, I scooped up, wherever she was, placed her on my lap, and brushed her. She sat perfectly at ease. Her fur was sumptuous, satin to the touch.

Charlie, my neighbor's cat from across the street, used to announce his visit with his bells. *Chink-ka-chink-ka-chink!* Had Charlie still been virile, I would have guessed him to have been Toby's choice for occasional frolic. His slender frame and white and tan markings resembled Janie's, whose paternity will be credited to a mystery gene.

On the Feast Day of St. Francis, I attended a local church without a pet in tow. I was the odd one in the congregation because the pet blessing event had brought every pet owner out on that Sunday. The aisle was crowded with dogs on leashes and cats in carriers. The priest beamed at everyone, and when it was my turn, he looked around for my visiting animal.

"I take care of feral cats," I said. "I could not bring them along."

The reverend saw the humor of my state as I stood alone in line. He blessed me. Then he quietly handed me a pewter St. Francis medallion. I loved this pastor instantly.

"Just one," he said, and it was my moment to beam. I had always wanted a pet blessing medallion.

The medallion was a gift for Charlie. He crossed the road more often than any feline in the neighborhood and had stayed unscathed all this while. I walked over to this home and gave the medal to the woman with whom he shared his house. Charlie was not home, she said.

The next time I heard the familiar *chink-ka-chink*, I looked at Charlie's collar out of curiosity. St. Francis was there along with his name tag and his bell. Charlie would never catch a bird, but he did not need to. He came into my kitchen and had a relaxed meal on the kitchen counter.

When Charlie's family moved, I went over to say a special goodbye. Not one for hoopla, he just sat on the porch steps and looked at me with his wide eyes, with his customary tranquil expression. I could never pass those steps again without thinking of him.

Partings

Partings are like punctuation marks. They are inevitable and essential in the grammar of life. No matter how many times you use punctuation, another pesky parting happens.

On the day off from work, I trotted over to Valerie's place to visit and to brush Ben, who now had me as his regular groomer. Valerie was in a despondent state.

"I feel like I have been beat up," she said.

"Why? What happened?" I asked.

"I'm moving."

"Just like that?" I said in surprise.

"Tom has been planning it for a long time." Valerie was abrupt. "I have a place opening up next month. They don't think I can live alone anymore."

When I spoke to Tom, I understood the foresight of this move. Valerie would have company and care around the clock. Lesley Terrace was an assisted living facility in Belmont, a city adjoining San Mateo. The apartment was pet-friendly and came with a meal plan.

I felt relieved that Valerie would be cared for where she was headed. I felt sad that I would be losing her nearness. I was without a car. This was not goodbye but merely the distance of miles that would make us less than neighbors.

"What about your outside pets?" I asked Valerie gently when I had her alone.

"Well, I can't take them with me, can I?"

We both sat in silence for a while. Valerie stroked Ben absentmindedly, and I stared at the television, my mind in turmoil. Valerie did not ask for my help. She had no plans to find anyone to replace her to feed the Seven Oaks ferals. They could survive on their own, but would they stop expecting the human who cared for them?

"I'll do it," I spoke aloud, cutting into Valerie's thoughts.

She immediately caught my intent.

"I can feed Tortie and Tiger. I don't know about the rest."

I shall remember Valerie's face from that moment forever. She smiled, and the shadows vanished. She smiled as if the world had come alive again. "The one with the limp, she has a name. I call her Meow. She is so pretty, I used to think she was a show cat."

I began to collect trays for outdoor feeding. There was a stack left over from Valerie's frozen meals. I thought of water and was stumped with the challenge of carrying a water bowl for the ferals. *Food enough for two. Where do they drink?*

The neighbors had a pool, and the thought of cats drinking chlorinated water made me recoil. Chlorine gives cats gastrointestinal irritation. At home, the cats got tap water, and I changed the bowls every day. When I learned more, I changed the San Mateo tap to filtered water. My feral companions had a different life.

Sleeping Arrangements

I had no secrets from my closer circle of acquaintances that I lived with five cats. I was happy but not without anxiety and thoughts of how I would sustain myself with my cat family in the years ahead. I had one income, and my expenses consisted of cat food, my groceries, and rent. The rent bubble with the influx of Silicon Valley techies had not affected me.

A colleague at the bookstore once chuckled at my getting a "Crazy Cat Lady" fridge magnet.

"I don't see you as one of those," she said.

I did not have the inclination to be one, but the accidental cat family would need to be explained someday.

The year was 2007. Toby had lost her sitting-on-a-mat "Gumbie Cat" look and was frolicking with her children as if she were one of them. She occasionally disciplined Inky if he misbehaved, but otherwise, all maternal displays had vanished. Toby had her favorite toy, a miniature plush gorilla, and her favorite perch by a windowpane overlooking the backyard. At night, she curled up on the bed with Janie by her side or indulged her instincts for nocturnal prowling in the living room. Inky, Flyer, and Tippy took the right side of my bed, occasionally migrating to the couch for night games.

Tippy stayed close to me. The habit continued through the years, and his sleeping spot close to my pillow or nestling by my belly was endearing. I called him "my lawfully wedded Tippy." He had grown from his littlest brother pecking order to a young cat of good standing. He could handle himself in a rumble with Inky and Flyer.

Toby's favorite animal, the gorilla, suddenly became headline news. The Congo's Virunga National Park, with its silverback gorillas, saw a massacre that shook conservationists. I bought a copy of *Newsweek* with the cover story and sat at the pine table at home, near to tears. The photographs of the rangers carrying the massive animal corpses away ripped me to the core.

"Don't Take It Personally"

I used to take Toby out to the backyard with me so she had a taste of fresh air and felt the rustle of the summer breeze. I usually held her on my lap, unsure of her swift movements and reaction to neighborhood sounds.

Once, I set her on one of the lawn chairs and blew soap bubbles to entertain her. She was fascinated by the descending shower of tiny globes in the sunlight. Back in the house, she appeared entirely settled into her comfortable life.

Nothing can ever be taken for granted with a true feral. Toby started making random darts to the back door when it was a crack open. During the day, I usually followed her out to hustle her back into the house. One afternoon she leaped off her window perch, dashed out, and found a gap in the wood fence. Into the neighbor's driveway, down the path— and she was gone.

I rushed out to the neighbor's yard and could not catch sight of her gray tail. She was gone. A stab of panic struck me. I sprinted down, calling her name over and over. There was no sight of the cat. *My Toby— gone?*

There was no one to call, no way to find the scamp in the row of backyards and shrubbery. This was her old turf, and she knew hiding places that I could never reach. Why did she go? *Boredom? Old wild instinct calling? Or just a prank on me?*

"Your mommy ran away!" I told the four at home as I came in distraught from my sprint. "What shall we do?"

I met the nonchalant gaze of Inky and Flyer. Janie looked at me with wide innocent eyes. I thought I saw concern in Tippy's face. They were all in the living room, scattered on the couch and rug in an impromptu family meeting.

The day rolled into evening. I fed the cats, my heart full of Toby. I was listless about myself but went into the kitchen to dish up my own dinner. On the kitchen wall was a calendar with a gorilla picture, Koko of California who lived with humans, the primate who could speak in sign language. Toby used to stare at that picture when she was in the kitchen. What she saw from the floor was likely a blur. Still, she stood, head lifted, fascinated by the dark form of Koko.

Pasta and sauce—my hasty meal did not take skill, but I made such dinners when my belly rumbled for comfort food. I still ate meat at this time and told myself I would turn vegetarian soon. My kitties remained an anomaly. They would always be carnivores, relishing Fancy Feast.

I was meandering, listless, around the house when I saw a dark shadow by the back door. *Mel*, I thought. I rushed to open the door— and *there was Toby!* She walked in as if nothing was amiss and headed for the living room. In her world, nothing was amiss.

Joy. I knew another meaning of the word that evening. As Toby ate her evening meal, I rejoiced at her return to my home. The world turned as it always does, and I thought of the million cats in kennels of shelters.

Every fifteen seconds, a cat or dog is put down—simply for being homeless. Healthy and adoptable but kenneled in overcrowded shelters— feral cats and feral dogs have a tenuous or no chance of survival in kill shelters.

Back at work the next day, I told my colleague Beth about Toby's escape.

With deep wisdom that comes with exposure to a humane shelter, Beth said, "Don't take it personally. Feral cats can love, but they can also live without us."

The words stayed with me. The home front fell back into place with my brushing Toby in the morning on the bed, the young ones waiting their turn. Fancy Feast was served as breakfast and the munchies for snacking in my absence. I did not make a prisoner out of my housemates, but Toby's movements made me tense.

"Something on your mind, Tobers?" I asked in earnest.

She looked at me as if plotting deeper plans.

One morning Toby sat on her haunches on the pine table after her breakfast. I had just stepped in after filling the squirrel feeder with sunflower seeds. The back door was open a crack. In a lightning flash, she barreled through the gap in the door. The next thing I saw was Toby clearing eight feet over the corner of the fence onto the wooden ledge.

"Tobers!" I raised my voice in shock.

Toby stood on top of the fence, a proud little tiger in the sunshine. She looked straight at me from the height as I stood at the back door. With a leap to the ground, she vanished.

Once more, I ran past the back gate to the neighbor's driveway. Hair askew, in baggy sweats, flip flops on my feet—I ran after Toby. It was like chasing the wind. She was nowhere in sight.

Gone. Again. I walked back home as a cold grip clutched my insides. This time, I could not face the young ones with the news. I picked up the phone and called my neighbor Don, and his quiet voice resonated.

"Sometimes mother cats give up their territory for their kittens."

Toby was wearing a pink collar with her name. She had had her rabies shot and had flea repellent on her. She had eaten and would not be hungry today. Tomorrow seemed far away, and I could not imagine my home without Toby.

I dressed for an afternoon shift at the bookstore and hugged Inky, Flyer, Tippy, and Janie harder than I usually did before I left home. For the first time, I was leaving them on their own without Mommy Toby.

The neat rows of bookshelves and the ten thousand titles were usually a pleasurable haven. That day, I was distracted by the events of the morning. I got off a few minutes early to catch the 11:00 p.m. El Camino bus home. The road was a cascade of streetlights and beams from cars, and my home stop was deserted. I quickened my pace as the reality of Toby's absence hit me again.

Three cats greeted me at the door. Janie usually hung back in the bedroom while her brothers raced forward at the sound of my key at the door. The ritual was never broken. Someone was missing.

I touched my cats as if my feelings were expressed through my hands. They milled around my legs, and Janie joined me, pattering up the hallway, her face very serious. Nobody was smiling that night. Cats do smile if given a reason.

The nightly practice of getting the family ready for bed was broken. Toby's movements were a lead for her children—a late-night game of hunt or cuddle time with the human. I turned the kitchen light off and felt the silence of the backyard. Not even the crickets could be heard. I decided to open the back door with a faint hope of seeing her finding her way back.

There were double doors to the backyard. I pushed the screen door open and surveyed the darkness. No one was there to lift the gloom in me. I stood in the semi-darkness like a soldier of the night, motionless.

Something prompted me to look at the bare earth behind the screen door. There was a silent, curled-up gray shape in the nook looking up at me. My heart leaped. *Toby!*

Time stood still. Neither of us moved. I slowly let the door go and bent down to touch her. She let me. As I grasped her, she resisted.

Refusal—Toby did not want to come in. The struggle to escape my grasp was insistent. She even nipped my wrist. I knew what she intended to do. I felt pain. I felt panic.

Wriggling out of my hold, Toby shot to the old escape route—the slim gap where the fence did not quite meet the ground. Flattening herself, she attempted to leave. I grasped her with one hand from behind. She was disappearing despite my hold. Her body slithered away until all I had in the grip of my hand was the length of her tail.

I lost Toby. She was determined to run. My feral mother had left me. I do not remember how long I stood in the darkness. I finally went in to face Toby's children. The pent-up emotions found no words, and in deep distress, I said nothing.

My pillow was exactly in the same place where Toby sat two years ago, the night her kittens were born. I lay there, with four cats around me. That night, the closest to me, by my head, was Inky. I held his large furry body to my face and wept. Tears came. Words came. I spoke of the deep pain within and why nobody could take her place. The young ones heard me, and I was not ashamed. Inky did not move from my side all night.

In the morning, I discovered a cut on my left wrist. The blood had dried, and the wound was not deep. In her struggle to escape, she left me a tiny memento.

Life without Toby

One word frees us of all the weight and pain of life. That word is love.

— Sophocles

Toby had left me four parts of herself: her firstborn and re-homed intrepid Inky, Flyer, Janie, and Tippy. I drew them closer to me for comfort, but Toby remained an indelible part of my "every days."

I had health plans for the family. The pampered life at home did not shield the siblings from the impact of the backyard. Their forays were always watched by the corner of my eye. Every darting movement—squirrels or birds—brought out the feral instincts in them. I pondered the possibility of bells on their collars to spare the sparrows surprise attacks.

One morning Inky walked in with a prize firmly clenched in his mouth. I looked down to see a bird clasped between his jaws. I pounced like a feral and prised his mouth open. The sparrow was still alive and flew up and out the door. Toby's nocturnal lessons had not been lost on her kittens.

Flyer was given to leisurely prowls, during which he discovered the gap in the bottom edge of the fence. He gave me a few bouts of panic when he set out on his voyages of discovery. He always came back home. Flyer and Inky were buddies. They seemed to tell each other the plans I never discovered until the deed was done. They were partners in cat capers.

Our next visit to the vet was a lesson in common sense: the battle against fleas. Flyer brought home the dreaded parasites. I took the cats in one by one, the short ride resonant with their tense meows. Janie was most overwrought from being taken out of the home front, and her protests grew louder as we neared the clinic. This little girl had an operatic voice. All this protest, and I had only found two fleas on her.

Janie was in fine health, like the others. A hardy brood, my cats were. The vet raised her eyebrows only on one count. With the exception of Janie, they all showed a tendency to be overweight. My fault—or was it in the genes? The boys were fully grown and impressive in size. Their physique was an echo of their paternal heritage. I did not carry a photograph of Mel, and I often wish I had proof in my backpack.

Janie had lost one tiny incisor from her lower set. Dr. Frank held her face in her hands and showed me the broken tooth. She was chewing on fronds again in the backyard. My Janie had less-thanperfect teeth. I felt I had let my princess lose a beauty contest.

Courage was not a quality Tippy displayed on the exam table. He turned around and buried his face in my belly as I stood next to him. Not hidden to his satisfaction, he leaped off the table onto my shoulder and refused all attention. Tippy's ritual resistance never changed.

Mel returned alone to the backyard many times. He was always passing through and stopped to sit near my feet when I sat alone on the lawn chair. I asked him in the English I used with him if he had seen Toby. I felt he understood my spoken language. His wide gray face stayed secretive. I lit a candle during my nightly vigils. The warbles of raccoon pups and rustle of branches broke the stillness of my yard.

Valerie Leaves the Neighborhood

Valerie and Ben were feeling the jostle of a move. The familiar paintings and pieces of furniture were disappearing. The couch was still in place. I brushed Ben with a sense of nostalgia for the two years we had spent together as friends.

"I feel as if I have been beat up." Valerie repeated her words to a point of pain. She loved where she lived. The new place in Belmont held neither joy nor anticipation for her.

I promised to care for the ferals she was leaving behind. Valerie's Alzheimer's had not affected her duties to her "outside pets." Valerie had said her goodbyes earlier in the day.

The next time I would see Valerie and Ben would be in their new place. They would both be comfortably anonymous. With time, Valerie's persona would fade from the minds of San Mateo's residents. I wondered how much of the neighborhood would stay with Valerie in the time to come.

When I started my walks to the Seven Oaks fence, cat food in hand, I was occasionally asked, "Where is your gray-haired friend?"

I would answer, "Valerie moved, not too far away."

"Did she find her cat?" a neighbor inquired.

"Which cat?"

"Her pet. The cat she had lost. She was standing on the sidewalk, asking people, 'Have you seen my cat?'"

"When?"

"Just the other day."

Ben never prowled outdoors, so it could not be him. Valerie must have been looking for Bear, Ben's predecessor. Her handsome Siamese who tended to slip out of her apartment door often put her in a frenzy. He was killed in a hit-and-run.

"Broke my heart," I remember Valerie telling me. We had been sitting on her couch, with Ben close to us.

On days when time and memories were especially blurred with her Alzheimer's, Valerie stepped out on the sidewalk in front of her apartment, looking for the lost cat, almost as if her yesterday had come alive.

Neighboring Fences and Glimpses of Hillsborough

I did not call the SPCA and report Toby lost. She was not lost. She could hunt and would probably find her meal in the bushes. Her rabies shot and vaccines were up to date. I was most worried that her flea medication would wear off.

Toby had chosen to abdicate as queen of her household to live outdoors. Contrary to a colleague's advice—"Don't take it personally"—I did take it very personally. Her absence hurt.

I made friends with Valerie's "outside pets"—at least those that came out to meet me. The little female tortoise shell began to answer to the name Tortie as if she had never been called by any other name before. Tiger, who I suspected was related to Mel, did not care for any name. He waited for me on a strict schedule and insisted on eating from his own feeding tray. I deduced that the feral colony hidden in the enclave descended from a clan of gray-striped tabbies. Tiger was unaltered. He had never been trapped. Tortie, who had not borne kittens despite years of outdoor living, had possibly been spayed.

Northern California brings rain in December and January. I was still an amateur who had no clue about keeping dry food from getting soggy in the downpours. My veteran neighbors Don and Vera talked about feral cat feeding stations, but Valerie's cats had always been fed on the borders of private property. I set up improvised feeding stations under two open umbrellas wedged between shrubs. When an umbrella blew away in a nightly gust, I chased the umbrella in the morning and set up the feeding spot again. This became my rainy weather ritual.

Tiger had a wide face and a broad neck, and his gray frame weighed about fifteen pounds. In wet weather, he slept under parked vehicles and fire escapes. I once saw him sitting on the hood of a van in a patch of sunshine. As I neared him, I noticed his eyes were watery, one eye with a streaming tear stain. Tiger had the cat flu. He needed food. I tried to think of ways to feed him pâté mixed with lysine powder. Tiger did not trust humans enough to sit at my knee, or else he would have gotten a dose of lysine from a feeding syringe. Tiger was unreachable.

At the eastern elbow of San Mateo is the prosperous city of Hillsborough, with its vast manicured lawns and prize real estate. The original homes were built by wealthy San Franciscans, and the acres of green spaces could camouflage a runaway cat or lost dog. The wooded slopes of the landscape could be a permanent hideout for Toby.

Instinct told me that Toby had settled within the borders of San Mateo after scouting her horizons. I started taking walks along a mile radius of my home and chatted with friendly faces I met along the way. On occasion, I wondered if I sounded like Valerie.

"Have you seen a small gray tabby with a pink collar?"

No one had. Not yet.

Before fall set in, I called Valerie to ask if she liked her new place. I wanted to see her and give her an update on our alley cats. I was delighted that Valerie remembered my name.

"Come brush Ben-Ben," she said as if we had never missed a day with each other. "I'll have Tom give you my address."

I felt a rush of anticipation. I would take cupcakes to mark Ben's birthday, which Valerie celebrated on July 17.

Fun, Games, and Matching Appearances

I enjoyed shopping in pet stores—little plush and catnip toys, feathered teasers, and laser lights. I browsed the aisles thinking of the family at home and how I would delight them with my discoveries.

Janie was an imp and an acrobat, the most agile and responsive to new attractions. She even tried her trapeze act by swinging on a single wool strand of a giant dreamcatcher, a cherished Lakota creation. I had acquired the dreamcatcher from a First Nations craft store in Canada many years ago. This became her entertainment for when I was not home.

Inky had been pampered with designer toys in his first adoptive home. My selection of playthings bored him.

Flyer and Tippy played their own games of chase and caught the taste of catnip early in their youth. I would come home to find the floor strewn with the toys of the day.

If they missed the presence of Toby, not one of them expressed it with despondence. Their own search for her may have been in places where she sat and where her scent lingered. My own feelings about Toby's new life would always remain mixed. I felt elation at her independence and grief for not having her furry self close by my side. Then there was relief. *My wild girl was spayed. She was relieved of nature's covenant of giving birth and raising her offspring.*

Toby's favorite toy, the little plush gorilla, became my treasure and keepsake.

Flyer and Tippy, with gray tabby genes in their markings, were now distinct in their appearance. When they were kittens, I could not tell them apart. Now they stood with the same stripes on their chest and forehead, legs and back, faces entirely unalike in features—nine black stripes on gray fur on the forelegs, three rings of white and gray on the chest, and five stripes on the forehead rising and merging to the back of the neck.

Flyer's face was narrower, his voice higher-pitched than Tippy's. The resemblance between mother Toby and Tippy was clear. In Tippy's eyes, however, there was a calm and an innocence that Toby never possessed. His voice was deeper and his meow more prolonged.

Inky usually had a double meow. In a fond and mellow mood, he would articulate one long sound. Janie's voice was sharp, and she had staccato meows. For her little self, she was loud when excited or annoyed.

I later found on the website *catster.com* a revelation on the voices of cats and humans.

"Every human has a unique speaking or singing voice, and we can differentiate one person from another by how they sound—*and cats are no different.*"

Susanne Schotz, of the faculty in phonetics in Sweden's Lund University's Centre for Languages and Literature, wrote a book, *The Secret Language of Cats*. She states that cats can imitate their owner's voices and create a private language with them. In eight years of research, Susanne Schotz recorded and analyzed cat vocalizations such as purrs, trills, meows, howls, growls, hisses, and chirps, studying how animals change the shape of their mouths to make different sounds. She discovered there was variety and range of sound in different breeds of cats, both male and female. The variety existed even in the same cat.

Each cat's voice is unique.

An American Aussie

My daily walk to the feeding ground became easier. I brushed and fed my own brood of four at home and had my own breakfast of coffee and cereal.

There was a row of townhouses close to the spot where I fed Tortie. Through my forays to feeding the feral colony, I met the owner of the townhouse, Trip, and his newly adopted dog, Aussie.

Trip was a Bay Area executive who got Aussie from the SPCA'S Hope Program. The program aims to rehabilitate animals that are difficult to place. An Australian cattle dog and husky mix, this animal had been picked up running along a highway by local humane officers. He had no collar tag or microchip. He was young and aggressive and showed all the behaviors of a trained guard dog.

He was magnificent—seventy pounds of muscle in a speckled tan-and-white coat, with the requisite curled husky tail. His elongated face, more elongated than his husky heritage should allow, was set off with intense, piercing dark eyes.

Trip got a new work schedule that kept him away from home for hours. The exuberant two-year-old Aussie needed a dog walker. I grabbed Trip's offer. In exchange for an hour of tending to Aussie during the work week, Trip would cover my feral feeding expenses for a month.

Aussie and I became a well-known sight, he with his blue leash and I in my teal-colored Gore-Tex. We walked many paths through the mounds and hollows of San Mateo together. He was frisky on some days, serious on others. He could be stubborn and a punk, up to tricks when guard dog memories surfaced.

He played mock games that I never taught him. He would attack my ankles and halt me on the sidewalk but never bite. He made wild dashes, almost tearing his leash out of my grip. His strength against mine—I would be dragged like a skateboard behind Aussie. Then he would suddenly stop and smile!

Aussie was an enigma. His feelings for me were inscrutable, yet we had a relationship. The affection was not the same as that between Trip and Aussie. I was the "girl next door" whom Aussie had decided to bring into his world to share his acumen.

Gramercy Drive ran parallel to El Camino Real where the San Mateo hills rose to make the Mounds. The backyards of the homes on Gramercy stretched to join the fence line of my own apartment building. On the way back from walking Aussie, I used to comb the area with my eyes for signs of Toby.

It happened one day. I saw a woman standing on the front porch of a home just off the corner of Gramercy. A small flight of steps led up to the porch. On my part, it was pure instinct. I had to talk to her.

"Do you have any pets?" I asked after introducing myself.

Her name was Marina, she said, and no, she had no pets.

"I have a cat that may have jumped the fence into your yard."

"A cat? We have a small gray cat who comes to sit on our porch chairs at the back. Is she yours?"

Toby! "Does she have a pink collar?"

"I did not see. I can't get too close, and she comes and goes . . ."

Still in the neighborhood and not far from home. I felt like shouting for joy. I did not. Instead, I walked home quietly.

Toby had been gone for three months. Her nails would have grown longer. Perhaps her forays in backyard earth and sidewalks had ground them down. Her ears would need cleaning. She could have tussled her collar off. I would never know.

Inky was near the doorway when I got home. Flyer and Tippy were rollicking in the bedroom and came out to greet me. Janie padded in last.

"Mommy Toby is still in the neighborhood!" I announced and bent to embrace my family.

I recalled the days when Toby was alone, my only housemate. Swollen with kittens in her, she would come to the door.

"Toby, are your kitties here yet?" I would ask in greeting. I was so happy she was mine.

Ben Gets the Best Grooming

Tom, Valerie's son, picked me up at Belmont Station as if I were visiting royalty. As the train pulled onto the platform, I hoisted my shopping bags, slung my purse across my shoulders, and stepped out in search of Tom. There he was, standing by his gray car, tall and smiling. He had Valerie's face and his dad Woody's height. Somehow the moment felt like a reunion.

"Val's doing all right," Tom said. "We got everything in place."

The road to Lesley Terrace took us up a winding incline. This was my first glimpse of Belmont's green hills. The senior living facility was pleasantly formal in the lobby. For the first visit, I had to sign a guest log.

"Take a look at the dining hall before we go up," Tom said.

I looked at the spread of tables with linen and flowers ahead of us. Glass doors on two sides of the hall provided a full view to the gardens.

"Not quite Valerie's little kitchen table," I said. Valerie always used linen tablecloths and real tableware even with microwaved meals.

We took the elevator to the upper floors. Tom and I walked down the hallway, and at Valerie's door, he did not ring the bell. He inserted his key and announced our presence.

Valerie was beaming. I had brought her favorite ginger thins from San Mateo's Trag's Market and cupcakes with vanilla icing. I wanted to remind her of her old neighborhood.

The apartment was sun facing, and the living room had the soft, pleasant hues of the late morning. It was the same furniture, placed a little differently. Predominant was the couch, a portrait of racehorses over it and a large-screen television. Her coffee table had magazines but no ashtray as she did in her old place.

Ben was in the bedroom, sitting on Valerie's bed like Leo, the MGM lion. He was staring out of the wide windows, and he looked content. My voice made him raise his head and look at me with his tawny eyes. I thought I saw recognition. I had a treat in store for him.

I had brought Earthbath foam shampoo with me and a widetooth detangling brush. My grooming kit was well stocked. All I needed were some bath towels from Valerie's bathroom closet.

I carried Ben to the living room couch. We sat together—Valerie, Tom, Ben, and I—and talked about the creatures and familiar scenes of San Mateo and brought the old neighborhood back to life. I had photographs of Inky, Flyer, Tippy, and Janie at play. I even caught a fuzzy focus shot of Tortie in the bushes. She remained the highlight of Valerie's recollections.

Ben lay stretched on a large pink towel and basked in the attention of two of his favorite people. The Maine Coon in him gave his fur a shagginess around the chest. He also had tufts of fur between his toes, and I had often imagined Ben walking on snow. I trimmed some of his paw fur, combed out his tangles, and gave him a waterless bath, with Valerie's hands helping me wipe and fluff his fur back. I remembered not to touch his back closest to his plumed tail.

The large brown ears were furry white on the inside, and Ben's ear cleaning was an exercise in persistence. A cat's ears work a double duty—hearing and an organ of balance. Cats also hear better than dogs and humans.

After a full brushing, Ben looked ready for a portrait. He got his picture taken while sitting on Valerie's lap. We started a tradition for each other on this day.

I came back home feeling content. Valerie had this effect on me.

Art and Disarray – The First Cat Artistry

Tippy was the first of my family to sit up on hind legs. There was no feather or snake teaser in my hand, just Tippy standing tall. He raised his front paws and made brush movements in the air. He looked as if he was blocking out a drawing or painting.

Cat almanacs say that cats stand up on their hind legs when facing a predator. The posture makes them look more intimidating than their size may convey to an attacker—not quite with Tippy. He was just frolicking about by himself.

I had a Matisse reproduction on my living room wall of a reclining woman. Matisse's women always fascinated me, and he was the sole Fauvist I cared to bring home. When Tippy stood tall and made his standalone brushstrokes in the air, I called him Matisse. Oddly, Tippy never approached a surface or bare wall while rendering his paw art. His motions were not erratic. He moved one paw at a time in rhythmic strokes.

I was still working as a bookseller through the years 2007 and 2008. I discovered a book that broke ground on artistic explorations in cats. Burton Silver and Heather Busch were hailed as newsmakers in 1994. *Why Cats Paint* was reviewed as a "seminal work in feline aesthetics which took the animal world and art world by storm." The theories on cat painting or "meow expressionism" were many, but all were rooted in the territorial marking instincts that made cats scrape grooves in earth for physical boundaries.

I never gave Tippy the luxury of paint because of my rental space. Often I was tempted to buy acrylic and upright art boards, but this would involve dipping his paws in color to see the results.

Paw-to-canvas results have been photographed for illustrations in *Why Cats Paint* and the results compared to Jackson Pollock's abstracts. One reviewer sardonically drew parallels to William de Kooning's work—the inverted shapes of abstract expressionism by the Dutch artist. Why inverted? Cats see the world lying on their backs, and hunt-play in this position makes them see reality upside down.

Less aesthetic in appearance are the radiating lines cats draw around their own feces in the wild or in litter boxes. With the earth still on their paws, they repeat the grooves on higher surfaces such as nearby tree trunks. Cat biologists have much to say on the arrowhead and line patterns observed in everyday pawings. Tippy stayed strictly within the realm of "air art" within the cat–human habitat. Whether or not he had a finer vision of color than his siblings, I did not know.

One thing, I did know. Tippy did not render his paw art simply to perform a "biological goal" of his species. Desmond Morris, who observed chimpanzees, had a perspective with which I resonated. Art "can be performed for its own sake." *Once an animal has "survival problems under control and has a surplus of nervous energy," art behavior finds an outlet.*

Janie's distinct pattern of being was lying on her back, paws up in the air—sheer contentment and an inverted world. I remember her days with her infant brothers next to her mother, Toby. The tiny Janie was on her back—the odd one out in the kindle. However, she did not translate her upside-down perception of the world she saw into "pawings." Tippy stayed the artist of the family.

Inky had one quality that might be compared to Vincent Van Gogh. He ran in diagonals and random circles around the home— hot in pursuit of imaginary prey. Van Gogh apparently, much like Inky, could not sit still. When Inky rested, he rested fully stretched on the bed or couch, the length of him from head to tail just under thirty inches.

Flyer was not a splashy fellow. He prowled and watched the birds at the window, and choosing his own leisure spot, he sat with his front legs crossed, lost himself in deep thought.

Pet Sitting and an Outside Pet of Our Own

I continued walking Aussie on weekdays. Within a year, he had grown calmer but graduated to a harness. His strength against my body weight needed more restraint than a neck collar.

Trip had a generous heart. He also had family that visited, and I mingled with them as Aussie's caregiver, celebrating Christmas and sitting at their table at gatherings. Among Trip's unique friends was Mike, who had survived a car crash. His injuries had resulted in a fused spine, through the length of his back to neck, that made him increasingly homebound. Mike refused to move into an assisted living facility and continued to live a solitary life. He was restricted in his mobility, entirely unable to bend and carry weights. He tended to spend time with books and his little black cat, whom he had named Baby. He had eclectic taste in reading and picked up used books from local stores.

Mike had had a string of social workers who visited to make his household chores easier. While I never got to meet any of them, I heard of a glaring shortcoming. Not one of his social workers did pet care as part of their duties. If Mike was unwell, none of Baby's needs—a clean litter box or a refill of food and water—were met. At Trip's request, I filled the gap.

Baby was a long-haired cat, fully black with reddish henna-like streaks around her chin and head. She was not the most amiable of cats and showed her suspicion of humans by disappearing under the bed or into an obscure corner of the living room, unreachable behind furniture. Mike's voice brought her out. She responded to no one else.

On my first cat-sitting assignment, Mike was away in the hospital for a while. I was urged to spend whatever time I could spare with Baby and make sure her bowl of Nine Lives dry food was full and her water bowl replenished. Mike had raised her on Nine Lives and Johnny Cat litter. Those requirements met, Baby expected nothing else.

Not discouraged by the first encounter and Baby's vanishing act, I tried an old trick to get closer. I sat close to her hiding spot and started singing, delving into a medley of songs in a voice suited best for a happy shower. I was beginning to run out of songs and enthusiasm when I saw a pair of green eyes appear from under the wooden credenza at the far wall of the living room. Baby had flattened herself under the credenza and heard my musical renderings, probably with some amusement. She pulled herself out and walked up to me as if she had known me forever.

Music has an effect on animals. Control group studies used to prove the effects of music on lab animals. The laboratory is a selfish ground for speciesism, and music does not make it better, yet I know that lab animals respond to music.

If I were to go by web wisdom, music to cats is just "sound," whether classical, jazz, rock, hip-hop, metal, or rap. However, a study done at the University of Wisconsin–Madison provides proof that cats do respond to music specifically written for them.

"We are not actually replicating cat sounds," said lead investigator Charles Snowdon in 2015. "We are trying to create music with a pitch and tempo that appeals to cats. By playing two specially written 'cat' songs, one based on the tempo of purring and the other on the suckling sound while feeding, researchers found that cats showed more positive responses."

They purr, approach the speaker, and rub themselves against the source of sound. One writer termed this phenomenon "Meow-Sci." This is not to be seen with classical music (Alexandra McNamara, *BBC Science Focus Magazine* (5/3/2019)). The cats in the test did not respond this way to classical music. I broke ground with Baby with my a cappella singing.

The presence of animals brings out the music within me. I used to sing to aggressive and depressed dogs when I volunteered at the SPCA several years ago. In the sick bay at the veterinary clinic, which was a pre-adoption holding for cats, I used to sing a cappella to cats. Before leaving for the night, I left a radio playing soft classical music for the cats. There were no recorded statistics for the recovery rate of cats that went up for adoption, but vet technicians often commented on the speed with which cats were moved to adoption areas after my musical ministrations.

My time with Baby took me away from my own family. One night at home—after hours of delightful play with Inky, Flyer, Tippy, and Janie—I stepped out to the backyard to sneak a cigarette in the semi-darkness. The canopy of trees overhead rustled with invisible nocturnal creatures. If I stayed out too long, I felt guilty. Toby, when she lived with us, was one to make an impatient appearance at the window as if to say, "What are you up to?" One huffy glare from her had me hurrying in.

Janie had taken her place. From the corner of my eye, I saw her silhouette at the bedroom window, which overlooked the yard. My immediate urge was to put the cigarette out and go back inside, but I did not.

My yard had a new visitor. A large black-and-white cat, its tuxedo markings in perfect contrast to the foliage of tree branches, walked into sight on the ledge of the fence. I was in full view of the cat, which did not deter him. He continued the tightrope stride and stopped in front of me, his night eyes staring down at me. He was fearless. To make his presence felt, he let out a full-throated meow and leaped off the fence onto the ground.

Food. He was feral. I needed to feed him. He was going to get Fancy Feast or dry Purina instead of his fresh catch of rodents.

Tuxedo Wakes the Neighborhood

The most remarkable feature about Tuxedo, as I named him, was his voice. Had he been human, he could have held an audience captive with his baritone voice. He was not shy about coming into the yard and letting out a few demanding meows at a time he presumed I was home. If he did not see me appear at the back door, he would sit on the threshold, peering in through the lower glass panel, and wait. While waiting, he would make the darkness resonate with his voice.

I still do not know how he discovered me. I could never explain his familiarity with me. While he did not come near enough for me to reach out and touch him, he would occasionally run rings around my feet and brush against my legs. If cats could talk, he would have given Mel's name as his personal reference.

Tuxedo and Mel were never seen together. Their personalities were in complete contrast. Mel was soft footed, quietly confident with a voice that is a countertenor. My own Flyer at home, Mel's son, had the same voice. Tuxedo was brazen but not aggressive. A certain strength emanated from him as he moved—his girth firm and medium-length hair swept askew from hustles. His lower face and underbelly were stark, unblemished white.

My neighbors across the fence, Don and Vera, both feral cat rescuers, were amused by watching Tuxedo's theatrical entrances into my backyard. The crescendo of meows and the great leap from the fence top became a routine. Why Tuxedo did not follow the feralfriendly path to Don and Vera's patio baffled me.

I started setting Tuxedo's food bowl at the far opposite end of my yard far from the baby raccoons and Marty the skunk. Marty's presence was peaceful, and he seldom left scents behind. Tuxedo only needed to be pointed to the whereabouts of his dinner once. His water bowl stayed filled all day.

He became Uncle Tux to my own family of cats. While Janie usually stayed out of sight, Tuxedo's meows brought her out to the window too. The boys found him a fascinating presence. If he was at the back door and I was playing floor games with teasers and laser lights with my cats, I would extend the game to him through the panels of glass. He would paw the teaser tail or light beam while sitting up on his hind legs—but leaped away if I opened the door even a crack.

Tuxedo could not come in even when cordially invited. If he had, he would have probably had a battle of territories with Inky, a relentless alpha. He was also very possessive about the backyard, but fortunately, Tuxedo only appeared at sundown. Inky ruled the daytime turf.

I asked Tuxedo aloud one night, "Do you know my Toby?"

He answered with a guarded expression.

I fed Tuxedo. I remembered Toby. I suspected fleas on Tuxedo. I thought of Toby. I did not see a clipped ear on Tuxedo. He was unaltered. I felt relieved that Toby was safely spayed. *This is her liberation. No more kittens.*

When I was near Tuxedo, I had an impression of nearness to water and flying birds. This was a recurring motif of a seascape I could not ignore. The feeling reminded me of the shoreline at Coyote Point in San Mateo. Perhaps Tuxedo had broken away from a feral colony in the area, but to get to our hillside, he would have had to walk miles through precarious roads. I would never guess his origins and stopped trying because Tuxedo had found his niche right where he was.

He reminded me of an Emily Dickinson poem:

> I never saw a moor
>
> I never saw the sea
>
> Yet I know how the heather looks

And what a wave must be

I never spoke with God

Nor visited in heaven

Yet certain am I of the spot

As if the chart were given.

I changed Tuxedo's nightly menu to wet food. He cleaned his bowl when he ate. This was not his only meal in a day. Looking at his forepaws and nails, I saw that he was quite capable of catching his own food.

I kept an erratic diary on his movements. Past 2:00 a.m., in late December 2007, I wrote to an absent Tuxedo, "It is raining, Tux. Where would you have been in the drizzle? I wonder where you go during the day."

An Epitaph for Tuxedo

Just before Christmas, while I was wrapping presents for friends and neighbors and preparing for a festive yuletide, Tuxedo met the end of his journey. He was killed in the early hours of dawn in a hit-and-run while crossing West Santa Inez. He was headed to my backyard for his nightly meal.

When I found him in the morning, I heaved his body over my shoulder and carried him indoors. As he lay, I stroked him, and my family of cats hovered around him. He was their Uncle Tux.

Don, Vera, and I drove Tuxedo in a carrier to the North Peninsula Veterinary Hospital, where he was pronounced deceased.

His ashes were scattered at the Bubbling Well Pet Cemetery in Napa. Tuxedo was not just another feral. He had been well loved.

A Notebook for Valerie

I never told Valerie about Tuxedo's passing.

Valerie and I kept our midweek "dates." Wednesday was my day away from the retail world, and I took the bus to Belmont Station as usual. After each visit, when I brushed Ben and filled Valerie's new world with snippets of cat tales, I bought a card from the nearby Hallmark store. I wrote about the old neighborhood with an illustration or two and mailed it to her. These cards were our "notebook" so Valerie did not lose the stream of our time together. I always addressed them to "Valerie and Ben," making her beloved cat part of our todays.

Tortie had begun showing signs of arthritis, and Tiger was thinner with age. New residents had moved into her building, some of them avid cat lovers who had encountered the "outside pets." Their feeding spots had moved from the Seven Oaks fence to a shrubbed back alley a few hundred yards away.

Seven Oaks mansion had finally been sold. I could see Valerie growing frail in health. She lost weight, and her gait was more measured. Her silver hair was still in perfect shape, as if her hairdresser had never left her side. On some days, her initial effervescence at seeing me wore out to disjointed conversation. She lost track of names of people she had known and jumbled the timeline of her experiences. However, Valerie never forgot her days at the Macy's department store.

"I worked, you know," she often said. "My life was not a bed of roses."

I sent Valerie pink roses on her birthday. I could not get away from work to celebrate her eighty-second birthday with her. Belatedly, I visited her with a cake and had her blow out a dozen candles in one breath.

In her old apartment in San Mateo, Valerie would occasionally sing. One of her favorite tunes was a 1950s melody by Eileen Barton— "If I knew you were comin', I'd have baked a cake . . ." She had a deep singing voice, and the Barton song accompanied the cupcakes I had brought Ben on his birthday in San Mateo.

The dining hall at Lesley Terrace was meant to be a place to get acquainted with residents who were open to conversation all through the three-course meals. I joined Valerie for lunch on one visit. For the first time, I saw Valerie's changing temperament. She was withdrawn and irritable with people despite sporting a good appetite. Before I could get too happy with the fact that she did not have to eat alone, I was informed that she sometimes forgot to come downstairs for lunch or dinner and fixed herself a snack in her apartment. Ben was oblivious to the transition in Valerie. She doted on Ben, and he remained her anchor in a home front where she sometimes lost her grip.

The year was 2008, and I remember it as the year in which I read very little. I juggled hard realities, and my enthusiasm for fiction paled. My consumption of a book a week had dwindled to skimming reviews and bringing home bestsellers with good intentions of reading in the backyard. I had stopped going to the library. Author Khaled Hosseini's *A Thousand Splendid Suns* was a new release I did read with the old fire of a fiction reader. The books I did not finish, I donated to Lesley Terrace's in-house library for Valerie's co-residents. Valerie had lost her reading habit too. She also lost her keys—often.

My young cat family encircled me when I was home. I could see sibling bonds grow stronger between Inky and Flyer, while Janie picked Tippy, the gentle one, as her favorite brother.

Given a chance, I would have stayed home and raised cats and forgotten the rest of the world. On second thoughts, I would need the *San Francisco Chronicle* delivered to my doorstep. However, being a stay-at-home cat mom was not in my stars.

Tom, Valerie's son, called one morning before one of my planned visits. It was not good news. Valerie had slipped in her kitchen and broken her hip. The impact of a metal transition strip between the kitchen and living room fractured her pelvic bone. Tom could not predict the length of her hospitalization.

Ben was alone, possibly stressed after the paramedics had left with Valerie on a gurney. I could not enter Lesley Terrace without Tom accompanying me. I suddenly felt inadequate. I could not reach Ben when he most needed a caregiver.

Three weeks later, after anxious phone calls and harrowing hospital news, I insisted I see Ben. Tom had arranged for a caregiver to feed him in Valerie's absence. Despite the reassurance, I felt compelled to visit Ben.

My first sight of Ben in Valerie's empty bedroom was a jolt. He was curled in a corner on the carpet, his face tucked between his paws. Tom picked him up and brought him to the living room couch. I had planned on grooming him, but Ben lay limp next to me, his beautiful fur a mass of tangles. He was thinner. My touch and voice made him raise his head—and I made up my mind that instant.

"He is coming home with me, Tom," I said. "He won't make it on his own."

Tom did not object. He quietly searched for Ben's carrier. I put the grooming paraphernalia away. The bag had room for Ben's dry and wet food and his blue bowl. I emptied the full bowl of food into the kitchen garbage and rinsed it. Ben had stopped eating.

As we loaded Ben onto the back seat of Tom's car, I had a premonition that I would never see this home again. I slipped into the passenger seat, and we drove in silence from Belmont to San Mateo.

Ben entered my apartment in a haze, unaware of his surroundings. As I urged him out of his carrier, Inky was his first curious host. Ben looked around bleakly and slowly walked to the center of the living room. Then he flopped down on the rug. Ben, Valerie's only boy, had broken his isolation. Tom looked on.

I induced verve in my voice. "Come meet Uncle Ben," I urged my cats.

Sensing Tom's presence, Janie did not appear. Flyer and Tippy succumbed to curiosity. Ben expressed no distress. He stayed motionless.

When evening came, I served my cats their dinner of Fancy Feast. Ben refused to eat. He was dehydrated.

I syringe-fed Ben that night—Esbilac to get fluids into him and then pâté mixed with warm water. I made Ben's bed in the living room to keep him away from the romping three-year-olds who had begun to hover around him. I spent most of the night sitting crosslegged by his bed, gently brushing him for comfort. He was fifteen years old and away from the only human he had loved for the first time in his life.

Being Valerie for Ben—and Being Me with My Cats

I never found out how old Ben was when Valerie adopted him. He once had a home before he had been brought to the SPCA. He had been a well-cared-for pet with no emotional or health issues trailing his adoption record. Valerie had not, in recent years, been a person with a knack for organizing paperwork, and I had never gotten around to asking for Ben's veterinary records.

My own vet who had known Inky, Flyer, Tippy, and Janie since birth became Ben's vet, and no eyebrows were raised at the senior foster in the family.

Ben recovered his strength and joined the family meals of Fancy Feast. I was his only familiar element in alien surroundings, and he did not refuse my attention, yet he did not cling to me. He explored nooks of his new home, always returning to his "corner" in the living room to curl up in his bed. This bed once belonged to Toby.

Ben's deliberate lion-like pace was a contrast to his young housemates, who were a galloping herd with furry legs. The backyard was a fascinating place for Ben, with the sparrows, ravens, and squirrels. He had seen very little outdoors, and he lapped up the sunshine as if he were thirsty for light. He was nosing the back door even before I had coffee brewing in the mornings.

Little did I expect a battle of "alpha" males in the months that followed. Inky was undeniably a dominant one in his kindle, and I had known his alpha nature since his kittenhood. I did not suspect the self-contained, serious Ben to be an alpha too. His benevolence with the young ones was enduring as Flyer and Tippy invaded his space to befriend him. Even the shy Janie was captivated by this large relative in her life. They matched coloring, although their markings were distinctly different.

Inky tended to be a troublemaker, finding moments to pester Ben in mock chases and rug wrestling. He had never been territorial, but Ben brought out an odd side in Inky. Ben did not stoop to battling Inky. He just stared Inky down—and if this did not work, he swatted Inky on the head with his right paw. I had seen Toby do that to this boy. Flyer and Tippy never got a swat.

Over the fence, my friendship with Don and Vera grew stronger. They had cared for several older cats, and I trusted their advice on Ben's well-being. Vera would often come to the fence just to look at Ben sitting in a patch of sunshine in the backyard. He was a handsome cat, his tan and white coloring vivid against the green shrubbery. Even without a striking backdrop, Ben was a work of art.

He had his own litter box, his own groomer, his own fan club of young cats, his play-pool in the yard in a blue tub. Ben loved playing with water. People said he had a good life, but someone was missing to make his happiness complete—Valerie.

Valerie's hip mended, but she was not allowed to live at Lesley Terrace anymore. She was transferred to a post-acute care facility where she would live indefinitely. I never got to see Valerie in a wheelchair, and Tom did not encourage me to visit her in this condition. I wanted to call and waited for the day we would have a conversation. I did so want to tell Valerie that Ben was loving the sunshine and the yard and that he was free of fleas. I wanted to say many things but did not know her phone number.

In the effort to keep Valerie's presence alive, I would hold Ben in my lap and talk about Valerie, taking her name in my monologue. Ben was not a vocal cat, but I did occasionally get a meow out of him if he resonated with my stories. Pets know the names of their human companions, an animal communicator once informed me. Ben, having lived alone with his human, seldom heard her name called out loud. Tom called her "Ma" and referred to her as "Val" in conversations. I still persisted with using Valerie's name with Ben at every chance I had.

Leafing through the pages of *The Natural Cat,* the cat lovers' encyclopedia by Anitra Frazier, I culled considerable knowledge on causes of stress in cats. "Stress is a cat's natural enemy." Should Ben have had latent stress for all the changes he had seen, his natural dignity was never shattered. When I noticed hair loss on his pristine white belly, I was upset and perturbed. Was this the impact of psychogenic or physiological stress? Ben was showing signs of alopecia. It was certainly not self-inflicted scratching behavior.

The vet and I ruled out all possibilities of hypersensitivity to food, hyperthyroidism, cutaneous lymphoma, infection, and parasites. Ben groomed himself in a mellow mood—and he certainly was not overgrooming. His Maine Coon breed was not prone to hair loss, yet his luxurious belly hairs kept thinning. On his nose, a bare hairless spot appeared, making the tip look pink. Ben was a baffling case.

When I studied the options of medications for feline psychogenic alopecia (FCA), I had the illusion of being transported to human health, not veterinary pharmacy. Cats with FCA may be administered Diazepam (Valium), phenobarbital, amitriptyline (Elavil), and megestrol acetate, among several other psychotropic drugs. Prescribed alongside, for human caregivers, is a large dose of patience because all medications take two to three weeks to have effect.

I increased my time and physical contact with Ben, holding him longer and sitting by his side when he ate. My attention did not rouse any rivalry in my young family, who now acted as if they had known Uncle Ben all of their lives. I chose not to medicate Ben. If we could not determine the cause of his alopecia, I was not willing to play roulette with pharmaceuticals.

Nine months after Ben came to live with me, Valerie passed away. "Val died this morning," Tom said on the phone.

I could not utter any words of condolence. "May I see her?" I asked.

"I would prefer you didn't. She is not the Valerie you knew."

I did not cry. Emptiness engulfed me. However, there was someone more important who needed to know of Valerie's passing. I walked into the backyard and found Ben, his back turned to me, sitting at his play-pool. With his right paw, he was stroking the water, going *swish, swish, swish!* I picked him up in my arms and brought him indoors.

Still standing in the center of the living room, holding Ben, I said, "Valerie has left us. She has gone, Ben." I said this over and over.

I set him down and sat with him for a while. I had no idea if he understood my words.

The next morning, Ben did something unusual. I usually woke up to the hustle of four cats in my bedroom, all bright eyed and hungry. If I did not wake fast enough, they climbed over me, snuck under my covers, and butted heads on my pillow.

Today I opened my eyes to Ben's voice. He was standing on the floor, close to my head. I looked to see a pair of intense, tawny eyes staring up at me. I sat up and lifted him onto my bed.

Remembrance

Tom and I talked on the phone after Valerie's last rites.

"I have her urn at home," he said.

Tom came by to see Ben, and the recognition in Ben's eyes brought me near tears. Tom sat on the couch with Ben by his side. Suddenly, it seemed like old times.

"Val did not remember anybody in the end," Tom revealed. "I was the only person she recognized."

On the hillside, setting down bowls of food for Tortie and Tiger, I spoke to Valerie's "outside pets" as if they would hear me and comprehend an absence. The news of Valerie's passing was scattered in the wind.

New Toys, New Friends

I would not describe myself as a "cat whisperer," but I can interpret cat moods and facial expressions from having lived alongside them. A treat, a toy, a bird in flight, a fly at the window, a spider on a tree trunk, an object, a movement, an occasion—each brings out a different reaction. The body and face reflect the response.

The brightest expression of excitement is with a toy that moves. Inky got his battery-run mouse as a gift from me on his fourth birthday. The mouse, once set in motion, would run across the hardwood floor, bump into objects, change direction, and run on. Inky, riveted by the toy, ran circles around the home with the speed of a skater, skidding, pouncing, and coming to awkward halts when the mouse did unexpected turns.

I was not being partial to Inky to have gotten him a mobile toy. He would share, I knew. He just had to have the first go at the steel gray robot with flashing red eyes. I got the first laser light with dual beams and catnip throwabouts and scratchers. This was splurging! I posted the birthday announcement on Facebook and made a festive hoopla just for the pleasure of it.

Ben, almost sixteen years old, showed perfunctory curiosity for toys. I knew exactly what would make his eyes light up like a kitten's: cat Greenies. He ate them as I would devour jellybeans.

My newest neighbor was Colleen, who had bought a condominium in the same building in which Valerie lived. She had two male cats and a heart like the ocean for strays. When we met, Colleen was strolling out to catch some sunshine by her poolside, which was surrounded by a scraggy circle of greenery. The residents rarely went for a dip in the pool.

Instead, they lounged, barbecued, caught a good read, and drank a beer or two. Colleen had brought her mat and a book and was planning to settle herself in for a quiet hour.

Colleen and her significant other had cats all their lives. Johnny and Bucky were touching on senior but not quite. For the first time, my own family acquired cherished hand-me-downs from their "cousins" next door. Colleen could not discard toys from Johnny and Bucky's youth. We inherited them.

I discovered that a toy, whether new or handed down, got the same reaction: excitement and fervent play and then disinterest. If I let a toy hibernate out of sight, it became new again.

Poolside leisure was rare for Colleen. Her commutes to work kept her busy through a four-day week. Her presence was a magnet for cats. She began to sight the ferals I fed, and Tortie made jaunty appearances for Colleen's attention. I could not witness this gradual friendship, but it progressed until Colleen had Tortie sitting on her reading mat by the pool. Tortie's limp was not her only distinguishing feature. She had a stubby tail. An accident, an attack, or abuse—we would never know. The tail got her a new name, "Ms. Stubbs." A new chapter to her life had begun.

Rendezvous Café in San Mateo was a tiny restaurant run by a local family. Had it been a bar, the ambiance would be a lot like *Cheers*, the television sitcom. There was Harry, a surrogate Sam Malone, and Nina, an attractive Diane Chambers for a barista. The cappuccinos were good, and the tall glass windows poured light onto the tables. Newspapers, secondhand books, and a community board with posters on the arts and social activism made this my hangout. I brought my guests here when I did not feel like entertaining them at home. Colleen and I made this our meeting place.

We were contemporaries in age. We had both spent years of our lives alone. Our cats were deeply integrated in our daily lives. We both had a love for books. Her degree was in medieval English literature, but her work was flung far from her academic passion. I still worked for a bookstore and had placed my writing career on the back burner.

Colleen was a Chicagoan of Irish heritage. Her journey to California was woven with explorations and adventures. Facing her across the coffee table brought a sense of being kindred, as if I had known her a long time. We talked of things in the present, occasionally coloring our conversations with the canvas of the past.

When we visited each other's homes, it was vital to get to know each other's cats. Both of Colleen's cats were "rescues" from shelters. Bucky was the shy one. A small gray tabby, a thinner version of my Tippy, he rushed off to hide in the closet. Johnny was bushy gray and open to conversation while he held his turf on Colleen's bed. By the window in the bedroom was a magnificent cat tree—tall, threetiered, made from real tree branches. For the first time, I coveted my neighbor's possession: cat furniture.

Colleen impressed my own cat family. I had mentioned in passing that "Auntie Colleen, my friend, will be visiting." I was never sure of being heard.

Her entrance was without fanfare. There she was, dressed in jeans and a summer top, her blonde straight hair down her back. Ben was there. Inky, Flyer, Tippy, and the very private Janie slowly gathered in the living room to check out the visitor. I wished Toby was at home with her grown-up kittens. I had talked endlessly about Toby and her unconventional entry into my life.

Connie Faust wrote a poem, "The Kittens' Tea Party."

> Mama Cat and her kittens
> decided one day
> to have a tea party
> while the folks were away.
> Mama boiled the water
> and made catnip tea
> with sardines and tuna
> (cats love fish, you see).
> They daintily nibbled
> each morsel and crumb
> then washed every whisker,

and when they were done,

Mama poured catnip tea

into each kitten's cup,

and they leaped on the table

and lapped it all up!

We shared coffee in my ceramic mugs, and I do not remember what we munched on (cookies?). We sat on the couch, the cats around us, Ben keeping some distance at first but dropping his guard to sit by Colleen.

Ben was the center of coffee table discussion. He did not mind his belly being looked at and patted. The alopecia did not make him any less handsome. He liked being coddled but, with typical hauteur, would not roll onto his back—no, not Ben.

Flyer and Tippy were in glowing health. Inky showed his extra three pounds. Janie was at the peak of her energy, defying heights, scampering on cats-do-not-touch surfaces, and ripping my Japanese rice paper lamps.

Cats do not protest when humans discuss their litter box habits in the living room. I believe they are secretly flattered. Colleen and I had notes to share.

Janie was coping with four males in the bathroom. I could never give her her own "potty." The language of her impatience with her brothers was simple. She peed outside the litter box. Testosterone in a male cat's urine makes it smell stronger, and not even Glade-scented Tidy Cat can hide the difference. Janie found her own solutions, and I had to invest in pee pads to curb the mess done in protest.

Colleen lived with an arborist who worked for the city of Burlingame. My working knowledge of Northern California trees was cramped by what I could see in the urban landscape. There was a medley of fir, maples, and white birch and a lonely redwood that may have been planted there by an ambitious property owner decades ago. Eucalyptus dominated some of the avenues, and groves of eucalyptus could be seen through San Mateo and Burlingame.

The older trees lining El Camino Real were getting the touch of chainsaws either for widening the road or for some rampant fungus that did not respect our landmarks. I was a literal tree-hugger when it came to bidding farewell to trees. I had personal relationships with the ones I walked by every day.

To Every Season . . .

By fall of 2009, Ben started showing visible signs of arthritis. The backyard was still a point of attraction, but he found a large wicker basket in front of the unlit wood fireplace, his cozy haven. When I sat by Ben and held his head in my palms, I could see his face had grown more childlike. The directness of his gaze stayed, but the arrogance of his youth had gone. Ben was tender.

I had altered Ben's diet to combat his inflammatory bowel disease, which interrupted his good days in the sun. He lost weight. I did not have enough time to experiment with naturopathic remedies. Prednisolone remained his only prescription, which I powdered and administered with water. Ben did not lose his taste for Greenies for treats no matter how rough a day his guts were going through.

I did not get invited out much, but I occasionally had a book date with Helen, a retired professor of philosophy who had moved from Texas to settle in San Mateo. We met at the library to browse shelves and talk about our current reads and bought ourselves coffee and pastries at the café inside. I regaled her with my cat stories, and she brightened my timid social life with tales of her students, whom she had educated in critical thinking with Descartes, Kant, and Hegel.

I had an unusual habit. When I came home, I always told my cats what I had done and what I had talked about with my "outside" friends. Inky was always an impatient listener. Flyer and Tippy hung onto every word. Janie was just happy to have me back home. Ben was amazed I talked so much. He had grown up with the sound of the television and a taciturn human.

He had crossed his sixteenth birthday. At first, his forgetfulness was unnoticeable. Ben was forgetting the location of his food bowl and occasionally searched a corner of the kitchen for his litter box. His playful tolerance of the younger males, even Flyer and Tippy, had lessened. He did not bicker with Inky anymore. Feline cognitive dysfunction (FDS) is the manifestation of an aging brain, akin to symptoms of Alzheimer's in a human. Ben's expression of affection toward me did not change. He also had a benevolent attachment to Janie, who often sat quietly near him with no other expectation but amity.

Halloween was not a big day anymore. I had relegated trick-or-treat to other people's frolic. There were years when I had carved pumpkins and a jack-o'-lantern had adorned my doorstep. That year, the Hallmark cards with arch-backed cats and flying witches did not make the mail. I had a lot on my mind.

Still, Michael, a bookstore customer, decided to propose a movie and dinner without a Halloween motif. We ate burritos at downtown's Tres Amigos and got tickets to see *Amelia,* a Canadian American biographical film on Amelia Earhart.

I relished the evening. Earhart was one of my perennial heroes. I had not eaten Mexican in half a decade, and I had no room for dessert. Beneath the enjoyment was a tug to go back to Ben and family. I seldom left them to tend themselves to seek a social life.

When I returned home, I turned the key to see two pairs of wide eyes staring back—Flyer and Tippy. They rubbed against my legs, and I looked around for the others. In full view of the front door was the dining area, dimly lit by the kitchen light. Ben was sitting quietly on his belly, tail swishing, looking back at me. He did not rise to come to me.

Slipping out of my shoes, I walked up to him. "I thought of you, Ben," I said. "I didn't stay out too long."

I gently lifted him to his feet. He seemed unsteady.

"How about a treat?"

I went to the kitchen cabinet for Greenies. I came back with a few in the palm of my hand. Ben had flopped down again.

He ate the treats, one at a time, until they were all gone. He showed no intention of walking to his basket or bed. Ben was losing strength in his back legs.

Inky and Janie were milling around us, and the presence of their scampering selves was comforting. I lifted Ben in my arms to settle him into his bed and then stopped. *Will he be able to walk to his litter box?*

I carried Ben to the bathroom, set him down, and waited. I did not take him back to his corner bed. Instinct made me place him in the wicker basket. I stroked him until he settled, kissed his forehead, and herded the rest of the family away to give him some quiet.

I had an uneasy sleep. Flyer, Tippy, and Janie curled up in their chosen places on my duvet. Inky stayed in the living room. Ben had company from no one else but his young alpha rival.

Daylight through my bedside window brought bird calls. I awoke before my mechanical alarm. I jackknifed out of bed and moved straight to Ben's basket. He was awake, his eyes wide and expression calm. I touched him. His response was slack.

I lifted Ben out of his basket and set him on the carpet. He sat. He did not rise but looked up at me with the same tender expression I had seen before. Ben usually followed me into the kitchen for breakfast. Today he did not move. His hind legs had lost their strength.

There were four waiting to be fed. Their bowls set, I mixed Ben's pâté in warm water to make a thin gruel and brought it to him. He sniffed the food but did not eat. Around him, Inky, Flyer, Tippy, and Janie burrowed their faces into their food, oblivious of Ben's lack of appetite.

I had a workday ahead of me. Today was a rare day to call out of my shift. I was engulfed in Ben and could not blind myself to the signs of the inevitable.

Sitting by him on the carpet, I brushed him. The white and tan fur on his back was soft and lush. His tail, having lost some of its plumed hair, was not moving in the typical half circles. I checked his mouth and the color of his gums. I knew he was mildly anemic. I saw clean ears and clipped nails. He was still immobile.

I picked Ben up in my arms and headed for the backyard. There were two favorite places where Ben liked to sit. One was a green bush behind the lawn chairs giving him a full view of the trees overhead. I set him down among the fronds, and he narrowed his eyes to the sunshine.

If cats could talk, I would have heard words of frantic worry from the family. There was a tense huddling that reflected a sense of uncertainty, anxiety in the air. Ben was loved. Ben was unwell. I wanted the clock to stand still.

Ben had not moved from his sunshine spot. He could not walk. This reality was undeniable. I picked him up one more time to take him to the shade of a small tree where two fence lines met. Fall leaves made a soft carpet at the roots, and Ben liked to play in nature's rustling rug. I set him on the leaves. He looked content.

Inside, I made two phone calls. First, I called Tom, Valerie's son. If Ben did not live through the day, would Tom like to be with him for the hours we had left? Tom was pained.

"You take care of him," he said softly.

I did. Strangely, I did not feel I was alone.

I called Ben's veterinarian with the brief words that I might have to see her today. There are appointments that are penciled in the book. They can be erased if fate changed its course.

As the morning rolled on, I made the day as normal as possible for Ben—walking in the yard, talking to him, and coaxing him with food another time. By noon, I was sitting on a lawn chair, Ben cradled in my arms like a child, his head resting on the crook of my elbow. He slept. He woke. I sang a melody to him. Valerie and I had sat here six years ago.

Ben slept again, his paws nestled to my chest. I watched him breathe—an hour, maybe more. Ben's breathing was growing shallow. I rose and set his sleeping form on the chair.

Gloria, my building manager, was home. She had gifted Ben blankets, fuzzy mats, and pillows and visited him through the year past. Gloria had a soft spot for Ben.

"Time to take Ben to the vet, Gloria," I said on the phone. "I don't know if I can bring him back without you." Many things remained unspoken.

I said, "See you soon" to the family as if I were headed for a walk in the park. I sounded fake to myself.

I went back to the backyard, closing the door behind me. Ben was still in the chair, awake, his eyes half closed. The breathing was now erratic. I wrapped my mauve scarf around him, picked him up in my arms, and sat down, waiting for Gloria to meet us.

Facing the vet, I placed Ben's drowsy self on the exam table. I felt as if I was ripping the skin off my chest. As Ben lay fully stretched on his side, the doctor looked directly at me.

"He is ready to meet his maker."

Ben did not need the phenobarbital. We nonetheless injected him.

I brought Ben back home and placed him in his favorite basket. I called this his "lying-in state." Before I cremated him, I placed two Greenies in his mouth.

Benjamin Lionheart lived on as a legend in my home. I told the young foursome many stories of their Uncle Ben, and I knew for sure they listened.

For the Love of Toby – Another Exploration

I cherish friends for having had so few in my life of constant change. In recent years, some of the most enduring friendships have come my way through work. A workmate at the bookstore introduced me to Hilary Renaissance, an animal communicator based in Seattle, Washington—and here started a friendship of many moons.

Cats measure time by the waxing and waning of the moon. A year has thirteen full moons. The age of a cat may be counted by the number of moons he or she has seen. This is a legend of the wild.

Toby, my mother cat, was now six years old, having lived seventyeight moons. She had lived outdoors for two years and was thriving as a free feral. I would sometimes stand outdoors at night and call to her as if she were near enough to hear me.

"Tobers, remember we sleep under the same sky."

I started tracking Toby through Hilary's talents. I had been a skeptic of an animal communicator's abilities, but Hilary's persistent work made me dispel my unwillingness to believe in the findings. Legitimate animal communicators work using an intuitive "gift" that science calls extrasensory perception. The exercise involves reaching an animal by communicating with his or her electromagnetic energy.

Hilary asked me to describe Toby. She always needed the name and as detailed as possible a physical description, age, and behavior patterns. Hilary began her "search."

Toby had moved from her settled location on Gramercy Drive to a gated home about a quarter mile away on Ericson Road. The front of the house was covered by a lush creeper with three-lobed leaves. From the sidewalk, the rear fence of the house was visible through a narrow path. The same creeping vine clung to the wood fence, creating a green backdrop. There was no sign of a dog on the premises.

The house was exactly as Hilary had described it in a "conversation" with Toby. Such conversations happened every year, where I could find the whereabouts of Toby through graphic landmarks. I got no clues in street names or numbers but merely visual descriptions of places in the vicinity of my neighborhood.

Toby could describe people she saw—Don, my next-door neighbor, slightly heavy around the gut with a cigarette on his lips, Pilar, the rotund maintenance manager on our premises, a woman of Asian heritage with a toddler child on Gramercy Drive. Marina had sold her home and moved away. Toby narrated her experiences in "images" to Hilary.

Thinking in Pictures

Animals think in pictures, Temple Grandin had said in her book by the title *Thinking in Pictures*. Professor Grandin teaches animal science at Colorado State University and, being autistic, gives insight into a cognitive realm very different from ours.

"I think in pictures. I translate both spoken and written words into full-color movies complete with sound, which run like VCR tapes in my head. When someone speaks to me, his words are instantly translated into pictures."

Animals think in similar ways. They also have emotions and wisdom that they do not share with humans.

My intense curiosity was embedded in the language of animal communicators. How does a versatile communicator like Hilary talk to a cat or dog? How does she ask questions?

Telepathy is a tool that needs no vocalized language. Penelope Smith is reputedly the founder of animal communication. The practice of "talking with animals" started early in her life. Unlike others who are endowed with this extrasensory gift, Penelope did not "shut off" her skills and took on an unusual profession.

In Penelope's Heart School of Animal Communication, telepathy is explained as an "energetic transference of information." "It is the ability to see what is in someone else's mind, to feel their emotional feelings, or to communicate with them mentally without using words or other physical signals." *The root meaning of telepathy is "tele-empathy," distance feeling.* It is a heart-centered exercise and certainly not mind control.

In the year 2010, Hilary and I repeated the efforts to track Toby. In the same neighborhood in San Mateo, Toby was hunting and thriving. She had also found a home with a younger male domestic cat who had a food bowl on his patio. Toby was sharing food as a "visitor."

There were no signs of injuries or illness. Relief was my reaction. I could never stop missing Toby. A sliver of pleasure came through Hilary's "reading." Toby remembered her way back home to me from her new habitat. Toby did not forget. She had also not stopped learning.

I continued the health plan I had started for Toby—just in case she chose to return and in case she needed medical attention. Hilary revealed that Toby was not wearing her collar and her identity tag anymore. Had she torn it off? Perhaps deliberately, in keeping with her feral nature.

Fat Cats, Shelter Seekers, and a Poolside Adoption

I was steadfast in my support of Alley Cat Allies, Becky Robinson's network for feral cats. The organization was a symbol of my deep involvement with ferals and a burgeoning respect for their survivalism.

I also started donating to no-kill causes, and I received a plethora of fundraising letters from national and local animal welfare organizations. The no-kill promise came from the North Shore Animal League of America.

The animals we save come from all over the world. Some are from small overcrowded municipal shelters. We also partner with over two thousand shelters and rescue groups to save even more pets. We rescue animals from puppy mills and from areas ravaged by natural disasters such as hurricanes, tornadoes, flooding, and fires.

I learned about the "nose-to-tail" wellness physicals that rescued animals receive when a shelter is compassionate—heart and lungs, eyes, ears, and nose, teeth and gums, legs, joints and abdomen, gait and stance, skin and coat, weight, and temperature. I had seen the brutal side of shelter life close up less than a decade ago. Now I saw the infusion of change.

Like their mother, Toby, my Inky, Flyer, Tippy, and Janie had Camino Real Pet Clinic in Burlingame for their health maintenance.

When I had a chance to be tongue-in-cheek, I called the clinic an "HMO." The services are on par with human health. The cost of health care is higher than the average Bay Area veterinary clinic, but I wanted my cat family to have the affordable best.

Among the veterinarians who tended to my young cats was Dr. Marilyn Frank, who did their nose-to-tail physicals twice a year. I ritually stood by the exam table, my mind lapping up every word on their development and health needs as if I were in a classroom with my favorite teacher. The visits brought about pride in my cats for how they had advanced. There was also anxiety over small things amiss and relief when I brought them back, each with his or her own agenda for progress.

The rabies shot and certificate were a formality. The combination vaccine FVRCP was a yearly routine. I always refreshed my working knowledge of the distemper vaccine as the vet administered the dose against feline viral rhinotracheitis, calicivirus, and panleukopenia.

Remembering my own stoical tolerance to needles, I watched the expression of each cat. Their reactions were never the same.

Inky was grumpy but mellowed with the presence of the vet and jolly technicians. He liked the touch and enjoyed human voices. He was a large cat and looked particularly endearing when turned onto his back for the physical. The expanse of fur on his belly was a light brown, and he looked like a little sea lion when stretched out. He forgot to be fierce and in charge at the vet's, and his face had the bemusement expression of a kitten. Inky always got "overweight" on his report card.

Flyer was a picture of bafflement. He never remembered visits to the vet, and each visit was a new experience. If he were vocal during the wait in the lobby, he could be easily calmed. His voice, rather high-pitched for a male, always reminded me of his father, Mel, who had left the imprint of his DNA on Flyer in several ways.

Flyer could purr at the vet's, although this was not necessarily at his being overjoyed at the attention. Nonetheless, he was the only one who would step out of his cat carrier without coaxing and step back in with dignity.

Learning anatomy, I found out that vocal "fold" cords in cats have a unique membrane called ventricular cords that are used in purring. This is not found in humans. Cats can rapidly vibrate the ventricular cords without closing the trachea and continue to breathe while purring.

Cats have a hundred different vocalizations. Janie's resentment at being taken to the vet reached the high soprano of Kiri Te Kanawa. The crouching and wide eyes were a pattern, and she had to be cajoled on to the exam table. Once out, Janie was the subject of awe for her cuteness and coloring. Undoubtedly, she was cute. She was also the perfect weight. She also had specific taste in veterinary staff. Dr. Frank could handle her like a familiar relative. She shrank from all else except a senior male tech who had known her since her earliest visit. This was a startling fact because Janie disliked male human presence. She even disliked male human voices.

Tippy was a classic case of "take me home," turning his back on the vet and leaping into my arms. At twelve pounds, he was the lightest of the three brothers. He insisted on staying on my shoulder and being stroked like a kitten until reassured that the vet knew him from many visits before.

This year, for all the details I had memorized of my furry family—personality, mind health, and anatomy—I noticed a mole-like bump on Tippy's neck, a tiny flaw that had grown bigger over months. I insisted on a biopsy. It was just a sebaceous cyst around a gland. I took worry off the checklist.

Back at home, I had good news from Colleen. She had started taking a cat carrier with her to the poolside on her days off. She had succeeded in coaxing Stubbs, the little tortoiseshell cat, into the carrier. Stubbs had stayed indoors with Colleen for a few days. These days could extend to a lifetime as Colleen had made up her mind to adopt Stubbs. Another feral in the neighborhood had crossed the borderline of wild to tame.

Book Lovers' Dilemma – E-Books Enter the Book World

The comfort of the brick-and-mortar bookstore began to crumble in the year 2011. The market was opening its portals to digital media, and e-books began taking their place next to the physical book. Those of us who loved paper began to feel the angst of losing the spirit of bookselling.

I had acquired a small library of books, mostly on animal welfare, before I succumbed to buying an e-reader. Several months passed before I was completely comfortable with opening an e-book and enjoyed the reading experience. In a "new releases" database, we could still see many books that had not yet been published in digital format. The physical book was still the chosen medium of reading among older readers.

One significant acquisition was Nathan Winograd's book *Redemption: The No-Kill Revolution in America*. Winograd, a lawyer, is the director of the No-Kill Advocacy Center and the producer of an award-winning documentary on the history of animal shelters.

Winograd's advocacy strikes at the betrayal of the ethos of animal welfare. Shelters are not a refuge. Shelters kill healthy dogs and cats in consensual killing because of overpopulation. These deaths are "by the thousands or by the tens of thousands" across the United States. Despite sensitization to the no-kill philosophy, four million animals lose their lives every year for the lack of homes.

An animal entering a shelter has a 50 percent chance of survival. Adopting out a few animals and killing the rest, shelters set their methods in animal welfare. This is where shelters lost their way. In a utopian shelter, every animal that enters should have a chance to live no matter the species, age, and treatable condition. Winograd, in a personal commentary in his video "The No-Kill Equation," describes a contrary picture of the fate of animals in "kill shelters." Those animals that do not find homes within a time-bound temporary refuge are gassed, shot, heart-sticked, or lethally injected, their bodies removed for mass cremation in trash bags. Shelter workers become "passive," no longer protesting or responsive to the brutality of policies. I have seen a small segment of this tragedy in my own volunteer experience.

The no-kill equation is a strategy devised by Winograd by which shelters can break away to seek a path to no-kill practices. The steps range from community outreach to involving rescue groups, attracting more fosters and volunteers, off-site adoptions, and creating accessibility through longer shelter hours.

A small part of the no-kill equation addresses feral cats in shelters. Winograd renames the feral as a "community cat" as they have no fixed "human address." Community cats, being unadoptable, are most vulnerable to being killed in an animal shelter. TNR resurges in Winograd's strategy as a life-saving population control practice, and a shelter needs to commit to returning community cats to their original habitat.

Toby, my notorious runaway feral, was now christened a "community cat." She had spent four years on her own in the outdoors. Tiger and Mel still prowled the backyards and hillside. I did not meet any new members of the gray-striped clan that year, but Mel did make a surprise appearance one morning with a gray kitten in tow. He looked like Mel's protégé, about six months old, and I named him Shadow. It was a brief meeting, and I never got to see Shadow appear on his own for a snack. Perhaps Shadow had been taken to other prowling grounds, and I wondered if he had indeed been Mel's own son, part of a larger brood.

Changes Unforeseen

San Mateo was changing. The economic recession that lasted until 2009 had hammered on certain retail sectors. Invisibly, the publishing industry was affected. Booksellers were running at losses, with a very large retailer declaring bankruptcy.

It was the age of the internet. Business commentators looked at the faltering retail trade of bookselling sardonically. "It is a large papercut." It seemed sensible to get away from the bookselling. Ironically, I met my new employer in the children's section of the bookstore, where he was browsing with his little boy.

The industry I was about to enter was a different kind of retail. My employer sold gas *fireplaces!* I sat cross-legged on the rug with Inky, Flyer, Tippy, and Janie around me. It was a semblance of a family conference. The wood burner in the living room had no fire.

"I got another job, guys," I said.

Silence.

"I got a job in the big city. I will be away from home in the mornings."

I believe I caught their attention. I had not gotten around to quite explaining what a "job" was except that it took me away from home. Wages, bills, and taxes were usually not part of our conversation.

Then came another whammy! My apartment building was turning into strictly "no pets," and my landlord made the call himself to get me all shook up. The neighborhood had dwellings with "petfriendly" writ large, but which property would take a family of five with only one human on the lease?

There are days on which I pray fervently. The fervent days had come.

Not So High on the Mountain

My first choice of a place for us was a duplex with a small backyard. The street was parallel to the main thoroughfare of El Camino Real, secluded from the traffic. My skills at presenting myself to a rental agent were rusty for having lived in the same abode for a decade. Nonetheless, I coped with the paperwork, stating that I would have a multiple-cat household. The duplex had just been remodeled, and my hopes of an easy move seemed reachable.

This did not happen. Quite alone, I continued to look further, with the deadline for the move growing closer. I talked to my cats, shrouding my tension in a joviality I did not feel.

"We are going to move up to the mountain," I said.

I did not hear anyone say, "Which mountain?"

I packed my books and kitchenware in boxes from the liquor store. More cardboard boxes came from the bookstore. The closets were emptied out, and the rugs were rolled up. The potted plants were in a cluster in the backyard, and I would have to take down the squirrel feeder someday later. I was hurting to leave. I still did not know where I would be going.

The classifieds were disheartening. Quite by fluke, I saw a vacancy sign on a low-rise apartment building a few blocks south of where I lived. Next to it was a scruffy path through which I walked to feed Stubbs when she lived outdoors. The building was strangely familiar.

I went in with no expectation of a grand reception. The place did not allow pets.

An idea that had been slumbering in me came alive when I walked into the rental office. *What if I had the cats listed as emotional support animals? I might get a foot in the door.*

Within the next three days, I had found a new home. The apartment overlooked the incline of the San Mateo mounds with a view of treetops and a vast glimpse of the sky—nothing ritzy. It had the feeling of a Soho loft with a tiny kitchen and a strip of a balcony.

The venture of moving my mishmash collection of furniture was not daunting. Having Inky, Flyer, Tippy, and Janie transform into indoor cats made my brows furrow. Some of the furrows are still there.

Love Thy Neighbor as Thyself

"Don't leave your cats behind," my landlord said on his last phone call.

Not funny, I thought. He had given me the option of staying on if I gave my cats up to the shelter. I was not up for any such charity.

There were my neighbors, Don and Vera, who were crestfallen at the news of my moving. Our friendship had grown stronger through hard times and shared joys. Mel's passing and the ritual of saying farewell to our gray-striped friend had brought us even closer.

I talked to my cats. Mel's living family, my cats, were told of their father's passing. They had only known Mel as a visitor in the yard, his voice at the window being a greeting to his kin indoors. Only once had Mel ventured into my home through the open back door. He jauntily walked down the hallway into the bedroom, where the family was gathered.

Mel stood very still and watched the young cats. I had very quietly closed the back door in the meantime. When Mel was ready to make an exit, he balked at the closed door. He backed several feet, made a lightning run, and crashed out, breaking the lowest glass panel with his body weight and head—a true feral. He could have waited a moment for me to let him out.

Mel died months later of a cardiac arrest. He was likely sixteen years old. With most community cats, their diseases go undiagnosed. I found him in full view of Don's balcony and carried our hefty warrior in my arms up the stairs to his favorite humans. I stood witness at Mel's cremation.

Vera stepped away in quiet grief. "He was like a child to us."

Mel took all my songs and poetry with him.

Don, with his handy toolkit and mechanical prowess, came over to help me undo curtain rods, take down pictures, and cover every hole and scratch with plaster. The only damage Don could not repair were little patches of stain on the hardwood floor under the dinette table. We saw them only after my handmade rug from Afghanistan was stripped.

"Cat pee," Don said.

Kitten pee was more like it. The stains had happened a long time ago, with color running from the dyes of the rug. I could now anticipate a squabble over my security deposit with my landlord.

Colleen and her partner, Sean, kept me glued together for the rest of the move. I donated all the plants I could not carry with me to the Burlingame city nursery.

My Ikea furniture was an easy fit in Sean's pickup truck, and after five trips up to the new place, I said, "Tell me how much I need to pay you."

"How about a cup of coffee?" was the reply.

Colleen and I put the finishing touches to the kitchen cleanup. I was teary-eyed with the memories of a decade that hovered around the kitchen—first Sam, the great orange cat from next door, Charlie from across the street, and Toby, the backyard guest who loved the corner bench for her meals. Her food bowl and kitty grass marked her spot long after she had left her human nest. Then there had been Ben.

Inky, Flyer, Tippy, and Janie spent perplexed days with their familiar surroundings in disarray. Delightful moments happened during the time I packed books. Paper and cardboard boxes meant fun. They began their own games of hide-and-scuffle, sometimes refusing to come out of their cardboard hideouts until the wee hours of the morning.

I remembered my early days here with Sam. He kept me company when I unpacked my boxes in the year 2000. He played his own game with half-empty boxes and forgot about going home on time.

In the transition between the old and new abodes, I settled most of the furniture in place and unpacked as much as I could before bringing the furry family over. I had three carriers. I coaxed Tippy and Janie together into the largest one. Inky and Flyer were carried solo. They all knew this was not a typical vet's visit. They did get time to say goodbye to the squirrels. The pickup truck took us all to the apartment by the hillside. I had Sean for a comrade on the elevator ride up to the third floor.

When I opened the carriers to let the cats into their new home, I saw consternation, not curiosity. I was told that cats are territorial. Taking them to an unfamiliar turf was no joyride for them. There was caution in every step they took on the carpeted floor. They looked like tightrope walkers who had just landed on terra firma. Not a meow was heard.

I said my goodbyes to Sean and turned around to seek the cats. They were nowhere to be seen—not in the living room, not in the bedroom. I passed the short hallway to the bathroom. There they were!

The huddle of four cats said many things. They stood pressed to the side of the bathtub, the white ceramic a wall of safety. Janie was in the middle. Her brothers were around her in a circle, their sturdy striped bodies protecting her from all that might come. They were all wide-eyed. No sound was uttered.

Welcome home, I thought. I said nothing aloud. Any sound would have shattered the moment.

Inky Takes Charge as San Francisco Beckons

There had never been a "man of the house" in recent years. Eons ago, I had been married. When I parted with my partner, we promised to stay friends. In the years of being single, I had taken all matters of everyday life on the stride as a "sole" decision maker. There was the friendly counsel of friends, but I did most things as I thought fit and lived by the rules of common sense. Now with the commute to San Francisco looming, I would be leaving my family in a new home for ten hours a day with no cat-friendly neighbor within reach.

I learned to read Inky's initiative after I started work in the fireplace showroom. I sometimes carpooled with the boss if he was passing by. On some days, I took the commuter train to San Francisco. The end of the Caltrain route on Fourth and King Streets did not bring me close enough to the workplace. I had to transfer to a bus to reach work. The way back to San Mateo was the same transit route in the reverse.

In my mind was the family at home whom I could not call to ask, "How are things going?" My new iPhone did not lend itself to such wonders. The wonder, however, was the adaptability of the cats to my new routine. Coming home, I found the foursome upbeat and playful, the boys meeting me at the door and Janie peeking out of the bedroom to make sure it was really me making an entrance.

Inky was a stabilizer. Whether or not he asserted his alpha personality is a conjecture. He nonetheless kept his siblings in a mindset of normalcy. If Janie felt him to be overbearing, she did not speak up. There were no chases or hissy spats between the two in the evening. Her temperament, belying her very dainty appearance, was spunky. Janie could handle life with her three brothers without losing her place.

I loved each one of them in a relationship unique to their personalities. Janie always had a lofty place as my "only little girl cat." Sometimes I pondered how the family dynamics would have been had Toby given birth to more females. Well, she did what she did. She gave me three burly toms and a princess.

At work, while I was immersed in fireplace technology and aesthetics in the most contemporary setting, Toby was an icon in my thoughts. My own relic of the wood burner had been a shrine of rescue with memories of Toby's escapade up the chimney. Now I discovered that wood burners were illegal in San Francisco because of their impact on the quality of air.

Contemporary fireplaces were fueled by gas or electricity—a domain of Pacific Gas and Electric. Glass, faux brick, faux logs, and decorative configurations of media for the fire basket brought an interior decor's dream to life. I was no designer but worked with those who could both imagine and sell home accessories.

Having never owned a home, I found the intensity of homebuilders and architects captivating. A crash course in construction lasted a month and included a glossary in fireplace terminology. Contractors are a tribe distinctive in their trade. Applied knowledge, multitasking, and deadlines given, the profession is quite dramatic.

Within a year, my office enclosure moved from the shared inside space to the front of the showroom. Sitting at a desk was novel after the time I had spent on the bookselling floor. The backdrop of my desk was a Mendota gas fireplace with a Zen sand garden in the interior and a streamlined sandstone mantel. To my left was the lifesize portrait of a dog sitting in front of a fireplace.

The scene was a welcome to homeowners. The phone rang often, and the day passed quickly. When the hustle of business peaked, I could break off for lunch and take a walk along the sandy paths of the San Francisco Bay shoreline. The waterfront had inlets and grassy patches with the full view of mercantile ships at a close horizon. If I got a ride to the big city with the boss and arrived early, I could catch the reddened sky of a bay sunrise.

I did not have a joyous beginning to 2012. My neighbor Trip was making plans to move to New York State. Aussie, his dog, whom I still walked intermittently, would be leaving with him. I could not imagine the neighborhood without Aussie, who had woven his personality and presence indelibly into my life.

At San Mateo's Central Park, I stood by and watched Aussie make runs with the frisbee I had bought him. He looked supremely happy, chasing the arc of the blue disk, quite oblivious that he would be living in Brooklyn soon.

When I said goodbye to him at San Francisco's airport, my prior attempts at practicing the farewell before the event fell to pieces. I just knelt by his carrier and held him as if he were my own.

Aussie and Trip headed off to live in Brooklyn. He would have another park, a hearth to call his own, and walks on different streets with brownstone buildings. The Aussie did not have another neighborhood dog walker. My "punk" dog had me for "one of a kind" and the only one who allowed him to playfully rip the sleeve off my Gore-Tex jacket.

I did care for a Doberman pup named Harley after Aussie left for Brooklyn. My friendship with the rambunctious Dobie was poignant. His young pet parent, though passionately involved in the life of his pedigree dog, was a bacchanal. Before allowing himself to go into detox, he rehomed Harley with people who were ready to adopt after their senior dog had passed.

My own parting with Harley happened in front of the new family. Harley, an expressive and affectionate dog, was entirely silent as I knelt at this side, arms around him. He seemed to give his consent to be moved to another home. I felt a sense of relief in Harley. His gait as he leaped into the cabin of the family vehicle was an exuberant one. He did not look back.

Emotional Support – A Spontaneous Act

My family of cats, born of feral parents, were born with an instinct for bonding, not merely among themselves but with the human who lived with them. Their "training" was not formal, but they were certified as emotional support animals in my home.

The first to display sensitivity to my health and moods were Tippy and Inky. Flyer, who tended to be passive in the face of his brothers, had quiet observational skills and picked up on stress and distress through my physical movements. Janie did not team up with the boys. Her compassion was expressed through physical proximity with me, lending her presence unasked.

For the first time, in a span of thirteen years, I was diagnosed with hypertension and went through my first hospitalization. Medication aside, the physical presence of my cat family was therapeutic. Tippy, resting on my chest, with his paws on my torso, was most endearing.

The Northern California chills brought out my latent asthma. On a difficult night, when my albuterol inhaler did not work its miracles, I stood leaning on the kitchen counter to stabilize my breathing. I was beginning to sound like a set of broken bellows when I was faced with Inky, Flyer, and Tippy sitting upright in front of me.

Their faces were intent. As I struggled to get rhythm back in my breath, they sat motionless. Every breath was an encouragement. I recall about ten minutes of effort when nothing was heard except my whistling breath in the stillness. I recovered sufficiently to get albuterol into my lungs. Night was a blur. I slept with my cats gathered close to me in a shallow slumber.

Years later, I became aware of a registry and support organization, U.S. Service Animals. Registering both cats and dogs as "ESA"—emotional support animals—brings them into the bracket of service animals. I do not dabble in "what if" and "what might have been" scenarios of housing, but I am certain that an early ESA registration may have spared me arguments made in my cats' defense. Mostly, the registration would have spared me an untimely move.

Juggling Tasks and Realities

I continued working at the fireplace showroom in San Francisco. The year 2013 was not without novelty in my workplace. I had to grasp within tight deadlines a new business software, NetSuite. My desk turned almost paperless. I sometimes pondered about becoming a salesperson on the showroom floor but never quite discussed the idea with my manager over coffee. We sipped Starbucks lattes at least once a week as a bonus for good teamwork. Our general manager was generous in his spontaneous acts of appreciation.

Outside the peak hours of sales, the fireplace showroom was a serene splendor. With each model fireplace lit, the flickering gas flames of a dozen installed units created a temple-like ambiance.

This was a rare workplace where I had to be cajoled to take a break. I did step out to smoke an occasional Benson & Hedges, which had lingered as a habit. The view was green. A native California plant nursery occupied one half of the land across the road. The other half was an open field where a trip of goats grazed. They belonged to a rent-a-goat collective.

I came home in a good mood. The family met me at the door. A fond greeting aside, they wanted a brief escape to roam the hallway. I was never a gourmet, and my own dinner was spun out of random shopping. Nonetheless, I could dish up something nutritious and aesthetic for myself. Inky liked to park himself on my wooden cutting board when it did not smell of onions. He was a kitchen Buddha like his brother Tippy. The cutting board took a lot of scrubbing.

Christmas 2013 was spent at a corporate party. I was invited to bring a guest or family.

"I have four cats," I said in the RSVP.

"Bring them!" came the response. "We bring our dogs to the gathering."

It so happened that my family stayed home. So did my boss's dogs. However, the hearths of lit fireplaces brought the season to life.

The year-end to-do list had one incomplete item. I had made time to browse John Bradshaw's *Cat Sense: How the New Feline Science Can Make You a Better Friend to Your Pet*. I did not finish the book.

"You Should Work at a Pet Store . . ."

My neighbor Valerie used to tell me when I visited, "You should work in a pet store." The words stayed in my mind even after Valerie's passing.

No pet store attracted me as a workplace, particularly those that sold hamsters and birds. However, when Michael Levy and Mark Vitriol gained local fame for starting Pet Food Express, retailers of holistic and organic food products for animals, my interest in the company surfaced. The owners gained further repute for partnering with 250 shelters and rescue ventures and for donating almost $1 million a year to animal-centered charities.

The nearest store location of Pet Food Express was in Burlingame within walking distance of my home in San Mateo. The store had a solar-powered self-service bath facility with fresh towels for pets. New product lines and over-the-counter remedies had a versatile retail team to encourage trials and sales. An array of human-grade products could be found for pet nutrition. If a pet did not like a product, there were no-fuss returns. This was an evolved retail scenario where I felt I wanted to belong. Inky's favorite Tiki Cat Ahi Tuna came from the shelves of Pet Food Express. Organic catnip, flaked fish treats, aloeand green tea–scented wipes—shopping was an elevated experience.

My first job application to Pet Food Express got an instant response. I was excited. I planned a day in San Francisco to meet a district manager and put my best paw forward. The interview lasted an hour and was one of the most enjoyable conversations I have had with a prospective employer.

Soon after, I was called for a store-level interview with the Burlingame manager. In familiar surroundings, with a familiar face, the interaction was like a coffee chat between friends. As a pet parent to four cats and a regular customer, I believed the job would be mine with no hurdles.

The blot on the hiring horizon was a sales partner who changed his mind on a transfer. The opening for hire vanished, and my pet store prospect went into limbo.

I tried again, twice over. Each time, the location was far out of my commuting boundaries. When I returned to my favorite store as a customer, I had an old sentiment in mind. I wish I could work where I shopped. So did the store staff who knew me well.

"Good Morning, World"

January 2014 crept in without a drumroll. We were adults in the workplace, and none complained of a hangover. I never had a Christmas tree to recycle. I put away the greeting cards that had come from friends and noticed with some irony that Ingrid Newkirk of PETA and Becky Robinson of Alley Cat Allies had put me on their season's mailing list.

I was on the Caltrain San Francisco at 6:30 a.m. on January 11 and had a window seat in a full car. My mind was occupied with Inky taking on his big brother duties and Janie being sassy with him. Flyer and Tippy usually stretched out after an early breakfast and kept themselves amused.

I browsed my iPhone for emails and Facebook stories as an alternative to watching the speeding scenery. On Facebook's notifications page, one post leaped out at me.

"Anna Bellin is no longer with us. She passed away yesterday of pneumonia."

Anna, my friend for five years—animal rights activist and rescuer, artist, and poet—was dead. Everything around me faded to an icy haze. I stopped feeling the motion of the train and was the last to leave the compartment when we pulled into the terminal. I spent the rest of the workday thinking of her.

Anna had a cat named Bella. Although Anna and I never met, our closeness was real, not a flimsy shimmer of pokes and posts on Facebook. She was in Los Angeles and connected with me, with us often discussing animal rescue, the state of the world, God, our own state of being. I had nothing artistic to show. Anna had her canvases, which she did not flaunt. I snuck a peek at her work outside our conversations. True, she did paint like Jackson Pollock, but there was more than form and color in her work. Anna's paintings carried a story from her life.

Anna was well connected with many friends; five thousand of them were people and groups on Facebook who were ardent animal lovers and rescuers. I was one among them. In the outpouring of grief and dismay, I could only write a few lines to express my loss.

I would miss her daily greeting when she embraced all her friends— "Good morning, world!" I would miss her encouragement when I expressed my feelings of not being able to do enough in animal welfare. I felt I was walking a lonely path in a tiny part of the world.

Anna replied, "The next time you feel this way, imagine me walking by your side, holding your hand."

Going back to messages from the year before, I found Anna's note:

Hey, my beautiful sis, just wanted you to know that I smile everytime I see your name & pretty pic on my wall; u have that 'effect' on me & it's so sweet...hope ur smiling today, my darlin.

The next week, I got off the train at the San Mateo station and started a brisk walk home. I was late feeding the family. Passing a corner store, I stopped to pick up a few grocery basics. One more set of lights, and I would cross the street to reach home.

Darkness fell early in January. El Camino was a swirl of headlights and homebound traffic. I was halfway into the crosswalk when I was knocked off balance. My view of the road suddenly became a worm's eye view. I had felt a blunt thrust, more like a shove, on the left side of my body. What had struck me was the side of a car moving slowly at a left turn.

I was lying on my side on the road, pain shooting through my right hip. I looked up and saw a fashionable woman in a short fur jacket stepping out of a BMW convertible. She was a picture out of Vogue. Pain had not muted me. Behind me, the headlights of stalled cars told me I had to keep my disgruntlement brief.

"Why did you do this to me?" I asked blandly as the Vogue lady helped me to my feet.

She did not answer but led me with my hobble to the passenger seat. She closed the door, got in herself, and hurriedly completed her left turn. Had the lights turned green? Perhaps because all the stalled cars were zipping by.

"I can drive you to the hospital. I have insurance. Don't worry." The voice had a slight accent.

"I need to feed my cats," I said. "I need to get home." I put the seat belt on. My right hip twinged in discomfort. The sharp pain had subsided.

"Are you sure?"

"Maybe you can drive me to the pharmacy for some painkillers. I have to go to work tomorrow."

The woman looked incredulous. "Which pharmacy?" She was not a San Mateo resident.

"Walgreens on Third Avenue. I'll give you directions."

We drove in complete silence. When we reached the parking lot of Walgreens, she took her keys out of the engine.

"What painkiller do you want?"

"A tube of Bengay will do," I replied.

The car doors clicked to lock. I was in a capsule of luxury inside the BMW. Sitting still, I felt no pain at all. One thought surfaced again. *I have to feed my cats. I am late for dinner.*

Good Samaritans
and a Bend in Time

Bengay and receipt in hand, the woman returned. I felt no animosity toward her. She was somebody who had made a trivial traffic miscalculation. She was making amends.

I was driven to my door. As fate prescribed, my neighbors from the apartment across got out of their vehicle. D'Marcus was an academic. He was a kinesiologist. His fiancée, Tomisha, worked for the SamTrans, the city's transit authority. I hobbled out and thanked the driver of the culprit BMW for bringing me home.

"I hope you will be all right. You have my phone number," she said before she drove off.

Facing the elevator, I shifted my balance to my left leg. My right leg felt wobbly—still no pain. By the time we reached the third floor, I began to feel a twinge. Five steps out of the elevator, D'Marcus and Tomisha took over as human crutches just so I did not strain myself.

"Can you tell a fracture by touch?" I asked D'Marcus.

"No. You are going to need an X-ray."

I convinced myself as I unlocked my apartment door that this was a sprain or a shade worse, a pinched nerve. I turned on the light. Three cats greeted me at the door. Janie was a shadow at the back. I shrugged my jacket off, slung the purse over a chair, and walked to the kitchen.

The pain hit me. I sank to the carpet. As I sat, the cats milled around me. I stroked them.

I remembered why I had hurried home. *Dinnertime.* I rose. My walk to the kitchen changed from a hobble to a crawl. I reached the Fancy Feast cans in a haze. I opened two and split them into four bowls. I placed the bowls on the kitchen floor within easy reach.

I returned to the living room and flopped back onto the carpet. Something made me avoid a chair. Perhaps I needed to be near the cats. Again, I felt the furry bodies around me but had no awareness of who was where. Janie was near. Inky was close against my thigh. Flyer and Tippy were a blur.

I groped for my cell phone. I had to report the incident. The pain was a warning. At the other end of the nonemergency San Mateo police line was a woman. The officer took down a shorthand account of the incident at the corner of North El Camino and Tilton Avenue in San Mateo.

At the end of the report, she asked, "How are you feeling?"

"I am okay. There is some pain on the right side where I fell."

"You are at home. Where exactly are you?"

"In the living room."

"Where in the living room?"

"Sitting on the carpet."

"Can you rise and walk?"

"No."

"I am calling an ambulance."

"I don't need an ambulance."

"I insist. I am calling an ambulance." The officer brooked no argument.

The police and paramedics arrived—no fire squad. I was spared the embarrassment.

I opened the door and descended to the floor again. Janie had scurried to the unlit bedroom. The three boys were sitting upright beside me. They were lined up as if in a military drill. Inky, Tippy, and

Flyer had their faces upturned, eyes fixed on the EMT.

The EMT towered over me in silence as the officer took my report. He then asked quietly, "Do you have health insurance?"

"Kaiser," I said.

"Where would you like to go? South San Francisco or Redwood City?"

"Redwood City," I said.

Inky, Tippy, and Flyer had not moved. Their stillness amazed me. The EMT was staring at the cats, bemused.

"My emotional support animals," I said. "I trained them myself."

A second paramedic was wheeling in a gurney through the open door.

"Is there anything you need before we leave?"

I looked at the cats. "Guys," I said, addressing Inky, Tipper, and Flyer, "I will be all right. Go in."

All three cats rose in unison and slowly walked into the bedroom.

"I need a jacket and my slippers from the closet."

The very tall EMT walked down the hallway and opened the mirrored closet door. The blue Gore-Tex was easy to find. The slippers needed some searching.

"One more favor," I said. "Will you please take the cat food from the kitchen and place the bowls in the bedroom?"

He did this solemnly.

I was being lifted onto the gurney when I said goodbye to my cats. "Back soon," I said.

I wondered what Janie was doing at that moment—most likely huddling under the bed, wide-eyed and nervous. She disliked strangers.

Housekeys, purse, and a bag of bare essentials—I was surprised, being wheeled out of my home. I did not like leaving the family alone. Inside the ambulance, my thoughts filtered the names of neighbors who could help with the cats.

Colleen. I could not reach my cell phone. I was strapped in, and my purse was out of reach.

One Leg, Four Cats, and a Walker

Not a sprain, not a pinched nerve—the X-ray showed a broken right femur. The ball of the thigh bone, the femoral head, had broken off in the fall. I was a candidate for major surgery.

The pale blue hospital gown had replaced my jeans and sweater. I lay in my hospital bed wondering if I could escape by climbing out of the balcony. I wanted to go home to the cats.

The ceiling above me was very bland. I imagined the faces of Inky, Tippy, Flyer, and Janie. Before sleep came, I made two calls— Colleen first to look in on the family and feed them, my office manager next with the dismaying news that I would be disabled for two months.

I met my orthopedic surgeon the next morning. Dr. Jonathan Lam was a person of quiet humor. He faced a patient who wanted it all done and wrapped up in a day. I was in a hurry.

"It takes forty-four days for the fracture to heal."

"Forty-four days? Why so long?"

"That is how long it takes. You are disabled for this time."

I was horrified. "What are you going to do?"

"I am going to make an incision and join the bone with three screws."

"No cast?"

"No cast."

This news had me almost dancing. "Are you using a scalpel?"

"No. I use a laser."

"No scar?" Not that I cared for a blemishless upper leg—I was fascinated by laser surgery. I suddenly realized that I was in a very interesting place. I had lost track of how far medicine had progressed. "Dr. Lam, why do you think this happened? The fracture? Is it because I am an osteoporotic hag?"

"No, no, no!" Dr. Lam was holding back laughter. "You are young."

Not so young, I thought, but I felt relieved. I was fifty-four years old. "May I please smoke a cigarette? I need one today."

"You can't." Dr. Lam broke into laughter. "You are at Kaiser."

I remember the anesthesiologist introducing himself before the surgical procedure began. In the hazy phase that followed, my distinct recollection was the faces of my cats and Dr. Lam's eyes. The rest of his face was covered with a mask. Then there was deep darkness.

Five days in the hospital—my impaired self, managed by blueclad humans, was a measure of unreal time. I was eager for discharge and afraid of what lay ahead. I could handle segments of each day with clarity. The other parts, I was thankful for sleep, which came with a painless needle. The ceiling changed from white to cat faces again. I shifted to soothing art and imagined Van Gogh's *Starry Nights*.

I ignored the television. I quibbled with the dietitian when I was served pork for breakfast. I thrived on orange juice and eggs. I wondered what Colleen was feeding the cats at home when there was no need for wonder. The foursome were being well tended.

When asked to step out of bed and try out a pair of crutches, I did so obediently. My right leg screamed as I stretched it. I quickly curled it off the floor like a flamingo. The kimono gown was still tied, knots in front.

I remember the walk well. I handled the metal crutches like a person using chopsticks for the first time. The two long hospital hallways had commissioned abstract art. They matched the fabric of the seats along the hallways. At the end of the exercise, I was fitted with durable medical equipment (DME), which, for me, was a fourwheeled foldable walker.

On the fourth day of my stay, I had a visitor: Penny, a therapy dog. The Golden Retriever was a Kaiser favorite who came from the Peninsula Humane Society, a San Mateo SPCA. Gratitude is a tangible emotion. I felt it flow as Penny jumped onto my bed and parked herself over my good leg. The contact made me come alive. I stroked Penny's head. I thought she smiled. Perhaps therapy for humans came from smiling dogs who do not talk.

I still had human friends. One of them, Jaime, drove me home after discharge. Before I got home, I had a request for my kind chauffeur. May I stop for a Starbucks latte and a cigarette? We stopped at the Starbucks at the crossroads of Peninsula Avenue and Delaware Street in San Mateo. The taste of good coffee and a cigarette felt good. I would not have this pleasure again in a long while. My DME lay folded in the trunk of the car.

Housebound and Healing with Cats

"I'm back," I announced at the doorway as I moved over the threshold with my walker. I felt as if I had been away for a very long time.

There they were, my three boys, alert and bright-eyed in the semi-darkness of the living room. I turned on the light switch nearest to me. The hallway flooded with light, and I saw Janie standing still, her eyes curious and wary. There was a visitor behind me. My friend and chauffeur had brought me to the apartment to make sure I could wheel myself freely through my living space.

I had the urge to sink down onto the carpet to hug Inky, Flyer, and Tippy, but I chose a chair instead. I kept talking to them in my normal voice, words of reassurance that I was here to stay. I would thank my neighbor Colleen once I had learned to reach for my family on one leg and learned to sleep with a broken hip.

Jaime puttered around on his own while I sat with the brood. He moved aside a small table on the narrow hallway leading to the bedroom.

"Your walker will not go through," he said quietly. He did not wait to be thanked. He left me in the midst of my cat family and shut the front door on his way out.

There was food in the fridge and in the cabinets. Colleen had been her usual thoughtful self. As I navigated my way over the carpet, the little wheels of the walker dragged. Inky walked beside me, leaving the others behind in the living room. The walker was a giant adversary. He swatted at the lower frame a few times and then ran ahead to confront it. Facing the walker headlong, he seemed to lose his animosity. It was just a metal contraption that made up for one disabled leg. Inky seemed to make up his mind to live with it as long as I was a one-legged human.

I sensed bafflement among the others. None had ever seen me in pain or impaired. The family was composed of little furry "people" with skills of their own species. Their instinct told them I was not in full form. I did not foresee that they would extend themselves to participate in my rehabilitation.

There are moments when the gestures of friends make indelible impressions on the mind. The cat bowls were full of dry food. Colleen had kept up a free-feeding household. Dinner had happened before I had arrived. My slow walk to the bathroom brought into sight clean litter boxes. I would figure out a way to scoop litter with a walker the next day.

I liked the huddle of cats around me when I settled into bed that night. Under the watchful eyes of Janie and Tippy, I folded the walker and placed it against the wall. Where were Inky and Flyer? I could not rush out to see. They were up to nightly games in the living room, quite content with the fact that I was home. I took my socks off in slow motion, sitting on the edge of the bed. My right foot was hard to reach, with my hip still sore from Dr. Lam's repairs.

Getting into pajamas was a contortionist's maneuver. Seated, I bent my body into a "U," hands holding pajamas, reaching my feet to bunch the legs in. After, I did not need hospital instructions to remember how to lie straight on my back. The body had developed its own chimes for comfort and discomfort. The light lamp could be reached with a dignified hobble. I turned it off and called out a familiar "good night."

"Come on, guys. I am off to sleep."

The bed was wide enough for all five of us. Tippy settled on a pillow closest to my head, Janie lower down beside him. Flyer jumped from the ledge of the bed and placed himself near my feet. Inky did half circles around us, stopping near my head to peer at me. He then headed for his basket, which was his alone, and curled himself in. I forgot to set the alarm. There was no need to wake up by anybody's clock except for the morning call for Fancy Feast. Even that had become flexible in my absence.

I awoke to sunlight through the window, and the California winter treetops were visible against a very blue sky. It was midJanuary, and there would be no rain today. There was no scramble for breakfast, and a calmness was visible in the cats.

I climbed out of bed without a nurse by my side. During the night, I had turned on my "good side" and felt no cramping soreness. I reached for the walker, and it was standing where I had placed it like a loyal friend.

Barefoot, with a walker in the kitchen, I moved in small steps, leaning heavier on the right, moving forward with the left foot. When I needed to use my hands, I let go of the walker and did the one-legged flamingo stance. If cats could laugh, they would.

Everyone in the family had a sense of humor, particularly Inky. Janie's humor had a wry tone. She knew how to laugh a quiet laugh and stare wide-eyed at the same time. Her breakfast was on the countertop, while her brothers ate from bowls on the kitchen floor. It was not a moment to criticize eating habits, but Inky ate too fast, Tippy nibbled, and Flyer spilled a bit. Janie, on her perch, ate just right.

I was the homebound Goldilocks who made her own porridge— oatmeal with milk. I missed the raisins. My spirits rose with breakfast and coffee. I had to feed myself to heal. A mountain of paperwork was waiting for me.

The pine table that now served as a dining-and-work table was a comfortable midpoint between the living room and kitchen. I realized I was within a scaffold of home care and social services. My workplace had gracefully accepted my disability leave. I filled in the application for short-term disability on my laptop and refreshed my memory of the accident with coffee and ruminations.

The phone rang a few times—friends, neighbors, and my home care nurse. I was going to have a professional come in to dress my wound—a luxury to which my health plan entitled me. I did not sit for too long because the cramps crept in, and the impatient "meow" near the doorway was Flyer wanting to stroll out for a change of scene.

"I can't walk with you, buddy," I said.

Flyer ignored me and persisted. I unfolded the walker, wheeled it to the door, and let Flyer out with a prayer. If he decided to run too far today, I would not be able to give him a sporty chase. Strangely, Flyer headed to the right, to a sunlit spot near the fire escape. He stretched himself out as if his day's plans had been accomplished. I shut the front door behind me and trundled to Flyer's side. He looked up with silent glee in his eyes.

"It's just you and me, and I made you walk!" he seemed to say. Flyer tended to be short in his conversations.

Physical therapy was not on my calendar until much later. In my six weeks of rest and repair at home, I would have a physical therapist come in once a week for a basic mobility regimen. However, on my own, the best workout regimen came every day with cleaning the litter box. It was a secret I never revealed to my cheery physio professionals.

I was careful not to pick up heavy objects. The walker, folded in half, worked like a cane. The litter canisters were eight and a half pounds, lightweight Tidy Cat. I could lift one while keeping my balance. Stooping with weight on one leg was easy. Scooping done, I straightened with the bagged waste. I unfolded the walker and took the bag down the hallway to the chute. I had a sense of victory over impairment. I also made sure Flyer did not follow me out for a prowl.

Those were the days I did not own a television set. I listened to the radio for news. The first day at home, the radio played jazz, and I was not hungry to catch up with the world. With Inky stretched out on the couch and Tippy curled like a croissant on his favorite chair, I started on a coloring book called *The Meditating Cat.* The central figure was a lone cat, cross-legged, in Zen meditation. I colored with wax pencils. The exercise of coloring empty spaces and with imagery of choice created a certain peace.

I could not procrastinate with insurance claims. The company of cats and the relief of being back home did not obliterate another imperative. I had to find a lawyer.

How Strangers Become Friends . . .

I looked ahead on the calendar and felt a lurch. I would be home for eight weeks, lending my body time to heal. The to-do list involved shopping for groceries and making a trip to the vet, and I had one scheduled visit to the hospital. The scaffold of social services became visible again. To each service, there was an application. An application meant wait time for approval. I became an eternal applicant.

"Hurry" was not a good word. I could not rush my body, and I did not push the system. From the depths of San Mateo's volunteer groups emerged two people whom I came to know by their first names alone. Maica and Clifford were on call for anyone who were homebound and needed groceries and simple shopping done.

"Goodness," I said to the family, "you will have your Fancy Feast and Tidy Cat delivered to the door!"

Surely, they did. Maica's favorite was Inky. I usually sat at my laptop with a cluster of cats and typed up a grocery list—my needs and their needs. I picked up health tips from whoever decided to counsel me on superfoods for healing: protein shakes, kale and almonds, black beans, brown rice, yogurt. I still drank milk and kept up the breakfast routine of oatmeal with raisins.

Maica and Clifford only needed reimbursement for the cost of groceries. Wednesdays were shopping days, and I eagerly waited for their company on the weekend. We sat around the pine table like old friends, with Inky perched in the center of human banter, listening to every word.

I would bring the introverted Janie out of the bedroom to meet Maica.

"We have a name in common," Maica told Janie at their first meeting.

Janie's expression changed from stress to interest.

"I am Mary Catherine. Nice to meet you, Mary Jane."

Clifford was not a cat person. Strangely, the petite Janie, despite her shyness, could charm Clifford.

One Saturday afternoon Clifford asked with some hesitation, "Have you made contact with the driver of the car?"

The woman with the BMW was never bashed in my cat–human household, but she became an adjunct to our conversation that day. My lawyer, handpicked by me after his phone conversation and home visit, had met with no resistance from her in the compensation claim made on my behalf for my injury. The aches and stumbles of recovery through eight weeks at home did not, even for a moment, carry a shadow of resentment or malice toward this stranger.

I had acquired an exercise mat some years ago to do daily stretches. Now, the fuchsia-colored mat, which clashed with the decor, became the mainstay of my physio regimen. D'Marcus, my kinesiologist neighbor, procured a yoga strap for me. When I did my wince-and-sweat routine to strengthen the muscles of the right leg, Tippy sat next to the mat, watching me with serious eyes until I was done. He earned the nickname "Zen Cat." If Tippy could have sat cross-legged, he would have. I, who could, had no way of bending the right leg any more than twenty degrees from the hip's perpendicular. My orthopedic surgeon had said my leg would take six months to a year's work to gain full strength.

"Too long! Why? You said forty-four days to heal." It was a moment of rare petulance.

"You have to rebuild your muscles."

I had quite forgotten a crucial fact: muscle–bone interaction. A fracture is not just a fracture. There is injury to the surrounding muscle, tendon, vascular structures, and other soft tissues.

An offbeat exercise was to study the musculature of my cats' hind legs to my two legs. My cats and I had the adductor group of muscles in common. They had the adductor femoris. I had the adductor brevis, longus, and magnus. The sartorius was a shared muscle. The biceps femoris, semimembranosus, and semitendinosus also appeared in both the cat and human bodies.

This brought me to a juncture of amused learning. Who came first on the anatomical naming board? The quadruped or the biped? Possibly the biped in the sixteenth-century terminology of Vesalius. My home physio routine became an interactive experience with the attentive Tippy listening to trivia on comparative anatomy.

The father of medicine, Hippocrates, had said, "The soul is the same in all living creatures, although the body of each is different." Well, not that different!

I enrolled myself in a subsidized transportation program, RediWheels, offered by SamTrans. I could book rides for errands and medical appointments and, for the most part, had pleasant shared rides in small buses. Occasionally, I had a cab to myself, and my walker came with me wherever I went. I still did not have the green signal to stand on both legs.

Inky's biannual vet visit came up in February that year. I booked a Redi-Wheels ride back and forth for the checkup. The bravest of the family, Inky usually made no fuss for vet's visits. He occupied our largest carrier, which was lined with a fuzzy blanket for his comfort. Our ride in a shared van was late, and I was tense about Dr. Frank's time window. I hoped Inky would not pick up on my stress, but his emotional radar already had done so.

The Redi-Wheels van rolled into our driveway. As the door slid open, I saw one other passenger with whom we were to share the ride. In my haste, I forgot to pick up my walker. I carried Inky into the van using both legs, feeling no pain. I used unequal weight, using my toes on my right foot for leverage. I was walking.

A few minutes into the ride, I saw Inky in the carrier, breathing heavily. He was open-mouthed, hyperventilating. Was it my stress or the presence of the co-passenger?

A female voice came from beside me: "I am allergic to cats. I cannot be with cats. I did not know I had to share my ride with one."

The ride was a short one. Redi-Wheels would have to hear from me later. At that moment, all I wanted to do was to get Inky as far away from the co-passenger as possible. I hustled Inky out of the van in the short driveway of the vet clinic. Once more, I forgot about the walker. I turned around and reached for it after I got Inky's carrier onto safe ground.

No medication was needed to get Inky's breathing back to normal. By the time Dr. Frank had him on her exam table, Inky had calmed down. He stretched his huge self out and let the vet roll him over onto his side.

He came out shining from his exam except for one observation by Dr. Frank. Inky was still overweight. He always enjoyed his food just as he did when he first invaded his mother's bowl when he was a kitten.

Two weeks after the event, I took another Redi-Wheels ride to see my orthopedic surgeon. Discharge was near. My healing had been a speedy phenomenon, surprising Dr. Lam.

"Start putting weight on your right leg," he said. This was a signal for full mobility.

I was allowed to return to work in mid-March with a "modified job description." On St. Patrick's Day, I went back to work at the fireplace showroom in San Francisco. I got an uproarious welcome with hugs, befitting the return of a surviving traffic calamity warrior.

"Are your cats okay?" was a question that came at the first encounter with my colleagues. I had missed their banter and camaraderie.

I blended into the workplace with one glaring difference. I stayed at my desk for a large part of the day, trimming all forays into the showroom. I did not carry the walker anymore. I left Inky in charge of the household for the time away from home.

Nine on the Calendar . . . How Many in Cat Years?

I had to believe the incredible. My cat family was now nine years old. On June 10, 2014, we celebrated their fifty-second birthday—and none of us cared how old we were.

Still, I noted that we were contemporaries. I was now fifty-five. Perhaps I had fallen behind on feline health education—or was it something pet parents ignore? Teeth and the subject of tooth resorption.

Teeth resorption or the erosion of teeth starts as early as five years old in cats. The phenomenon was startling to me because I had stayed unaware of the process until I saw the physical erosion of teeth in my cats during a physical at the vet clinic. I had to take photographs of the gum lines of Janie and Flyer to make myself believe that resorption was happening.

None of my four cats showed signs of discomfort or pain. None had difficulty eating. Inky, who always tilted his head when he ate as if keeping his eye on his food, made me suspect that he might have a problem with a tooth or a lesion. He did not.

I could not afford cat dentistry. My knowledge came from routine visits to the vet and from delving into the web for direction on what to anticipate in dental care. Cat ancestors in the wild experienced the same resorption, I learned. Animal science describes resorption as a "common condition." From the wild to domesticity, this erosion of teeth happens at various speeds.

The Cornell University Feline Health Center describes tooth resorption for the pet parent. The anatomy of the feline tooth is very like the human tooth.

Within each cat's teeth is a chamber or root canal that contains tissue made up of blood vessels, lymphatic vessels, and nerves. This tissue, which communicates with the rest of the animal's body, is surrounded by a bony substance called dentin, which accounts for the bulk of the tooth's structure. In a condition known as tooth resorption, the dentin in a single tooth (or several simultaneously) erodes and eventually becomes irreparably destroyed. Over time, all areas of an affected tooth, from root to crown, may become involved.

Inky disliked toothpaste. He drooled for several minutes after I brushed his teeth. I used a finger brush. Janie could not be caught when she saw the tube in my hand. Tippy and Flyer made funny faces when the paste touched their gums. They looked like little humans tasting castor oil. I was in a quandary.

Then I realized my mistake. I had bought mint-flavored cat toothpaste. Toby, their mother, had better luck. Her toothpaste had been salmon flavored.

The kitchen was now stocked with Greenies for dental health. The boys expected Greenies when I came home from work. Janie, with her tiny mouth, had to maneuver the treat with effort. For her, SmartBites came into the household. To each his or her own, and that is the way the menu worked.

The year was not without novelty in my workplace. I had to grasp within tight deadlines a new business software, NetSuite. My desk turned almost paperless. I occasionally pondered about becoming a salesperson on the showroom floor but never quite discussed the idea with my manager over coffee. We sipped Starbucks lattes at least once a week as a bonus for good teamwork. Our general manager was generous in his spontaneous acts of appreciation.

Outside the peak hours of sales, the fireplace showroom was a serene splendor. With each model fireplace lit, the flickering gas flames of a dozen installed units created a temple-like ambiance.

This was a rare workplace where I had to be cajoled to take a break.

I did step out to smoke an occasional Benson & Hedges, which had lingered as a habit. The view was green. A native California plant nursery occupied one half of the land across the road. The other half was an open field where a trip of goats grazed. They belonged to a rent-a-goat collective. There was never a dull moment.

I came home in a good mood. The family met me at the door, eager for an escapade from the living room—and I truly believed in fond greeting. I was never a gourmet, and my own dinner was spun out of random shopping. Nonetheless, I could dish up something nutritious and aesthetic for myself. Inky liked to park himself on my wooden cutting board when it did not smell of onions. He was a kitchen Buddha like his brother Tippy. The cutting board took a lot of scrubbing.

Christmas 2014 was spent at a corporate party. I was invited to bring a guest or family.

"I have four cats," I said in the RSVP.

"Bring them!" came the response. "We bring our dogs to the gathering."

It so happened that my cat family stayed home. So did my boss's dogs. However, the hearths of lit fireplaces brought the season to life.

The year-end to-do list had one incomplete item. I had made time to browse John Bradshaw's *Cat Sense: How the New Feline Science Can Make You a Better Friend to Your Pet*. I did not finish the book.

More Change and New Directions

Convalescence is not a vacation. I do not remember taking vacations away from home in my adult life. When I had time off from work, I did all that I loved to do in my own dwelling place, which was a refuge from the outside world.

I was fit and mobile in 2015. The last vestige of my time with the physical therapy routine was a purple resistance band from Kaiser. I used it around my knees and ankles to build and strengthen the muscles of my right leg. The band had teeth marks on it from Inky's curiosity.

I was sprightly as spring when I walked into the CEO's office the morning I was summoned. Work had peaked in the Northern California winter, and the fireplace showroom and service operations were facing hectic days. I least expected a reorganization.

The agenda was a complete relocation and a departmental split. The fireplace showroom was going to be moved and reconstructed. Service operations were moving to another city. My place in the big picture was fading as I listened to the corporate plans.

When I first joined the establishment, I had stood in the midst of the dancing flames in the showroom and said out loud, "This could be the last job of my life." I had been imbued by beauty and aesthetics.

The day I left the showroom, the fireplace behind my desk was still lit. I had a substantial severance check. The paperless desk had nothing to clear out. The only fun object I carried out with me was a personal item. It was an enormous pink eraser with the words "Use for very big mistakes." I boarded the train from San Francisco to San Mateo. I had one thought in my mind. I would have time to spend unhampered days with my cat family.

No walker, no work schedule—I deposited the severance check in my bank on the way home. I had a bigger nest egg. The insurance compensation from my accident was on hand after almost a year of negotiation. After all the bites taken out of the sum, I had enough to survive one year at home. As habits went, I would look for work—but not on that particular day.

Coffee in a Siren Cup

I liked my morning cup of coffee. I liked to brew as a ritual. When I visited a coffee shop, I ordered an espresso. No handcrafted coffee drink matched my own cup at home.

I had once rescued a raccoon whom I named Coffee. In the darkness, I found Coffee wounded on the sidewalk. Still alive, she made it to my backyard. I carried her in my arms knowing she would not be able to survive her injuries. I sat by her in the early hours of the morning, my cup of brewed coffee growing cold. She died as I sat on the patio chair by her side. The motif of the coffee cup became sacred, a symbol of connection and friendship. However short our meeting was, Coffee became an abiding inspiration in my life.

After a week at home, spending waking hours watching the antics of Inky, Flyer, Tippy, and Janie, I opened the window in search for a job. The classifieds looked uninviting. Remote work-from-home jobs were not fashionable in that year. I was torn between returning to familiar retail ground or trying something entirely new.

I walked through downtown San Mateo one morning, and instead of my usual double shot of espresso at Peet's, I walked into Starbucks. To a coffee connoisseur, there is a difference in the taste of the shots.

A store manager was at the bar, and as I tasted the coffee, I said, "This is good. It makes me want to work for you!" The remark was casual.

The manager did not stop her line of drinks and talked as she worked. "You should apply here. We are hiring. You might even be a coffee master someday."

"A coffee master?"

"Someone who researches the taste and origins of coffee and everything else you need to know about what you are drinking . . ."

"You might find me too old for your crew."

"There is no such thing as too old." There was a smile hidden somewhere in her voice. "You can apply online."

I applied to work as a supervisor at the Fourth Avenue Starbucks sometime around Valentine's Day in 2015. The call for an interview came from a different store. Burlingame Avenue captured my résumé first.

Before I went for my first interview, I brushed up on the romance of coffee.

"Recipe for Happiness in Khaborovsk or Anyplace" by Lawrence Ferlinghetti

> One grand boulevard with trees
>
> With one grand café in sun
>
> With strong black coffee in very small cups.
>
> One not necessarily very beautiful
>
> Man or woman who loves you.
>
> One fine day.

A large green orb with a twin-tailed mermaid dominated a corner of Burlingame Avenue. It was the siren, Starbucks' totem from Herman Melville's Moby Dick. My interview was conducted on a barstool overlooking a team of baristas at work.

"Why do you want to work for Starbucks?" the store manager asked. He was a heavyset, cheery man.

"I am a coffee drinker. My beverage of choice. I understand the coffee drinker. For the first time in my life, I have the opportunity to learn something I have wanted to for years."

"What is that?"

"A handcrafted coffee drink. I want to learn how to work the bar."

"What else?"

"I want to be in a happy workplace. Starbucks has this reputation."

I was hired. There was no room for a new supervisor. I agreed to start as a barista. A foot in the door was the right foot.

I could not wait to tell the family. I would be working very close to home. I could walk to work in the mornings.

All Grown Up, Keeping Up with Tomorrow

Inky and Flyer grew closer as a pair. Inky's alpha personality became subdued, but his playfulness stayed unchanged. If siblings could be best friends, the two were a pair worth watching. Still as heavy as a sumo wrestler, oblivious to efforts to control his weight, Inky frolicked as if he were half his age. Flyer, more restrained in his antics, was stout but showed brawn. At play, the siblings resemble two carefree highschoolers who had been let out of school.

My family consisted of educated cats. They could not count, but they did appreciate music and being read aloud stories. I talked to them just as I would to a human family. Family conferences aside, my conversations and everyday banter was with the individual cat. Tippy, being the most attentive of the brothers, had an impressive grasp of vocabulary. His closest companion was his sister, Janie, whose personality was impish and restless compared to Tippy's sedate, selfcontained demeanor.

Being ten years old did not slow anyone's gait. With the exception of Janie, who always was slender and small, Inky, Flyer, and Tippy seen together inevitably got an exclamation from guests: "You have big cats!" The boys, born of the small gray Toby, took after their father Mel. That mighty gray feral had left his legacy with me.

Feline intelligence as a subject is well discussed. Most commentaries are about domestic cats. From my own observations, I can corroborate several of the findings of cat behaviorists on cognitive abilities in feral cats. Learned behavior, retention, memory, and the application of acquired skills are clearly manifested in a small group of domesticated feral cats such as those in my household.

Rebecca Marek, in an article entitled "Feline Intelligence: How Your Cat's Brain Works" (*Cats Life at Home,* 2018), says,

Like humans, cats learn by observation and doing. Examples include opening (cabinet) doors, turning on light switches, ringing doorbells. This is procedural memory, and cats excel at it. Research shows that these memories last 10 years or more. Cats associate memories of an event or place with the emotions they expressed in the surroundings or locations. They will remember traumatic stress or fear as in a veterinarian's exam room. Fortunately, they will also remember positive experiences with food or play.

I did not need to be convinced that cats are among the smartest creatures in the animal kingdom. They are capable of rational thought and problem solving just like humans. The cerebral cortex of a cat contains 300 million neurons or nerve cells, dogs have 160 million neurons, and humans have 21 to 26 billion neurons.

Rebecca Marek goes on to say, "Cats clearly have a superior ability to learn new information, mesh it with existing information, recall it, and use that information in other situations. This cognitive ability makes them card-carrying members of the highly intelligent class. We may never know the full depth of feline cognitive abilities, but their keen aptitude continues to surprise us."

Individual differences in ability and aptitude exist in cats as they do in humans. Inky, regardless of his alpha personality, was the quickest learner. Janie, when out of the shadow of her eldest brother, had the same mental alacrity. Flyer was physically more agile, aggressively curious, and combative. Tippy, a quiet and observant learner, was the gentlest of the siblings. He also had the most expressive face and the only cat I have known who could smile.

Vanishing Boundaries

I liked working close to home. The walk to work was brisk. On the way back, my pace slowed after several hours on my feet. The Starbucks barista role was more creative than working the bar and being creative with espresso beverages.

My morning shifts gave me time to do exactly what I had put aside in the year past: my dance, my reading, and my being a stayhome companion to my brood of four with no pressure of a commute. I shopped for my own groceries and cooked for myself. Housework became enjoyable. Four curious, furry helpers followed me around as I went about the chores. I played music and read aloud to them. The home front was lighthearted.

The occasional closing shift at the store brought no complaints. My welcome at the door was uproarious. I had to herd an impatient family back into the apartment, and dinner for five was a ritual.

I had no notion of how long I would work at Starbucks. My plans were fluid, and I looked at the company as a place to grow. There were days when the role of barista did not fit. I worked with a crew of people who were seasoned on the job. I was older than the average barista and the newest hire. It was a hat that felt floppy on my head.

I tended to be reticent about my previous work and skills. I was candid only when asked what I had done for a living before joining Starbucks. "I have left two careers behind . . ." I usually stopped midsentence. I was not given to being an enigma, and I knew I would be asked again.

Starbucks was not my kitchen. Six months passed before I could work the bar at peak hour. The company still stood tall with its employee benefits. I had a health plan, disability and life insurance, and the start of a retirement fund. Our tomorrow had some shape, and I was willing to wait for opportunities to unfold.

Cat People and Dog Lovers at Work

My crewmates were curious about me as they trained me on the simpler tasks of the workday. There was a culture of camaraderie peculiar to the workplace. The simpler tasks were heavy. My highlight was people. I liked the interactive customer contact. What I did not anticipate was the labor-intensive workplace with minimum mechanization. The maintenance of equipment and the food area was a process of meticulous breakdown and assembly. There were no shortcuts in the routine.

My mind was in two places when I worked: my family at home and my output on the work floor. I did not have to take work home, but I brought the presence of my cats to the workplace. They brought meaning to my work.

Phil, my supervisor, was my worst critic. One day, standing at the bar, having memorized a dozen recipes for hot and cold drinks, I felt Phil peering over my shoulder. He was monitoring my steaming milk in a pitcher for a latte.

The steam wand in an espresso machine is used to heat and froth milk. The wand is best submerged a centimeter below the surface of the milk. Some say half a centimeter if you want more frothed foam. The wand should stay steady near the side of the milk pitcher, not against it. I could make good textured milk for a latte. I had not yet learned to make the best microfoam to draw on my lattes, and Phil was not looking for latte art. He was critiquing a flat white, an Australian recipe introduced into the Starbucks menu.

"That is not the right foam for a flat white," Phil's deep voice spoke with authority.

"See, there is almost no foam at all . . ." I said, tilting the pitcher of steamed whole milk.

"There has to be foam, light foam. Your milk is so thin, I cannot see a bubble in it."

He was right. Before I could say another word, he tipped the freshly pulled ristretto shots and the milk into the sink. I was aghast.

"That was training milk. We waste training milk."

I was also miffed with Phil. "Are you going to do your own flat white to show me the right kind of foam?"

"Another time. Just hop on the register and take care of the line for now."

The flat white had to wait for the next day. I smiled at the customer who had heard our interchange. It was my lucky day. I did not go back to the bar.

The next time I stood next to Phil, we made drinks at different paces. He was a veteran in sequencing orders; I was an amateur. He was "Bar One," and I was "Bar Two." I bore less pressure. We did not have time to discuss making the perfect flat white.

Phil broke the silence. "Indrani, my cat died."

I felt a wrench. "When?"

"In March. His name was Nico."

"I am sorry."

"I loved him more than I loved almost all my relatives."

"I have four cats."

"I heard."

"I raised them from the day they were born. Their mother Toby gave birth in my home. They are my relatives."

There was another silence.

"Tell me about them."

Phil and I became friends that day. The story of Toby and her kittens became part of my Starbucks chapter.

I had started using Instagram around this time. Pictures of Inky, Flyer, Tippy, and Janie as keen viewers in the crew room, portraits and paired antics, sleeping, leaping, daydreaming cats in their apartment habitat—they made my photo gallery come alive.

Phil's Nico had been a Norwegian Forest cat. He was large and long-haired. How such a beautiful creature became a stray remained a mystery. Nico was a foundling that found his own family. Phil carried pictures of him on his smartphone. Cat lovers are timeless in their devotion.

Cayla, a young colleague, was a whirlwind barista, an artist, and a fashionista. I suspected she might change her major in college to fashion design. Her home had a cat and a dog, and she divided herself between the two impartially. The cat was older and in a household of mixed species where seniority had a lot to do in keeping peace and being happy. Cayla was an oracle of pet stories. I was content to listen.

My boss, store manager David, was a devoted dog owner. He would have loved to bring his dog to work if Starbucks allowed him to. I sometimes imagined Inky sitting in the crew room, perched on a chair. He would have basked in the workplace attention. With a green apron on him, he could pass for a Starbucks mascot. The best part about backroom fantasies is that no one stops the other from dreaming.

Secret Santa and Retail Festivities

The green apron days change color with the nearness of Christmas. Cups turn festive with holiday motifs. A new array of espresso drinks stretch the coffee menu. Red aprons and a retail hustle go together for the months of November and December. The peak of the season brings a Christmas party with the company's top brass and crew. We tended to forget hierarchy and exchanged gifts and bonhomie at the store.

A long time ago, Starbucks was a small store in Seattle's Pike Place Market. It sold superlative coffee. The Moby Dick seafaring theme was meant to create a historical backdrop of coffee traders on the high oceans. Howard Schulz, then CEO of Starbucks, was my metaphorical Captain Ahab. Starbuck, his first mate, was not a member of the Seattle leadership. Howard used the name for his flagship.

I went shopping for Christmas of 2015. It was an unusual exercise. I had not indulged in ritual gift-giving in years. I also had a bit more to spare to make family and friends and neighbors happy. My cats got new carriers. They looked like little spaceships that could be top-loaded or sideloaded. The rest of the list was easy to complete. Holiday coffee and drinkware from the home store were irresistible. Burlingame's shopping district, "The Avenue," was glowing and intoxicating.

My secret Santa stayed a mystery for a week after Christmas. I had taken home cups and cards with cat motifs. One cup was handpainted with the Starbucks siren with whiskers: a cat siren. The artist was Cayla. She made my heartstrings twang many carols and a crescendo that day.

Happiness according to Charles Schulz

Charlie Brown said, "In the book of life, the answers aren't in the back." He also said, "Life is better with a dog."

I had neither dog nor cat growing up. Until Toby the mother feral barged into my life, I did not expect to have a cat in my life, least of all a brood of kittens.

Today, I say, "Life is better with cats." I truly believe their entry into my life was not by chance but an act orchestrated by a mystical hand. I did not "own" my cats. They grew up to be an extension of myself. When I looked at my grown-up cats, I had a singular thought and feeling: "You make me happy."

Charles Schulz wrote many "Happiness is . . ." lines to go with his *Peanuts* characters. The most famous is "Happiness is a warm puppy." I wrote a few of my own:

- Happiness is a kitten on your shoulder.
- Happiness is a nap with a cat.
- Happiness is a meow in the morning.
- Happiness is a cat under your blanket.
- Happiness is four cats on the couch.
- Happiness is sharing string cheese with a cat.

- Happiness is a cat sitting on warm laundry.

Simply, happiness is different for different people. This too is a Schulzism.

The year 2016 was uneventful. To me, being uneventful was good. Work shaped itself in a predictable pattern. Inky, Flyer, Tippy, and Janie now made visits to the vet twice a year. They were "senior" cats who believed their years. At home, they were as rambunctious as they were as five-year-olds. Small changes in their dry food diet went unprotested.

Fancy Feast remained the menu of choice for all. It was only to please Inky that I shopped at Pet Food Express for the "ahi tuna" in the Tiki-Cat offerings. Sitting on the kitchen counter, Inky devoured his ahi tuna with a gourmand's relish. He ate with his head tilted to one side, as if he expected an ambush on his bowl.

In a book, *Animal Blessings*, is an anonymous ode to the furry relatives at home:

> If you can start the day without caffeine,
>
> If you can resist complaining and boring people with your troubles,
>
> If you can eat the same food every day and be grateful for it,
>
> If you can understand when your loved ones are too busy to give you any time,
>
> Then, my friends, you are almost as good as your dog—or cat!

My cats taught me a few good things. However, I still needed my morning coffee.

Janie Speaks Out on Three Brothers

A friend who is a young father of two once declared, "I do not have favorites among my children." Some do. I never understood why.

When Toby lived with us, her nurturing behavior toward her kittens was impartial. She indulged, played, groomed, and disciplined her brood. On rare occasions, I saw her spend time nestling Flyer as if he needed her more than the others. Janie received no special treatment for being the only female.

The household stayed without gender bias even after Toby's departure. Janie could keep up with her three brothers without effort. She had short spurts of temper that made her stand out. She also had enormous energy in her tiny frame. The boys were laid back to the point of being languorous. They had all been altered at about the same time, and even prior to the necessary event, I had seldom seen male aggression in Inky, Flyer, or Tippy.

Inky was one who could irk Janie. Their sibling relationship, blurred because of Inky's time away from home with his first adoption, made Janie confront her own femaleness. Inky never stopped seeing her as his little "girlfriend."

Janie's relationship with Flyer and Tippy was a deep sibling bond. Any nearness would prompt her to groom her two brothers, and she often slept flanked by Tippy and Flyer.

There were days when Janie pulled away from her brothers and chose the solitude of her own hideout under the bed. There was a certain pensiveness in her that worried me, and I wondered what was going on inside her agile mind.

I had bought a set of cat stairs that gave them a view out of the bedroom window. I sometimes saw Janie silhouetted against the panes, quite oblivious of her brothers. These enigmatic moments drew me closer to her. We developed a "talking" relationship, more eloquent than I had with her siblings. I came to respect her occasional aloofness. I also recognized that growing up with three brothers had needed some endurance.

The litter box was a male domain. Janie disliked Inky's scratching and scattering. She found the boys messy. A litter box set apart for Janie was quickly invaded by the others. They just did not perceive her need for privacy. The girl was miffed.

No one disrupted her meals. While the dry food was a family eating hub, Janie had her own bowl for Fancy Feast. Janie was a dainty eater. She saw her brothers as gobblers.

Janie stayed small and compact in size. A neighbor who had caught sight of her through my open door once said, "You have a very cute cat." Janie was the essence of Barbie and Hello Kitty combined. Not even a wild stretch of imagination could make one guess her feral heritage. She looked pedigree to the tip of her tail.

I have tried to find a cat in literature who came close to the personality of Janie. I never found one. At her most content, Janie would lie on her back, paws up and face in a near-smile. Perhaps Lewis Carroll could have borrowed her to augment the mysterious Cheshire Cat. The Cheshire in *Alice in Wonderland* was never seen lying on her back. The only tree that Janie climbed was the designer cat tree I had bought that year.

Personally, I had no favorites. I had no chance to build a gender bias. Love at first sight makes for no favorites. I must admit that my relationship with each of Toby's kittens as they grew up was unique, each developing a bond peculiar to his or her personality. Janie, without doubt, stayed my "only little girl cat," our interaction colored by uncanny nuances. We were like siblings together.

Four "Obligate" Carnivores and a Vegan Wannabe

The fact that I had spent two years at Starbucks with the effort to become vegetarian amused my colleagues. One colleague, a pescatarian, noticed my dilemma with café food. While I was obliged to taste the food on the menu, I never could make a meal out of Starbucks fare. In an honest appraisal, only two menu items out of ten listed were vegetarian. A vegetarian sandwich with egg and cheese was knocked off the menu for its unpopularity. Sausage, bacon, and ham were best-selling sandwiches. A beef wrap and a chicken bistro box entered the menu. Should I have excluded eggs, I would have made sprouted grain bagels my staple.

I lost count of how many spinach feta wraps I ate before I started buying lunch from the Le Boulanger next door. An in-house alternative—the PB&J box with a wheat bread sandwich, string cheese, and chocolate-covered raisins—was one of my favorites.

I occasionally brought a chicken wrap home because Inky loved shredded chicken. Flyer and Inky loved cheese. Janie and Tippy were less experimental with "outside" food. Had I told the family I intended to go vegan, I would have been considered insane. The era of the non-dairy had not yet arrived. No one in Starbucks attempted to be vegan with milk flooding the bar every day.

Cats are carnivores, as nature made them. Like eagles, seals, dolphins, seals, and walruses, cats are "obligate" carnivores. Meat is a biological necessity and an ancestral trait. Jim Scott, author and co-founder of RAWZ, states that the anatomy of a feline is designed for hunting and eating raw prey. The four front canines are extremely sharp, and the jaw is strong. The ears are forward-facing and have twenty different muscles that can locate the sound of prey. The eyes have many rod cells in the retina, making it easy to see in low light.

RAWZ is natural pet food. Jim Scott, on the RAWS blog, explains that "a meat diet offers vitamins and fatty acids in a preformed state. Since cats can get these nutrients from the animals they are eating, their bodies no longer have the ability to make certain vitamins and amino acids like herbivores or omnivores can. Cats have a dire biological need for niacin, taurine, vitamin A, and arginine, all of which can be found in meat sources."

I, the mere human in my family, continued to ponder the omnivore's dilemma. I had browsed Michael Pollan's book titled *An Omnivore's Dilemma: A Natural History of Four Meals*. I committed myself to healing my own eating habits. A plant-based diet did not seem too ambitious.

A Meaningful Bath

Many years had passed since my volunteer days at the local SPCA. I had bathed a few cats in my time, but the ones that were picked for baths were those chosen to go up for adoption. A typical bath was a shallow sink filled with warm water and hypoallergenic cat shampoo. We towel-dried a petrified cat and then used a human blow dryer on the fur. I learned early that cats do not like water. The cats who came into the shelter had never had water baths before.

The cats I wanted to bathe were the matted, downhearted ones, and I was hoping that a makeover and a human touch would make them happier. More importantly, they would be more presentable for adoption. My wishes were not always heeded.

When I had a cat family of my own, the weekly waterless bath was as much a ritual as dinnertime. The nail clip was once a month, with Tippy and Inky wrestling me on the grooming seat. I saw sullen faces for half an hour before I was pardoned for picking up the clippers. Flyer did not yell at me. He just looked mournful on my lap and turned around to put his free paw around my neck, just like a human child. Janie's nails were pale and soft, but catching her as she scurried under the bed was a maneuver I never could master.

Janie disliked baths. They were not real baths. I used Earthbath wipes for a thorough rubdown, down to between the toes. She had unique pigmentation on her paws on the right side. The pink paw pads on her right fore and hind legs had dark brown markings. They matched a thumbprint-like patch on the right of her nose. Janie was a calico, except her coloring lacked black patterns. She was white with orange and dark brown.

No matter how many times I groomed Janie, I never tired of admiring her orange-striped flanks. The diagonal tiger stripes stood out on white fur halfway down her back legs. Her paws were pristine white. Inky was a brown tabby with a buff colored belly. Like Flyer and Tippy, who were predominantly gray, he was a blotched tabby. A pattern of circular smudges around the neck and upper torso resemble a haphazard bullseye.

Bath time inevitably brought musings on the gene pool of feral cats. Every time, I recalled Toby's simple gray coloration and the array of colors she brought to her kittens. Coat patterns were meant to be camouflage in the wild. This skin-deep coloring, acclaimed in pedigree cats and scrutinized at adoptions, is a functional heritage for a hunter. Feral cats do not look any different from domestic cats. Behavior sets them apart. I usually run the wipes against the direction of the bristle. I could moisten and clean their skin this way.

Flyer basked at bath time. If I bathed him twice a day, he would ask for more. Inky was skittish. He tolerated the moisture of the wipes on his back but did not have the patience to stand still for me to finish his feet and expansive belly.

Tippy sat still like a baby seal in the sun. I always felt he was critiquing my efforts at grooming him. He watched my movements with a half-closed gaze as if he were grading my skills. Once I had bathed him, he would move away and groom himself all over again, reorganizing his fur the way he wanted. He had his own comb, his tongue.

"Tabby cats are almost as old as Mother Earth," wrote Franny Syufy in her blog, *The Spruce Pets.* They were the first domesticated cats of Egypt. "The most consistent markings of tabby cats is the magnificent 'M' centered on their foreheads, just above the eyes. This 'M' is the stuff for legends. It may stand for 'Mau,' the original name of cats in Egypt."

If color patterns were all a matter of genetics—and I had long thrown Toby's lineage out of the window—I took the rainbow of the eight kittens she had birthed in my home as a lottery of nature. From Toby, I saw kittens—three tabby-stripes and a calico who became mine, an orange and a snow-white kitten, a speckled white and gray, and a gray with white socks, little feral miracles.

Inky and the Medicine Chest

The firstborn, Inky, the eldest, seemed to be responding to his weight management diet—only so, under my watchful eye. He made a beeline for the communal kibbles bowl whenever I was not around. He saw no reason to eat different food.

Inky had lost weight, but with the approach of fall 2016, the weight loss seemed a little too rapid. Still, he showed no signs of fatigue, and I was not looking for signs of any health issues. His mood remained exuberant, and he continued to be the de facto boss even when the household did not call for one.

One evening, sitting with him in a bear hug, I felt a tangible reduction of his girth. His skin was less taut than usual. Earlier, Inky had made three trips to the water bowl. This was a sum of something unusual happening. Inky was twelve years old.

I waited a week, debating with myself as to whether I should book a routine physical or take him in with critical concerns. Without a veterinary background, I speculated that Inky was ailing from a condition related to his kidneys. I cleaned the litter box with zealous frequency. Inky's urine made enormous maps on the clumping litter. He was paying more visits to the bathroom quite casually. If I were not tracking him, I would not have noticed.

I did not delay the appointment any longer. Camino Real Pet Clinic had his charts since 2006. Inky had grown up in their care. He had even been neutered in their surgery. Every hair and sinew on Inky's self had a record in this bastion. Still, I stood by the exam table on tenterhooks.

The physical was complete, and the ambiance of the room was somber. Inky was ill. The vet tech came in to take him to the back of the clinic to draw blood and urine. I went to the lobby to wait. The most agonizing waits of my life have been in such lobbies.

There was no second-guessing Inky's illness. The blood glucose reading shouted out diabetes. The signals I had read at home were all tantamount to diabetes mellitus, a disease of the pancreas. The beta cells in his pancreas had stopped producing the hormone insulin to regulate sugar in his bloodstream.

My head sifted through memories of a diabetic with whom I had lived in my childhood: my much-loved grandmother who did not know how to inject herself with insulin in 1973. Here was my hefty alpha, my mascot feral kitty, in 2017, looking bereft of zest and buoyancy, diagnosed with the same disease. Inky was not going back home in his condition. He and I were headed to the North Peninsula Veterinary Emergency for an overnight stay.

I looked at the vet, seeking the blunt truth. "Is he critical?"

"Yes and no. He will be if he is not treated immediately."

The carrier shaped like a spaceship was full of Inky—a despondent, irate one. It was a short ride to emergency.

Inky had been on prednisolone for a mild case of irritable bowels. My verbal description of symptoms at intake matched Type II diabetes. The emergency intake fee was waived, and I barely heard the details of the estimate given to me.

The emergency clinic repeated an in-house urinalysis and a comprehensive panel for blood glucose levels. Insulin Humulin was immediately rendered with IV fluids. Inky's plasma ketones were high, a typical indication that his cells were not getting enough glucose. Ketones are the byproduct of fat metabolism. Inky's diabetes was edging out of control.

Inky was treated for DKA or diabetic ketoacidosis. Was he in pain? He felt dull pain and discomfort. He was given buprenorphine and Cerenia for controlling discomfort and nausea. Veraflox suspension was added to the list.

In the two days he had spent in hospital, Inky's blood glucose level was measured thirteen times. His discharge came with instructions on a lifetime of insulin injections and a diet low in carbohydrates. *I could handle it,* I told myself. I knew without a crystal ball that Inky would never have a diabetic remission. I would learn to handle needles and craft my work schedule to be home to feed him before his shots.

Insulin glargine and four-millimeter needles are human health products used for felines. I did not realize until much later that veterinary science ran in tandem with human health. Health care is where the two species meet. The cost of treatment is not trifling. My Inky deserved the best of care.

Something had not changed. Inky was still overweight. I brought him home feeling as if I had rediscovered my kitten who was born in the early hours of dawn in the crook of my knee. He looked like an enormous kitten as he hurried to his favorite nook under the bed. On his left foreleg was evidence of the fluids that had gone into his body. The shaven inch of fur had a blue patterned bandage wrap.

I became a regular customer at Walgreens after Inky's diagnosis. His prescription for Lantus insulin glargine, a long-acting insulin, was filled every three months. The supply of insulin needles came from the same pharmacy.

Every time I approached the counter, I had to say aloud, "The prescription is for my cat."

"For Inky Sircar?"

"Yes."

For his insulin supply, Inky took my last name. The surname "Catwings" stayed an unofficial record.

The Special Brother

I did not expect Flyer, Tippy, and Janie to understand the nature of Inky's illness. Still, the serious family conference had me sitting cross-legged, talking about Inky in hospital and how his pancreas was not working fully to produce the much-needed hormone insulin. I had to give him insulin twice a day with a needle. I had serious eyes staring back at me.

Whether or not my words had an impact on sibling dynamics, I shall never be quite certain. Inky maintained his boisterous presence with his brothers, and Janie gave him no special treatment.

In early spring, Inky looked bright-eyed and content. My own prowess with the delicate insulin needles had grown. For the first weeks of Inky's injections, I sat beside him on the couch with a full syringe and metal comb in hand. I gently parted his fur at the back of his neck to find a strip of skin. The grip of the syringe was tentative in my fingers. My clumsiness lingered for a short while. If I heard a mild "meow" from Inky, I was quick to apologize.

"Better the next time, okay?"

Inky took the needles stoically—no protests or hisses. The ritual was unhurried. My hands grew steady with practice. Flyer, Inky's constant companion, watched in avid curiosity. He had a way of showing up when I approached Inky, just after a meal. Flyer looked as if he were making notes for his own journal.

In solitary repose, Inky made an imposing sight. The sunlight poured in through the wide glass doors of the balcony, creating highlights on his brown fur. His first dose of insulin was given in the morning before

I left for work. When I returned, Inky was fed first. I filled the syringe from the glass vial in the kitchen and walked to him as he planted himself on the couch. I did not need the comb anymore. I parted his fur with my fingers and gave him his second dose. The tiny needles grew in a cluster in my homemade "hazmat" box.

My Inky was a tough boy. The regimen of insulin was conquered. Convincing Inky to eat a DM diet was a battle I never won. Three kinds of prescription diets with high protein and low carbs got nonchalant responses from him—Hills, Royal Canin, and ProPlan. Hills got an outright paws down. I had ProPlan samples from our vet. The pâté was too bland. Royal Canin interested him if I held his bowl to his mouth. After the first few nibbles, he turned away to find Tippy's or Flyer's bowl and helped himself to Fancy Feast.

I could never separate the bowls of my foursome. Janie was the only one who stuck to her own platter. The boys were a jumble of "free for all." Setting Inky apart with his prescription diet became impossible. My turn to be a stoic came when I threw uneaten Royal Canin down the insinkerator, watched by an unrepentant Inky.

There was quiet amusement in his siblings. They knew something I did not know. Inky loved his food. He ate what he liked when I was not watching.

Changes within Us

I had a set of two green lawn chairs on my apartment balcony. Before my property manager declared the building to be a nonsmoking abode, I used to sit among potted plants and smoke my favorite menthol Benson & Hedges on these chairs. I tried not to smoke with my family of cats around me. Secondhand smoke was not for them. I went a step ahead and stopped smoking in front of my plants too. I doubted cigarette smoke was good for them. It reduces photosynthesis.

Inky's favorite seat was the chair closest to an enormous jade plant. It was the sunniest spot, and he curled up into a half circle of fur and wrapped his tail around his hind legs to snooze. He was an artist's vision of the sleeping cat. I sometimes had to wake him from his cat dreams to bring him indoors.

Tippy liked the other chair, my chair in the shade. He was a jumper and had attempted to climb the balcony ledge a few times. He rested with his eyes wide open, his chin on his front paws. When he was done sunbathing, he would come indoors without bidding.

The sky was a short expanse of good weather as seen over the solid balcony guard. The tops of evergreens and high-rises at a distance were in constant sight. On a windy day, the swaying trees would make me wonder if Zephyrus, the god of gentle winds, was angry. When we would hear the shrill hiss and whistles of little Northern California storms, we would huddle together for comfort.

Within me, there was a heightened appreciation of the presence of my cat family. Flyer, Tippy, and Janie were in good health. Twelve years had passed with days full of ordinary acts and routines. Time did not blur special moments or the underlying happiness of our everydays: mealtimes, messes, sniffles, sneezes, fleas, upset stomachs, broken china, smashed lampshades, and spats.

My collection of cat hair from the daily brushing had grown. I started picking up shed whiskers because they had been part of cherished faces.

Inky's diabetes, the vet stated, was being well managed, yet his illness brought within me an awareness of mortality. I had loved him since the day he was born. Claiming him back from his mismatched adoptive home had been an emotional turmoil. The event had faded in my memory, but the chronic nature of his diabetes raised a hypothetical question in my mind. What would have happened if he were still with Talia? The word *chronic* had deep implications. In the health of people and other animals, it means a recurring condition that lasts a long time and may not have a cure.

I continued working at Starbucks, keeping a five-day week and coming home with no other plans but being with Inky, Flyer, Tippy, and Janie. A few of my friends jibed about my absence at social gatherings. I did not fall away from everyone's calendar. I did not find pleasure in the afterwork bar scene or random distractions.

Another realization reared its head. If I were to take care of Inky, I needed to stay fit myself. No premonitions were delivered to me, and no packaged wisdom reached my mental mailbox. I just knew that we were all aging, and a new preparedness began to grow in me. I began to watch my own eating habits and took mental health more seriously.

Sugar – Friend and Foe

The best way to check blood glucose at home was drawing blood from the lateral ear margin—the lower edge of the ear. I did not have the skill to use a handheld glucometer. I was also reluctant to bruise or scar Inky. I chose to take him to his vet and leave him in nursing care for half a day and pick him up on my way home from work.

Inky was a trooper. His eating habits were still topsy-turvy. He needed to be coaxed with his platter of DM. Otherwise, he did not protest the visits. His short absences did not worry his siblings. Tippy and Janie were steady playmates, and Flyer found a place to make a contented gang. When Inky got home, Flyer separated himself and attached himself to his favorite brother. He may have been the only one who noticed the ups and downs in Inky's behavior after the hospitalization.

Six months passed. A normal stay-at-home evening took an odd turn. The evening shot of insulin was rendered, and I had pulled less than 1.0 mL in the syringe. An hour later, I pulled .25 mL to complete the dose.

I had known a vital fact when Inky was diagnosed with diabetes mellitus. "Hyperglycemia is better than hypoglycemia." Inky seemed slow in his gait. I was in sweats, sock-clad, and finishing chores when I saw Inky standing by the balcony glass doors. For a split second, I saw his hind legs buckle. Then he was up again. Something was amiss. This was my first encounter with hypoglycemia—low blood sugar.

Inky had had a full meal. Was he reacting to an overdose of

insulin? Hypoglycemia is a side effect of insulin therapy. I called the vet emergency with one question. Did I do something wrong?

The staff nurse calmly asked a question in turn. "Do you have corn syrup at home?"

"Corn syrup?"

"Yes, the kind you buy in grocery stores. Just apply some to his gums. His glucose levels should improve."

Inky was now sitting, an awkward limpness in his pose.

"I don't think I have time to buy any." I described Inky's behavior.

"Bring him in. You have a diabetic emergency."

Inky spent a night in the hospital. He was administered dextrose, a simple sugar made from corn, chemically identical to glucose. The bill was $1,500 for the emergency nursing care, urinalysis, and routine blood glucose monitoring.

A bottle of good-quality corn syrup in Safeway costs $12. The bottle I purchased after Inky's critical overnight emergency stayed in my refrigerator as a landmark purchase. It was part of a hard chapter of education in home care. The chapter was not without humor.

"You Have Never Been a Mother"

Honestly, I do not know what it is like to be a mother. I have watched animal mothers tend their young, but it is not quite the same for human mothers raising children they have brought into the world. I did not see myself as a mother to my family of cats. I was a caregiver of a species with two legs. I loved my four-legged family with a deep, protective love.

"You have never been a mother" came to me from a woman who made the fact sound like a social shortcoming.

I never had human children. I had never been a mother. However, I took my undefined role among my cats seriously.

A colleague of mine had once described an incident with her infant that gave her a taste of true motherhood. She had to probe her severely constipated six-month-old son with her pediatrician on the phone. The experience dulled the beatific side of parenting and brought her headlong into the role of a homespun nurse.

"So this is what it is like to be a mother," she said.

When Tippy was eight years old, he suddenly stopped eating, and his water consumption went down. On the second day of coaxing, I sought an appointment with a vet. My surmise was constipation. My full work schedule could not accommodate a time window. I turned to my neighbor Colleen, who was Auntie Colleen to Tippy.

I was on the phone on my break to get an update on Tippy. Every muscle on my forehead was furrowed. Colleen's report was brief, but she wrote the details of the visit and left it on the pine table at home.

Tippy has seen a new vet, affectionately known as Dr. G. He was the new owner-practitioner of Camino Real Pet Clinic. Tippy's X-rays were good. There were no stones in his bladder, no signs of any type of blockage. The urine test was to come back the next day. He had two prescriptions: a pain management medication for straining and an antibiotic in case of a urinary infection.

When I came home, Tippy looked calm and at ease. The medication had begun to take effect. He ate a little, and I breathed relief. He used the litter box, and I almost shouted with joy.

I will never know how mothers feel when faced with inexplicable dilemmas. I do know that the comfort and cure of being well loved is more than duty. The mixed feelings of fear, insecurity, and relief are part of an emotional journey.

At age twelve, Tippy stayed his tender and uncomplicated self, the most demonstrative in his attachment to me. His physical exam with Dr. Frank, his vet from kittenhood, had a moment of reminiscence. I had carried with me two photographs of Tippy. One photograph showed Tippy, six years old, perched on a lawn chair on my balcony. The second was a recent portrait where Tippy looked seriously at the lens, his expression similar to that of a high schooler at his graduation.

"It is the same face. He is just a little grayer," Dr. Frank said.

The pun was intended. Tippy was a very handsome gray tabby, as perfect as a cat on a Hallmark card. He was slightly overweight and came home with a prescription of a metabolic diet of dry food.

Bowl Scrabble

The family now had two members eating normal food. Fancy Feast and dry Purina were for Flyer and Janie. Inky and Tippy had their own prescriptions served apart from the routine menu.

Tippy took to his metabolic diet instantly. Inky began playing thief and snuck portions of Hills Metabolic when no one was looking. He was irreligious about his own prescription of DM.

I fumed a little about the chaos and chided Inky. He looked penitent. He sat on my lap on my swivel chair at the desk at home as if to make up for my distress. I usually held him while plodding through my online course work, his head resting on my elbow, his body upright on my lap. When he got bored watching me work multiple choice answers to self-exam questions, he leaped off to sit on the couch behind me.

Inky was a quiet fellow. Flyer would saunter in to join him. Tippy and Janie had their nook in the bedroom. They lay intertwined in the evenings as if their world was complete.

I could not, despite frequent advice, leave their bowls empty for timed feedings. There was always a choice of dry food like an allday buffet. None saw a meal as a special event. However, my serving wet food was a moment much awaited. For me, this was a cherished moment of my day as I had my foursome eat together.

Janie Holds Her Own

The home front had not seen a frenzied sibling chase in a while. Inky was less frisky with his sister, and Janie's flat-eared hisses had vanished. The two sat together on the couch, with Flyer as a conciliator.

In her thirteenth year, Janie was self-possessed and picked her own company among her brothers. I had always seen her as a precocious imp, and her maternal streak came as a surprise. Janie took to grooming Tippy and Flyer as they sprawled on the bed in the mornings. She expected no attention in return. I tried to capture them together in snippets on video, and I soaked up the scenes to make them indelible in memory. Janie was beguiling. My only little girl cat had two sides to her personality.

Inky's new hideout was a furry bed under my own. On occasion, Janie nosed into this private turf by some unknown instinct. This instinct surpassed mine. Inky was acting apathetic. His glucose levels had no upheavals. His meows were lower pitched. What was bothering him was deeper than my eye could see.

April was chilly in San Mateo. I made sure the windows were closed and preserved the heat from the electric heaters in the bedroom. I had fed the family and given Inky his insulin shot. I was on my way out to work when Inky stepped out of his bed and made a half circle to come into view. Looking at me, he let out a soft moan. I have never heard a sound so alien from him. It was a prolonged deep-throated meow that indicated pain.

Cats do not show pain. Crying out in pain in the wild attracts predators. Their immense threshold for tolerance makes it hard to figure their state of health. I held Inky to me. He took some comfort. I spoke softly to him, promising to be back home soon.

"We are going to the doctor when I am back," I said to Inky, planning an urgent trip as I spoke.

People speak. Every day and even in a crisis, I used simple English to speak to the cats.

I finagled an appointment at Camino Real Pet Clinic with a relief vet. Neither Dr. Frank nor Dr. G was on call. I spent a tense half day on the job and came home. There was a deceptive quiet in the living room with Flyer and Tippy. I found Inky under my bed on his favorite furry spot. Janie was in the bedroom with him.

While scooping Inky up into the carrier, I was conscious of his weight loss. He was fully alert and did not resist being zipped into his space age capsule.

We had the last appointment of the day. The vet was unfamiliar to Inky. I described the morning's incident.

"You wanted a routine exam done?" he asked. The question was loaded.

"There is something wrong with him. It is more than his diabetes."

"He has kidney failure."

I stood by the exam table in stunned silence.

Cat Anatomy – A View from Crisis Point

The cephalic vein runs on top of the forearm, under the elbow. Inky had a twenty-gauge IV catheter in the right cephalic vein, and I was looking at him through the open door of his kennel at North Peninsula Veterinary Emergency. He was suffering from azotemia, an elevation of blood urea nitrogen and creatinine levels.

Creatine is found naturally in muscle cells, helping muscles produce energy. Creatine is protein waste, and kidneys filter creatine from the blood. Vets measure creatinine levels because it is a good indication of kidney function. When kidney function is lost, creatinine levels soar.

Inky was anemic. His weight was barely twelve pounds. He had uremic breath, a metallic smell that happens when excess urea in the body encounters saliva. The cocktail of drugs rendered included Clavamox, an antibiotic. An ulcer had been found under his lateral tongue, a symptom of renal failure.

I could afford to keep Inky under hospital supervision for a day. In the twenty-four hours after Inky's diagnosis of chronic renal failure, I learned a skill that would last for years afterward.

My initiation into subcutaneous fluid therapy was a daunting venture. Dr. Hovde had gently held Inky on the exam table before his discharge. A bag of water, a fluid line, and a needle composed the first step in fluid therapy. With two women standing beside him, Inky submitted to his first "subQ." He had been entangled in IV catheters for a day. The vet gently pinched the skin between Inky's shoulder blades, talking to me all the time. In a perfect textbook demo of rehydration, she inserted the small needle and released the water in the fluid line.

Inky did not flinch. He was being irrigated with water containing electrolytes and dextrose. He would go this once a day, every day from this moment on. The fluids formed a small bump under his skin. Vets call it a camel hump, which flattens out as the fluids are absorbed.

Dr. Hovde conquered the day. Tomorrow would bring my turn with subQ , and the thought made me a nervous wreck. I brought Inky home like royalty, knowing that this apparently simple regimen would prolong his life.

Time Together Alongside Nitty-Gritty

Living together for more than twelve years had been my delight. The kitten who had grown into adulthood and had given me his trust and love was now on a timeline. Every day with him was acutely precious, and whenever I thought of forever, the word took on a temporal quality. The future was today. The future was whatever we imagined ourselves to be with or without needles and catheters.

Every day I imagine a future where I can be with you.
In my hand is a poem that will write a poem of me and you.
Can you hear me?

(A doki doki verse. Doki doki is onomatopoeia for a fast-beating heart. Such verses are love poems in Japanese.)

"Inky, can you hear me?"

He was under my bed again. His latest acquisition, my gift to him, was a short shag dog bed that could hold him stretched out. He loved it.

It was time for his insulin shot. He separated himself from Flyer and walked out with curious eyes. My voice still had its effect— dinner first, insulin next.

As I set out four bowls, I divided Fancy Feast into three of them. Inky got Tiki Ahi Tuna, his favorite. Flyer and Tippy did not care for it. Janie thought it smelled nice but tasted weird. She walked away after a dainty nibble.

I tried not to think of what happened earlier in the morning. My work schedule had put me in the opening crew, and I had to be at Starbucks at 5:30 a.m. I had set my alarm for the crack of dawn. I had to give Inky his subQ before I trudged to work. I was a nervous wreck even before I went to sleep.

My alarm went off at 3:00 a.m. It was pitch dark outside. The neon lights from the backstreet made streaks on the ceiling. Flyer, at the far end of the bed, was oblivious to the sound of the alarm. Janie stirred. Tippy, closest to my pillow, sat up. Inky was asleep in his wicker basket.

I went about getting the hydration gear in place. I had made a nest of towels in one of my open-topped cat carriers. The carrier sat on my pine dining table.

I had no hooks to hang a fluid bag. A makeshift coat hanger made a good suspension point. I placed the bag flat on a high shelf and pulled the line to the carrier. I fitted a new needle. Then I went to get the patient out of bed.

Inky meowed. It was more like a growl. I lifted him into my arms, one hand flat under his belly, and carried him to the table. I let him settle. From the corner of his eye, he saw the fluid line and needle. Up he was on his legs, ready to leap out of the nest. I gently pushed him into a sitting position and steadied the needle. This time, he hissed.

The sight of the fluid gear upset him. Being confined in the basket even for a few minutes angered him. He was not a compliant happy camper, not with me. I placed the corner of a towel over his head to distract him, leaving his shoulder blades and the active fluid line bare.

A mother cat lifts a kitten by the scruff of his neck. The loose skin at the back of the neck is hardy. Inky's scruff had felt Toby's teeth. His scruff now felt my fingers. The same scruff felt the pinch of insulin shots and subQ needles. Whoever pondered on a cat's scruff did not give it due importance.

When two minutes had passed with the irate Inky and 100 mL of solution had entered his body, I pulled the needle out and turned off the fluid line. Inky leaped out of the nesting basket and bolted. Beads of water trickled down his neck onto his back.

He headed for his feeding bowl in the bedroom. He ate voraciously for a while. As I stood behind him, trying to gather my wits and calm, Inky turned to give me a look that said, "I am mad as heck, and I do not want to speak to you."

I made it to work on time. The sun was not out. In my mind, I was still apologizing to Inky. I was apologizing to all of them. Flyer, Tippy, and Janie had watched part of the "watering" with anxious eyes. They were confused but not afraid.

Did Inky feel fear? I was pummeling him as instructed. I was pummeling him day after day.

Path of the Warrior

I have heard this being said—"Feral cats never die of old age." PETA, in a web alert on free roaming cats, stated, "These cats have short, hard lives."

What if Inky, like his parents, had been an outdoor cat?

Zoonotic and contagious diseases affect feral cats. Zoonoses are caused by germs that move between animals and people. Contagions like feline AIDS, leukemia, and infectious peritonitis are common among outdoor cats who are never seen by veterinarians. In their own encounters and squabbles with other animals, small cuts and puncture wounds become raging infections.

Cat flu causes deadly upper respiratory infection, caking the eyes and nose with mucus. It becomes hard to breathe. Cat flu epidemics kill kittens in a feral clan. Worms cause anemia. Mites cause ear itches. Urinary tract infections lead to fatal blockage, taking the lives of male cats. Rabies also makes the list.

More cruel than nature's adversaries is human indifference. People destroy feeding grounds. They kill with poisons and shotguns. Hit-and-run victims are left behind, untended.

Having picked up still bodies of wounded and dead ferals and mourned alone, I have come home to four cats who occupied the core of my existence. They were progeny of two ferals who followed the path of the urban warriors, brave and independent, uncompromising in their ways of the free.

I named the remaining ferals in the neighborhood, sometimes after they were dead. Meuzzah, Katie, Tamara, and Little Dot were killed by passing cars at night. White Tuxedo, who occupied the green grounds of a church, still roamed the lawns, looking for prey. He sometimes sat on the flight of steps, overlooking the traffic of El Camino. He was white with black markings, his coloring the reverse of a true tuxedo cat.

I never fed White Tux. He was a hunter. I used to catch sight of him cross the breadth of El Camino when there was a lull in the whizzing cars. This was the "thunderpath" that cats feared. On the other side of the thunderpath was more prey.

Walking to work, I saw White Tux walking on the highest step of the First Church of Christ. It was early morning, and his pace was slow and deliberate. His sturdy frame looked small from a great distance. He took a turn at the edge of the stairs and vanished into the shrubbery.

A few days passed. I was home early, and having fed the family and given Inky his insulin, I stepped out to run an errand. El Camino, on my side, had a row of parked cars. Between two parked cars, I spotted something pristine white. I felt my heartbeat rise. White Tux had been hit by a car. How long ago, I did not know. His body had been flung by the impact toward the sidewalk and had landed between the standing. Next to his still frame was a patch of mottled blood. The injury had been internal and fatal.

I picked him up in my arms and stood all alone on the sidewalk.

"Will anyone miss you?" I asked him quietly.

I did not care if anyone saw me carrying a dead feral home. I was not going to leave him for an anonymous funeral on the grass. I called a cab and wrapped White Tux in my blue Gore-Tex jacket. I did not have time to get a carrier. I was headed to my old stomping grounds—the SPCA I had left behind many years ago.

I cremated him as if he were mine. Before the SPCA staff took his body away, we checked his teeth. They were a strong and perfect set. White Tux was seven years old. He had spent his life as a mouser and bird hunter, drinking from sprinklers and puddles, sleeping in a gazebo when it rained and on stone steps in summer. Perhaps he had known human kindness as well.

Prognosis – A Dreaded Word

"Px" on a health chart is prognosis. In April 2018, when I brought Inky home from the hospital, his discharge was done by a guru in kidney disease, Dr. Wolf.

"Prognosis is poor," Dr. Wolf had said, looking me straight in the eye. "I would say six months."

"Can I have him for a year?" I asked.

"No promises."

When vets put their heads together, the truth is like a rock that cannot be chipped by sentiment. Inky's family practitioner, Dr. Gyulassy, called me at home from his after-hours desk.

"How is Inky?" Dr. G opened a difficult conversation.

"Up and about. Getting his insulin and being unhappy about his daily fluids."

"Has he lost weight?"

"No."

Dr. G was following up on Inky's lab results in late April.

"Will you tell me how much time he has? I need to know."

"About one hundred days."

I was sitting on my bed, surrounded by four cats. I felt a chill but no other emotion. Inky's in-house urinalysis did not show the decline of his kidneys. His anemia was acute.

The day after, I bought a card with a picture of a kitten in bed. The words were from Colleen Houck, author of the book *Tiger's Dream:*

A tiger needs only three things to be comfortable.

Lots of food, sleep, and . . .

Actually, no. It's just those two things.

On the inside of the card were milestones measured by tally marks. A tally was each precious day spent with the family. The first tally mark was placed on April 27, 2018.

Inky spent his days with sublime pampering. I kept my workload contained. Flyer and Tippy stayed by his side, jostling his occasional languid days into play. Even at their age, my boys were still young in their romps. Janie remained a serious observer. She never lay by Inky or groomed him. She remained his closest sentry through their days together.

Early June, four days before the birthday of my foursome, I came home from work. It was a humdrum Tuesday, and I stopped to smoke a cigarette before entering my front door—five minutes of peace and reflection.

I opened the door to the apartment. My family of four were milling at the threshold. This moment of joy, I have cherished, no matter how the day has taken shape. Dinner for the family was Fancy Feast oceanfish.

Inky was a little slower than the rest of the family. I stroked him and set his bowl down close to the kitchen. As I moved to the living room, I saw a stain on the carpet that made my heartbeat pound. The stain was the size of a saucer, crimson red. It was blood.

I sought Inky out and checked his body with my hands—no wounds. I went to his furry bed. What was I looking for? My hands encountered the wetness of blood. Inky had thrown up. He was bringing up blood. Kidney disease sometimes brings up blood in vomit.

I had not changed out of my work clothes. I picked up the phone and called the emergency clinic.

"I am bringing my cat to you. He is vomiting blood."

I did not rush Inky to the hospital. It was sheer instinct. Rushing him was not a cure. There would be no more cures. In that moment, the three others at home vanished from my mind. Only Inky remained.

I talked to Inky. I sat on the carpet by his side, talking in a low tone. He was sitting still.

"Shall I read you a story? We are going to be apart for a while."

He looked at me as if it were an ordinary day. I brought Ursula Le Guin's Catwings from my bookshelf. I started reading aloud.

Overnight without Inky

The intake diagnosis was no surprise: diabetic kidney failure. Dr. Hovde was on call.

"He is going to need a transfusion. He has lost a lot of blood."

"Give him a transfusion."

The amount of $600 was not a concern to me. I wanted Inky to live.

"We are going to keep him overnight."

I consented.

At this previous hospitalization, the vet nurse had taken him away, saying, "Tell Mommy you will be better."

"Fight back, Inky. Fight back," I had said to him.

As he disappeared, carried in another woman's arms, I saw there was no fight in him today. He was tired.

"May I see him in his kennel?"

"After we have set up his IV."

I waited.

There he was, on his pink blanket, his green eyes wide. I hugged him, the kennel door wide open to make room for my presence. I did not want to leave him and held his gaze as I walked away.

At home, I lay awake until the early hours of the morning and then slept fitfully. I picked up my cell phone and called the emergency clinic.

"How is Inky?"

"Holding up."

The assessment was severe: hemoptysis, severe anemia, uremic gastritis, and ulcer. He had complete renal failure.

When I picked Inky up in the morning, I had called off work for a family emergency. I sat with him in the empty intake room, where we had been given time together. I took my hairbrush out of my backpack and brushed him down. My hands stroked him as if to memorize every inch of him. I did not wish Inky to leave from the threshold of emergency.

An hour later, I faced Dr. Frank at Camino Real Pet Clinic. "I shall take him home again, if you say so. But if this is not possible, I will accept your decision."

The emergency vet had left his catheter port on his left foreleg. I looked at Inky's face. He knew. His eyes had lost their brightness. As Dr. Frank laid him on his side, I held his paws with both hands.

"Inky, I am setting you free."

Vets use phenobarbital in euthanasia. I took the storm in my soul without tears as Inky departed.

The day was June 6. He was thirteen years old.

Not Quite Normal

Mark visited us after Inky's passing. Inky, the most sociable of my foursome, usually rushed to Mark as he stood in the living room. Mark forgot his allergies when he came to see us. Even if his chest tightened after playing with Inky and he started to sneeze, he never distanced himself from Inky's presence.

Today it was Tippy who came out to say hello. We talked about Inky as if he were still with us. The past tense did not pass our lips.

Flyer sat in the hallway, curious about the visitor, but did not venture into our midst. Janie hid herself under the bed at the sound of a male voice. The ambiance of our home front was subdued. We were mourning the eldest.

Mark drove me to Camino Real Pet Clinic with a case of Inky's DM diet. I donated the prescription food and the insulin needles. I had a million thoughts running through my mind about the health of my family as I reviewed Inky's health history. Caring for Inky had not been a chronicle of love. It had also been a grueling education. My thirteen-year-olds now came under the scrutiny of what might be typical health challenges in their senior years. I had learned what to look for, but I had no crystal ball for the unforeseen.

I held on to the subQ fluids and spare needles. Then I started talking to Dr. Frank about Janie's kidneys. Something made me believe she resembled Inky more than his brothers. The word "chronic" on the health frontier had become indelible.

The Day in Rained Worms

Summer had passed. A few surprises in my own health cluttered my calendar. Quite by chance, doctors discovered an aneurysm in the basilar artery at the base of my brain. The CT scan that revealed the aneurysm was done for an entirely different purpose. It was my turn to cling to my family for comfort. Affection came spontaneously to Flyer, Tippy, and Janie. The generosity in their affection moved me. They seemed to need no explanation for my strained behavior. Their nearness was a healing touch.

I took a long bus ride to Kaiser for an MRI. For the time I spent on the road, I had one recurring thought that turned into a prayer. Whatever my own fate was likely to be, I wished that the life of my family would not be unsettled by my condition. Between thoughts of survival and sustenance, I missed Inky.

The day was cloudy. I caught a shuttle to the hospital, and the drizzle that had started turned into a downpour. It had rained the night before, and the front lawn of the outpatient neurology clinic was sodden. Large, robust earthworms had surfaced with the heavy rain and were on the edge of the grass and in puddles on the concrete path. They seemed oblivious to passing feet and human presence.

I checked myself in and was relieved when I had a short wait time before I was due in the imaging chamber. The rain had dwindled. I stepped outside and started moving the worms from the concrete path onto the grass—one by one, picking up one worm at a time. They felt squeaky clean, washed and scrubbed by the rain. I must have rescued a good two dozen worms when I saw other people coming up the path.

No one thought I was doing something odd. They barely noticed the human bending over the puddles. I kept on going until all the worms were out of the danger zone. My good turn for the day was done.

The MRI chamber was akin to a dwarfed spaceship. The control room was out of my view. Inside the cylinder, the hum of the machine was deafening. I lay on my back, my head in semi-darkness. I took the name of God. I took the names of my cats. I saw the face of my mother, who was not with me. I did not feel so alone.

An oxymoron is a stable aneurysm. I presumed that all aneurysms were prone to rupture. When I reached home, I slept in relief. Tippy parked himself near my pillow. Janie and Flyer played hopscotch over me a while and napped to follow suit.

Sharing Tippy

Tippy, with his half smile and wide eyes, was loyal in his devotion to me. We were both unashamedly clingy, and between the two of us, this tenderness was okay. I had named him Tipper Tenderheart at birth. He was all about true love with a little bit of mischief thrown in.

One day Tippy stepped out of the apartment and met my new next-door neighbor, Pallavi. Another fan was added to Tippy's calendar. Auntie Pallu, who always wanted a cat, fell for Tippy, lock, stock, and barrel. He seemed to have a crush on Pallavi and made it a point to sit at her door whenever he had a chance.

No doorbell was ever rung. Pallavi was home, he knew. Some instinct made her open her door and melt over Tippy. I had some competition in the tiny neighborhood. Tippy roamed every nook and cranny of Pallavi's home as they unpacked. When sated, he would return and sit at our door, letting out a mellow meow—"I am home now."

Flyer was curious about the new turf Tippy had discovered. He had never intruded. The relationship with Pallavi was entirely Tippy's own. He had his space in building his own social life.

The Hills Metabolic appeared to be working. My new portraits of Tippy on the kitchen counter, with the domestic backdrop of cereal boxes and mixing bowls, showed a thinner Tippy. In truth, I liked his chubbier version.

Outside, the hillside changed color. I would hold Janie up in my arms so she could see over the balcony rail, and I would point the yellow and gold leaves to her. Her face had a look of wonderment. When the sun went down, Flyer would stretch out on the couch on the gray blanket, which was his and Inky's. Inky's presence was still tangible, and I thought of him every day.

Janie and Tippy would find their favorite corner in the bedroom and huddle in companionship on their fuzzy pea-green bed. I would find them entwined all evening, stepping out only for a nightly treat or a game of laser light.

October came, and I had suspected that Tippy was losing weight too quickly. He was also nibbling at meals, yet his movements were jaunty, and he was as nosy and social as before with the neighbors. With some consternation, I started watching his intake of water. He was drinking more frequently.

Water bowls aside, a clear glass of water stood on the kitchen counter in case one of the cats decided to climb a favorite perch. Tippy drank from the glass often. I began searching for telltale signs. His skin felt less than taut. I held him to me to check his breath. There was the mildest odor that put me on guard: halitosis, the onset of kidney disease.

Day Care and a Health Revelation

I told myself that proactive is better than reactive. Before I went to work, I took Tippy to Camino Real Pet Clinic. He was to be monitored all day with IV fluids. Diagnostics and a blood pressure check were scheduled. The vet techs knew Tippy to the core. I stood by his open kennel set up for his fluids and kissed his gray forehead.

"Back soon," I said.

His bewildered eyes stayed with me.

Tippy's primary diagnosis was renal failure. The report indicated uremia, an elevated level of blood urea. Oral neoplasia baffled me. What was affecting his gums? The likeness of gingivitis and the beginning of ulceration—all connected with the syndrome of kidney failure.

My Tippy was ill. The kitten who leaped onto my shoulder from the vet's exam table and buried his face in my neck was grown up. At thirteen and a half, he was precariously facing a chronic disease. The most worrisome news came in a low voice from the vet tech when I came back in the evening.

"Tippy has a heart murmur."

The heart has four valves. When one of the valves is damaged, the murmur is heard. Midway through Tippy's health report was the revelation: valvular heart disease.

He was happy to see me, and I watched as he was disentangled from his fluid lines. He eagerly climbed into his space age basket and came home.

"He is going to need another day of fluids to bring the numbers down," Dr. Aki was in charge.

Back in the familiar living room, Tippy showed no signs of illness. He was hungry. Flyer and Janie flanked him in welcome. I fed and brushed them. I held Tippy on my lap on and off all evening as if he were a kitten again. I wanted him to meld head to tail with my own energy. I knew I could not heal him, but I could give him strength for the time ahead.

The next morning, Mina, a familiar vet tech, was at the door of the clinic long before office hours. I had brought Tippy for another day's fluids. Mina set up Tippy's kennel, and he did not look so sad when I headed off to work. Mina had a way with him.

The vet met me in the clinic lobby. I had worked a full day and remembered nothing of the workplace. Tippy was on my mind, with flashes of Janie and Flyer. The conversation with the vet was a déjà vu of my time with Inky.

"He is going to need subQ fluids till the end of his life."

"How long, Dr. Schmidt?"

"I cannot tell."

The words were spoken yet not uttered. No one was willing to give my boy a timeline. Alert and eager, Tippy came home. My own heart was full of undefined emotion.

When Tippy slept that night, he stretched out next to Flyer on the living room couch. I spent a few hours of light sleep with Janie, who decided to curl up on her box-bed in the "underneath." It was lined with a cat-patterned duvet.

In the early hours of the morning, I moved to the living room, laid a blanket on the carpet, and camped out next to Tippy. I fell asleep holding his nearest paw.

This was the first of many nights with Tippy. He slept like a baby, and I wished upon the stars outside that I could lend him a decade of my own years just so he might be with us longer.

How Do I Love Thee . . .

I made good friends during my time in San Mateo. The others were acquaintances who came and went and fell off the horizon when good times were done. My life at home was of some curiosity and banter among those who stayed in touch with me.

I was involved, deeply involved with my cat family. They were not compensation for human progeny. Nor were they a substitute for blood relatives who were lost on the map of the grand diaspora. The sentiment I had for Inky, Flyer, Tippy, and Janie was expressed in everyday presence and quiet commitment.

If I were to bring forth the emotion, I would have to borrow words from a forgotten sonnet from my adolescent years, Elizabeth Barrett Browning in "Sonnet 43":

> How do I love thee? Let me count the ways
> I love thee to the depth and breadth and height
> My soul can reach when feeling out of sight
> For the ends of being and ideal grace.
> I love thee to the level of every day's
> Most quiet need, by sun and candlelight.
> I love thee freely, as men strive for right.
> I love thee purely, as they turn from praise.
> I love thee with the passion put to use
> In my old griefs and with my childhood's faith.
> I love thee with a love I seemed to lose
> With my lost saints. I love thee with the breath,

Smiles, tears of all my love; and, if God choose,
I shall but love thee better after death.

In late October, I was homebound from work when I saw my former neighbor D'Marcus driving down El Camino Real. He drove me back to the apartment, talking about his newborn son and his new career as a personal trainer. He had spent his early career as a coach at the University of San Francisco, and I still called him "sir" to remind him of his days as a kinesiologist on campus.

D'Marcus and Tippy had been friends. Tippy had needed no invitation to barge into his bachelor apartment when he lived across from me. D'Marcus walked up the stairs with me, ignoring the elevator. He had to see Tippy again.

As we entered the apartment, I called out to the family, "Guess who is here . . . Uncle D'Marcus!"

Flyer and Tippy appeared in the hallway. They stood side by side, staring at D'Marcus in recognition. One look, and I knew something was amiss. Tippy had a hazed expression. Around his mouth was a film of froth. *Saliva? No. Something more serious.*

D'Marcus walked toward the cats. I overtook him and pulled Tippy to me. As I knelt, his meow was low, with a tone of distress.

Neither D'Marcus nor I debated the decision. Tippy needed medical attention. On the phone to the pet clinic, I found a window in Dr. Frank's book. The last appointment of the day was Tippy's.

A hurried hug for Janie, a touch on the back for Flyer—they seemed to be getting scraps of my attention that day. Tippy had all of me, and before placing him in his carrier, I stood at the glass doors of the balcony with him in my arms.

"Our balcony, Tippy. Remember, we stood here together." My words were whispered. A lot remained unsaid.

D'Marcus navigated the rush-hour traffic while I sat in the back seat, with my hand on Tippy. He was quiet.

The lines between urgent and emergency became blurred. Standing in the waiting room, I waited for Dr. Frank to emerge.

"Do you think he had a stroke?" I asked.

"Possibly." Dr. Frank did not make a firm statement.

I had suspected the froth around his mouth to be pulmonary edema. If Tippy had indeed had a stroke, it was a mild one.

"Is it time, Dr. Frank? I do not want to lose him."

I followed her into the critical care area. Tippy was on the exam table.

"Look at him," Dr. Frank said. "He is so alert."

I picked Tippy up and put him to my shoulder. I held him and buried my face in his fur. I was unashamed in relief. I did not cry.

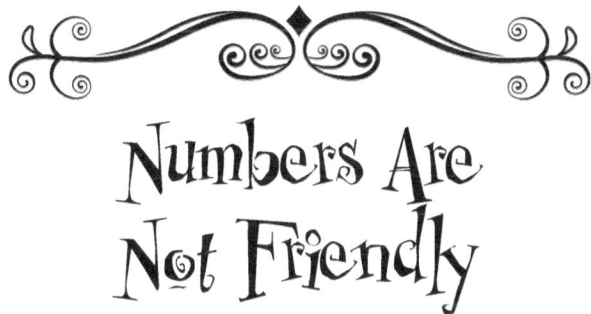

Numbers Are Not Friendly

Visitors galore—neighbors, friends, workmates. Tippy was popular. Tippy was not well. He handled the social circle well, still full of verve, and circled the humans in conversation as if there were no clock in the picture.

When we were alone, we both struggled with his subQ fluids. Tippy hated being confined to the fluid line and hissed out of character when I inserted the needle. He was huffy with the regimen and often stalked out of his confines, dragging the fluid line with him, and left the needle with his surge of water dangling.

I toweled his wet back dry. I faced his annoyance the next day. Then he stopped eating.

"Try baby food. Get food into him," the vet said.

Tippy clamped his jaw on the feeding syringe, and I spattered food all over his face. I held spoonfuls of food to his mouth. He turned away. On the second day, when I could not bear the tension any longer, I took Tippy into emergency.

I was hoping to spare him a night away from home. I could not. I could not tear myself away from his kennel door. His face was so dear, my mind snapped a picture of him through the crisscross of the mesh. I counted his whiskers close-up, saw the anxiety in his eyes, and knew that he was not smiling inside.

Nausea, typical of kidney disease, kills appetite. Tippy's inpatient medication was a smorgasbord of Cerenia and famotidine to fight his nausea. Mirtazapine tablets were given to increase appetite. Baby food and kitten kibble made up his diet.

"He is eating for us," said the vet tech finally.

His blood pressure was high. I brought him home with a prescription of amlodipine, a calcium channel blocker to relax his blood vessels. I stood slightly frozen in front of a familiar face, Dr. Hovde, at Tippy's discharge.

"We are fighting a catch-22," Dr. Hovde said.

Heart disease and kidney failure—the treatments contradict each other. I had to be careful with his subQ fluids. A fluid overload could cause congestive heart failure. I was taking a fragile patient home with me.

A Time and a Season for Every Purpose . . .

For the next two weeks, I slept by Tippy, holding his nearest paw. If he chose to sleep by Flyer on the couch, I would place my blanket on the carpet by him and fall asleep listening to him breathe.

The evenings were never broken by my silent heartache. I held him as he lay on his favorite blanket, occasionally pulling him onto my lap as I did when he was young. When Janie nudged her way in, I let her claim her brother as if she had more right to his presence than me.

Fancy Feast was served for all, and Tippy's appetite faltered. I used subdermal mirtazapine on the pinna, the outer part of his ear, to boost his hunger. We both knew that a day would come to part. I wished we could live together forever.

"What are you thinking, Tippy-O?" I asked silently.

"I wish I could live with you forever," he answered without words.

He was unnaturally thin. He prowled the kitchen and every nook of the home front. He even climbed the kitchen counter on better days. The bowl of water on the coffee table was close to the couch. I watched him drinking, his tongue making little ripples on the surface. His gait back to the couch was slower.

I never imagined I would set a date to say goodbye. I had an ominous sheet of paper in my binder. It was called the "quality-of-life checklist." I read it many times over.

I made many promises to Tippy. I would feed myself and paint my face in front of the mirror. Putting on my warpaint is something he liked watching me do. I would not let him fall apart with his illness. I would go on with life because the end was not an end.

"I shall write to you every day," I promised. This was the most solemn promise I ever made.

On November 16, Tippy spent a day with Flyer, Janie, and me. I followed him around, absorbing every moment of his presence, talking, singing, reading to him. When he decided to sit on the fleece mat at the bathroom door, I sat by him and wondered if he had something particular on his mind.

He had watched me from this very place—brushing my teeth, putting on makeup, drying my hair. I got my handwritten journal out and began reading pages out to him—my thoughts and feelings after his mother Toby ran free, Inky and Janie's rampages, Flyer's escapades, and descriptions of his own endearing personality.

The hours went by, too fast and then in slow motion. Janie and Flyer napped in the cozy underneath, and the bedroom was silent. Tippy sat on the couch in the backdrop of the greenery of the balcony. The afternoon sun streamed in. His eyes were half shut. I wished we could talk more.

When Marge, my friend and minister from the local church, arrived, she stood at the door, gazing at Tippy in the sunlight. "Shall I take him in to say goodbye to Janie and Flyer?"

"No. Just pick him up from where he is."

Marge had had nine cats in her life. Today she was standing by me to do what she had done nine times before. Marge was driving Tippy and me to the clinic.

Dr. Schmidt and the techs came in to see Tippy. He protested with a meow when I hoisted him onto my shoulder. I let his fur brush my cheek and then set him down on the table. I bent over his body before the needle reached him, holding his paws in both hands.

"No one has ever loved me like you." My words were said in front of an audience that seemed invisible. The words were not the whole truth.

"I love you," Marge said quietly.

I picked Tippy up and held him on my lap for a long time. Dr. Schmidt had placed a blanket on my knees.

"He might wet your lap. It happens when the body relaxes."

He did wet my lap. In his stillness, he etched himself on my heart.

I would not let him go. Scott, the bespectacled vet tech who had known him since he was a kitten, came to me.

"We will take good care of him," he said. He waited.

I surrendered Tippy to his arms. I sat down again.

"I have sobbed like a child," Marge said. She was giving me permission.

I did not cry. I was tearless all the way home.

A Different Kind of Love

Flyer was the first to come out to greet me. Janie stood at the bedroom door. There was something somber in both of them.

I remembered the moment for a long time. They knew. I did not need to say more. They had lost a second brother.

"I said goodbye to Tippy. It is just the three of us now."

Instead of my casual conversation, there was silence. I did not go into the kitchen. I went into the bedroom and sat on the edge of the bed. Janie and Flyer came to me, and I held them close until it was time to turn on the lights.

Pallavi knocked on the door late in the evening. We said nothing but embraced each other in shared grief.

There were days when I wished cats could talk. Perhaps we would have all wept for the missing brothers and remembered them in a "wake." Inky had had a wake with Maica, Clifford, and me drinking. Tippy's departure struck us with an inconsolable note to our grieving.

The festivities of the year-end were blurred, and we faced one another every morning with a different kind of love. Love infused with loyalty makes healing easier.

I did not want to grieve forever. I wanted to remember without the sharp sensation of pain. I wanted to rejoice in the time we had had together. Then I read the words by the authors of Grief and *Grieving:*

The reality is that you will grieve forever. You will not "get over" the loss of a loved one. You will learn to live with it. You will heal, and you will rebuild yourself around the loss you have suffered. You will be whole again, but you will never be the same. Nor should you be the same. Nor should you want to. (Elisabeth Kubler-Ross and David Kessler)

These words are debatable, but I had no one with whom to debate.

I have learned that animals cope with loss with greater resilience. I, a mere human, grappled with grief in my own way. I did not join a grief therapy group. I did share photographs of Inky and Tippy on my Facebook page but refrained from sounding shattered in my stories. I had dropped in at Camino Real Pet Clinic to pick up fluids for Janie and Flyer when I saw Dr. Frank come out to greet me.

"I lost two beloved cats in one year . . ." I said to her, my voice trailing off.

"It happens." Dr. Frank's words were not without emotion. She had been in veterinary practice for two decades.

I went home to find Flyer at the door, and Janie came out softfooted. I brought out the bite-sized Greenies. Janie used the cat stairs and stood on the kitchen counter with an insistent meow—"Me first!"

She was on her last morsel before I moved to Flyer. He preferred it at floor level or on the coffee table. I patted both as if to reassure them I was all theirs for the evening. I had left the burden of the workday outside.

The next course was Fancy Feast. I did not really want to nap but liked the quiet hour with Janie stretched out on the bed by my side. Flyer jumped up to my left, finding his spot by my ancient teddy bear. The bed was a tranquil place, with the evening sun in a half-blaze through the window.

Just the three of us—we spent many evenings this way. I never seemed to remember that Janie and Flyer were "senior" in the measure of cat years. I had a few years to go before I would be a senior too. Human seniors had to be sixty-five to have the honors of aging.

Not many of my friends had young children, and those who did had not yet explored the emotions of letting offspring go from the nest. I fell back on a recollection from two decades ago with my friend and colleague Joanne. We were having dinner at her home when her toddler son Jeffrey climbed onto her lap.

Joanne hugged him and broke our conversation, saying, "I love you. I shall love you this way even when you are an old, old man."

I tried to imagine the red-haired little boy as an old man. My mind could not generate little Jeffrey at seventy-five. I do not believe his mother could either.

I have since used the words with Flyer. "I shall love you even when you are an old, old man." I could never think of Janie as a dowager cat. I said no such words to her.

I acquired a television set. Our habits changed a bit because we clustered in the living room after dinner. Before the invasion of the television, I used to watch my favorite serials on my tablet, with Janie and Flyer sitting with me. I propped the tablet on the pillows, and we sat in a row in front of it. If we had popcorn, we could have called it movie night.

I realized that cats do not "watch" TV. They look at the moving pictures the way they respond to a laser light thrown in front of them. Janie sometimes leaped onto the glass-topped surface in front of the TV set and touched the screen with her paw. She was sometimes content to sit with her back to the TV screen, enjoying the ambiance of LED lights.

Inky and Tipper had not seen the couch-potato culture in the home front. Flyer took to being the typical male on the couch but without the can of beer. He looked, eyes half-closed, at CNN news. When bored with the program, he dozed off.

Family nights at home had one other facet. Janie and Flyer got subQ fluids on every third day of the week. Janie's kidneys had shown mild deterioration. Flyer was still holding strong. SubQ was precautionary for Flyer.

The Next Birthday

June 10, 2019—my specialty was tuna cake on Janie and Flyer's fourteenth birthday. The candles did not stand well, and the humangrade tuna made a wobbly cake. I visited Pet Food Express on the way home to pick up something particularly special. Gigi, my longstanding friend and manager, gave me salmon fillets as a treat—a gift for my birthday girl and boy.

I lit four candles. I blew them out with some fanfare and watched the two burrow into the tuna. This festivity had an inevitable poignancy. The song was sung to Inky and Tippy as well. In my heart, I was convinced they could hear me. I tried not to sing off-key. I had lost my singing voice ever since I stopped attending Sunday church.

Flyer was a heavyweight with the manner of a mature male. His face had taken on a worldly look, as if he had seen much and done much. Janie, however, looked as if she were five years old, untouched by time. Every time I looked at her, I wondered if I would ever see another cat who matched her beauty.

July came with a heat wave. The squirrels disappeared at noon, and I saw deer descend from the hills to search for greenery in backyards and lawns. Although the sprinklers came on at night to wet the grass, there was no rain to bring solace to the parched ground.

I was home, kidding around with Janie and Flyer about their smorgasbord diets. I became the butler, carrying a selection of prescription and non-prescription platters at dinnertime. Royal Canin kidney diet morsels had entered the menu for Janie. Flyer ignored Hills stews for weight control and ate only Fancy Feast.

One day, while seated at the edge of the bed, I watched the two of them come back to their half-full bowls for round two. Janie was headed out to the hallway when I noticed a slight limp in her gait. One foreleg seemed to be bothering her, but I could not tell which one.

By the end of the evening, I confirmed the limp to be in her left foreleg. *A sprain?* She leaped from the pine dinette table to the kitchen counter and landed like a bird—no chance of a sprain there. She easily climbed in and out of her box bed under the bed. The favorite hideout was made out of a rollout clothing drawer. Did the high edge pinch a nerve?

Two days passed, and the limp did not go away. Janie showed no signs of pain. I made an appointment with the vet and took a protesting Janie for a ride. Her meows were indignant. I still thought she needed a checkup.

Dr. Aki did a probing physical and found nothing startlingly amiss. Janie had an enchanting effect on her with her wide-eyed shyness. Dr. Aki gave Janie a free nail clip and sent us packing with bupenorphine as a painkiller. The assessment said "soft tissue trauma." My vigil on my girl's gait did not cease.

Although the limp got deeper, it seemed to have no effect on Janie's movements. She still leaped on tabletops and climbed the cat stairs. The limp caused no impediment in jumping on the bed and climbing the cat tree. Janie was uncomplaining and relaxed. She lay on her back, paws up in the air on the duvet, waiting for a belly rub. My touch on her left leg did not make her flinch. The exact location of the injury was still a mystery.

The next visit to the vet brought Janie and me to Dr. Frank. Three weeks had passed. There are days that stay etched in the mind despite the wear and tear of other events. I had walked into one such day.

Dr. Frank examined Janie for ten minutes. It seemed like an eternity. There was a hard mass where Janie's left foreleg met her chest.

"This could be a sarcoma. I would like to take an X-ray."

Instinct told me I did not have to wait for a biopsy for the verdict. This was soft tissue sarcoma—a large mass.

"Can you operate?" I asked Dr. Frank.

"I could not," she said. "There are too many nerves in this area."

We were still standing in front of Janie's X-ray. I was transfixed with the view of the hidden anatomy of my girl.

"Call Sage." Dr. Frank was referring to the best veterinary specialization in the Bay Area. "Make an appointment with an oncologist."

Anything for Janie. I would walk to the ends of the world—not quite. I was headed for Redwood City, where Sage Veterinary Center was located. Nothing happens fast enough when you need it to happen. We had to wait a week to see an oncologist. I did not know at the time that Janie had a fast-growing sarcoma that had no regard for veterinary schedules.

On August 6, 2019, Janie and I met Dr. Brian Marker at Sage. I took Janie out of the carrier and placed her on the exam table. Her tension was palpable. Her face had "baseball" eyes, expressing fear, and she moved closer to me as Dr. Marker began to speak.

"I am going to run some preliminary tests on her," he said.

Dr. Marker had a very pleasant voice. My hands were stroking Janie's back, and she seemed to ease a little.

I sat alone in the room, ruminating on the decisions I would need to make. I cleared my mind of all the other nitty-gritty and focused on what was impending. The cancer was not a matter of speculation. Dr. Frank's assessment had given me options of chemotherapy and radiation. Nothing Dr. Marker could say would be as a surprise.

In that half hour, Janie's life cascaded through my mind—Janie as a kitten, an imp crashing my paper lampshades and ripping my dreamcatcher, the hissy girl confronting Inky and the wild chases through our living room. Most vivid was the loving Janie sitting on my chest or lying curled by my side as I rested.

When Dr. Marker walked in with Janie in his arms, his first words startled me.

"Where did you get her?"

"She was born in my home. I rescued her feral mother."

"She is beautiful. I thought she was much younger than fourteen."

Janie had gone through an ultrasound with Mr. Marker. My girl had fibrosarcoma. She was in the first stage of chronic kidney disease. The diagnostic imaging revealed gallstones in her bladder and cholangitis. Cholangitis is an inflammation of the bile duct, which carries bile to the gallbladder. I took in the news unflinchingly.

Dr. Marker was at his computer, looking up available dates for an appointment with radiology. Radiation therapy and a prescription of ursodiol for Janie's inflammation were on the chart.

"I would give her a year of good life with treatment," Dr. Marker said.

This time, I flinched. If I had promised myself to walk to the ends of the world for Janie, the trip would take me to Campbell on the other side of the peninsula. Sage's bastion of pet cure oncology was a long ride with hope.

Dr. Marker gently placed Janie in her carrier. I had the urge to get Janie out of there in a hurry. There was no panic in her. I wanted her home with Flyer. I wanted to tell her nothing had changed. I wanted nothing to have changed.

Still, everything had changed. The afternoon suddenly seemed less bright. I had the first taste of a battle with an unknown assailant.

The Promise of Human-Caliber Cancer Care

The MRI was scheduled for mid-August with PetCure's Dr. Quarterman.

The MRI chamber was identical to the one I had seen for my own MRI. I was not allowed to enter. Instead, the oncology nurses carried Janie inside. MRI machines are large tube-shaped magnets, and lying inside the machine, I was claustrophobic, as if locked into a space capsule. I lay still, but animals are anesthetized. Janie would not remember the experience. Her little self would have lain on the back, the radio frequency currents realigning the water molecules in her body.

A human body is made up of 65 percent water. I did not know how much water a cat's tissues contained. I had to look it up—67 percent water. The newly aligned atoms produce signals that can be captured by imaging. Later in the day, I saw the cross-sectional images of Janie's thorax.

The diagnosis was fibrosarcoma, a large invasive, rapidly growing cancer. The treatment plan was stereotactic radiation therapy or SRT. Three sessions of treatment would take Janie into September— three fractions of radiotherapy. Fractionation divides a full dose of radiation into parts. Neither Dr. Quarterman nor I wanted to prolong the sessions. Janie would receive three fractions in one day.

Janie was a quiet observer to this discussion. Her sedation had worn off. I looked at my little girl. She was hardier than I had anticipated. I scooped her up like an infant and headed home.

The cost of the MRI had been met. The estimate for SRT was intimidating, but I did not stop to ponder over a veterinary budget. I used every source of available funds for the procedure and applied for a grant with the Joshua Louis Animal Cancer Foundation.

Except for the limp on Janie's left foreleg, Janie had not changed. Her expression was less impish, and that was the only difference. She still asked for belly rubs. Her colors were vivid and her fur immaculate. The impending radiation would lead to some hair loss on her shoulder. I tried to imagine a bald patch but could not.

Flyer treated Janie as if she were normal. His sister of fourteen years, she had become his playmate. He still scruffed her in his tussles and snuggled next to her in their box bed when he felt brotherly. He was taking Tippy's place with great aplomb. Animals have an emotional resilience that unfolds in the way they accept loss and pain.

My own world shrank with Janie's illness. All else faded but my family of two. I turned entirely mechanical at work, performing with a distanced state of mind. I was not without the empathy from my coworkers, who pitched in with a purse of $350 as a pre-Christmas gift dedicated to Janie.

Despite oncologist Dr. Marker's letter of reference, the Joshua Louis Foundation did not contribute to Janie's cancer care. The foundation was blunt. The patient's prognosis was not good. I spent a moment in resentment and then went ahead with my own plans with Sage.

"Sounds Like a Plan"

During the MRI at Sage, the oncology team made a body "mold" of Janie that would allow the curative beam of radiation to accurately target the cancer while protecting the healthy tissue. The mold was made of a foam product that hardened into a full-body shield.

A fraction of external beam radiation takes fifteen minutes to render. I assumed three fractions would take less than an hour. The procedure took half a day. I surrendered Janie to the scrub-clad technician.

On the ride to Campbell, I gently stroked her back all through the ride, and she had not been vocal in her irritation of distances. Her fur was soft, and she purred in comfort. Perhaps the purr also had a note of bewilderment. Her right foreleg was curled under her as she sat in the carrier. The left foreleg was stretched out, a bit unaligned. The mass was impeding free movement.

Before Janie's treatment unfolded, I did my own research and sometimes talked aloud to her about what I learned. I needed to know for myself every step of what she would endure. A full dose of radiation is typically divided into smaller portions—fractions. While informing myself from human health websites, I discovered the unit of measurement "Gy." Radiation doses for cancer are measured in "gray," the symbol for which is Gy. SRT was a gamma knife, the procedure replacing surgery. I could not visualize Janie in the linear acceleration vault. I had nothing to do but wait. I longed for Dr. Quarterman's reassuring presence, and the Sage lobby grew oppressive.

I sat a while in a corner seat, my backpack by my side. Next to me was a dog owner who was also biding time for his pet's discharge. We exchanged our stories and shared the lives of our pets. I looked around the lobby. It held half a dozen dog owners and one woman with a cat. I looked into the carrier at the large gray longhaired cat. He meowed, looking me directly in the eyes.

"My boy," the woman said.

That was all she needed to say. I knew exactly how we were all feeling.

What to Do with Nothing to Do

The Pruneyard Mall was two miles away from Sage. I asked the receptionist for directions and left the hospital.

The sprawling mall had Peet's. I sat down for a cup of coffee, and a sliver of tension vanished. I walked down the cobbled path, looking at window displays. Shopping was not on my mind. There was a grassy patch with benches on the northside of the mall, and I sat down to smoke a cigarette. I could not remember the taste.

I was hungry. I was still in touch with the clock. It was past the noon hour, and the lunch places were filling up with an office crowd. I went into an Italian sandwich counter to see the takeout menu. The salad servings were large, and the sandwiches were hefty. I suddenly lost the patience to sit down for a meal. Within me was an anxiety I could not quell.

I began walking again, this time to the outskirts of the parking lot, where I spotted a Pet Food Express. Flyer and Janie were running low on bath wipes. I crossed Campbell Avenue and entered the store. The small purchase made the day a bit normal.

I had two more hours to see Janie. Meandering past the outdoor sculpture of four life-size blue gorillas, I stopped to take a picture of a young girl sitting on a gorilla's back. Her mother smiled her consent.

The face of Dora the Explorer stared at me from the posters of Pruneyard Cinemas. It was a human Dora, not an animated one.

Dora and the Lost City of Gold had a matinee showing. On an impulse, I bought a ticket and went into the theater. The darkness was a relief, and I sank into a seat. I watched the movie as if on mute. However, the green Peruvian jungles and antics of Dora and Boots made pleasant pictures. Janie stayed on my mind, and I lost track of the storyline.

When Doctors Say "Hope"

I faced Dr. Quarterman with the eagerness that comes on Christmas Eve. I was not expecting Santa to walk in through the door, just the person who took on a battle against the spindle cells that had become the enemy inside.

The radiology tech had placed a sheaf of radiology images in front of me. The sarcoma, in graphic form, was intimidating. The treatment was going to shrink the mass, but the nerve damage to Janie's left leg would never be fully reversed. Janie was still to be brought back to me.

I took the moment to ask Dr. Quarterman a potent question. "Do you think the treatment will have full effect?"

"I hope so," she said cautiously.

"Just hope?"

"I always say 'hope.' We can only hope."

The door opened. The technician walked in with Janie in her arms. Janie's carrier was slung over one shoulder. Her face looked a little sleepy, but she brightened upon seeing me. Soundlessly, she stood on the examination table, three legs firm. The left foreleg was tentatively off the surface. This was where the damage lay. I touched her gently, biting back many words.

Dr. Quarterman picked Janie up and set her on the floor. Janie walked across the room to the window where the sun poured in. Except for the visible limp, Janie was exactly as I had brought her in.

"Let's go home, Janie. Flyer is waiting," I said aloud.

She willingly climbed into the carrier.

I spent five minutes with the discharge papers and an online questionnaire, giving Sage permission to use Janie's case for their patient profiles on web.

"I would recommend physiotherapy for the leg." Dr. Quarterman's voice was calm. "Redwood City has physical therapists on staff."

I suddenly had more to do. Providing love was a busy pursuit. I had had plenty to do with Inky and Tippy at home. Janie still needed subQ fluids. Flyer was going to get his fluids that evening. I sat by Janie, my hand stroking her neck and back during the ride home.

Flyer greeted us at the door, his face curious and anxious. I never underestimated his understanding of illness. He knew what I could not explain. I unzipped the carrier, and Janie stepped out, quite unheeding of the weak left foreleg. The two met and touched noses, and Janie made a beeline for the bedroom.

The same night, I resized some baby clothes my neighbor had given me. I made short-sleeved T-shirts for Janie. The spot on her shoulder that had been radiated needed cover. She looked so cute in a shirt that I had to take photographs to capture her fashion statement. We learned to make our moments memorable.

Finding Scout's House

Scout's House is a landmark in San Mateo. It is a physical rehabilitation therapy center for special needs and disabled pets. I chose to take Janie to Scout's House after a veterinary tech at Camino Real Pet Clinic spoke about its services with accolades.

Janie's left foreleg had the same unaligned appearance as before her radiation therapy. She did not touch the leg to the floor when she walked. It was likely she felt discomfort from the radiation and the continued presence of the sarcoma. Janie had a prescription for Pregabalin to control neuropathic pain. She paid no attention to the radiation site on her shoulder, and there was no hair loss on her body.

Before I met Krista, Janie's prospective physical therapist, I delved into the story of Scout, the dog after whom Scout's House was named. Janie was my cherished companion. In contrast, Scout was an abandoned black pup who was found in a Petco parking lot. She was seven weeks old, hearing-impaired, partially blind, with hind legs severely weakened by distemper. Miraculously, she survived the viral disease. Lisa Stahr, who had rescued the abandoned Scout, rehabilitated the pup with extensive orthopedic manipulation, acupuncture, and swim therapy. Scout was finally able to walk. She lived for three years.

Krista became "Auntie Krista" to Janie, who saw her once a week. Perhaps it was love at first sight for Janie because she was delighted by Krista's company. The first assessment of Janie's physical abilities was done by a resident veterinarian and Krista.

I was allowed to sit in for the examination. Janie seemed so tiny with three women surrounding her. She sat, walked, lay on the therapy mat, looked around, and walked around the room. There was a spontaneous ease in her movements. If I blinded myself to the left foreleg, I would have found Janie her flawless self—only I knew that Janie had never had a day of illness in her life, not even a sniffle.

It was mid-September. After each visit with the physical therapist, I brought Janie back with a home exercise program, written in Krista's own handwriting.

A Yoga Mat and a Paddle Board

After work each day, I sat on the living room floor with Janie and Flyer. I used my own yoga mat for Janie's exercises, with a towel thrown over to give her a comfortable surface.

We simulated "bicycling" movements with Janie standing. I supported her under her belly with one hand and made pedaling motions with her left foreleg, giving her foot and paw a sensory experience.

My hands played a vital part. I tapped, tickled, and spidered my fingers along her carpal extensors. I gently pinched her toes to energize her when she stiffened. It relaxed her leg. I became part of the small cat anatomy for the half hour we worked together.

One exercise stumped me. Krista prescribed weight-shifting with Janie lying down. I could get her to lie down, but rolling her side to side with my hands met with protest.

"Get a Bosu ball," said Krista.

A Bosu ball was a balance aid. I searched online and found one on Amazon for $119, and it was bright blue. Delving further, I saw a used Bosu for half the price, but I did not want Janie using a secondhand product. Whether Janie would take to something so new made me think of other strategies.

I had a paddle board in the closet. I had intended to use it myself but never made time to go to the pool in my apartment building.

Besides, I hated cold water, and the pool did not have solar heating. The paddle board was now Janie's. I made her sit on it, belly flattened against the board. I lifted the board two feet off the floor and tilted it side to side in a gentle see-saw. She could stay steady in the sway, even with her left foreleg impaired.

All the while, I got calls from the oncology team at Sage, following up on Janie's progress. I reported the progress in physiotherapy. I described mild hair loss on the radiation site. I was uncertain if the mass was shrinking. Janie's upper left foreleg still had a visible mass. To my eyes, the position of the mass seemed to be shifting, diminishing above and growing bigger in the lower leg. Krista had noticed this shift during our last appointment at Scout's House.

There were alarm bells from Sage. The radiotherapy had floundered. In November, I called Dr. Marker and scheduled a physical for Janie.

The Road Less Traveled

Two roads diverged in a wood, and I
Took the one less traveled by, and that has
Made all the difference.
                              — Robert Frost, "The Road Not Taken"

When Janie and I drove into Sage for her post-radiation assessment, we were both attached in our movements and emotions like conjoined twins. My tension made Janie tense. Janie's fidgeting made me fidgety. I would have meowed to echo every one of her meows.

I had a brave conversation with Flyer as we left home. He may as well have berated me with the words "How many times do you need to take her to the hospital?"

Too many.

"I am very worried" were my first words to Dr. Marker, Janie's first oncologist at Sage, Redwood City.

"So am I" was his response.

Janie's mass, instead of shrinking after stereotactic radiotherapy, had tripled in size. Dr. Marker's prognosis was grim. Janie was diagnosed with a second type of cancer on the same leg. Osteogenic sarcoma is bone cancer, common in children and dogs. Osteosarcoma rarely occurs in cats. Now I was really ticked off with Mother Nature.

What I had tried to avoid became the only choice: amputation of the left forelimb. Something within me churned in protest. The drastic solution would be a violation of Janie's independence and beauty. How long would she live as a rehabilitated tripod?

Candor is a necessary ingredient in an oncologist's conversation with a pet parent. "Without amputation, she has three months. She has already lost use of the left leg."

The silence in the room was laden with unspoken decisions. The decision was my own. I looked at Janie, who sat between us. She seemed distracted and had lost track of the conversation.

"If she were my cat," Dr. Marker was saying, "I would not choose amputation."

"Why not?" I asked.

The prognosis was gloomy. Janie was fourteen years old.

I decided to go through with an amputation. For all the care Janie had received, I was determined that Janie be free of cancer. Dr. Marker did not dissuade me. He just opened the surgery schedule and found the first available date for Janie.

I took my treasure home. As I gently spoke to Janie, the roads of Redwood City blurred, and so did my sense of time. I spoke a human language. I wished I had the communication skills of my friend Hilary. Animal psychics communicate in images. Janie seemed attentive, but I had no pleasant mental pictures to offer.

Red Letter Day

When we drove to the hospital, I held Janie's left paw all the way to Sage. The day was December 13, 2019, and my friend Joyce was my stalwart companion at the wheel. We talked about Lily, Joyce's beloved dog whom she had nursed through Cushing's disease. Janie's impending surgery brought back memories of Lily's critical stages, but Joyce had words of encouragement despite her experiences of difficult caregiving. We both shared an intense love of animals. They were our families.

Dr. Colleen McCoy was Janie's surgeon. When I checked Janie in at Sage, Dr. McCoy took her out of the carrier to take her into a preoperative exam.

"I shall take good care of your child," Dr. McCoy said.

I would be without Janie for almost two days. I made an unorthodox request to Dr. McCoy before she disappeared into surgery with Janie.

"I would like to preserve Janie's leg."

Dr. McCoy did not look surprised. "I know," she said. "You mentioned this to Dr. Marker. We will freeze it for you."

This was the left forelimb that Krista at Scout's House had worked on for three months. I had massaged this precious leg every day between the physical therapist's labors. This limb was now going to be separated from Janie. Joyce drove me home and hugged me before she left. We had both run out of conversation.

Flyer and I spent the evening feeling the absence of Janie wordlessly. He and I had a connectedness from overcoming hard times. Flyer was more of a stoic than I and seldom showed stress. I held him close and lay on the couch, and the CNN newscast was the only resonance of reality in the living room.

I talked at bedtime. I remembered Inky and Tippy, and their absence became painfully pronounced. Flyer's expression did not change with my monologue. He just moved closer to my pillow, and I fell asleep with my arm around him.

A Terrible Haircut

Veterinary techs specialize in surgery. They do not specialize in cutting a cat's hair. When I saw Janie at her discharge on December 14, I did a double take. Her gorgeous fur on her left side was gone. I expected the shave but not the clippers of a clumsy barber. I was horrorstruck. The incision was covered by a body sock, beneath which was a heavy dressing. Janie was a tripod. She was awake.

I was fighting mixed emotions. The child I had left with Dr. McCoy was mine again. She saw me, and her eyes changed expression. She was euphoric under anesthesia, but this was a different reaction. Janie was alert. I saw recognition.

The postoperative care had a sheaf of instructions. I ingested most of the facts facing the surgery technician. I did not have my glasses with me, and the papers went into my backpack.

Along with Janie's oral medications came a waterproof freezer pack—her left thoracic forelimb, now mine to keep. A fentanyl patch was on Janie's bare skin. I had never seen Janie's bare skin before. With the fur shaven, it was pale pink, soft as velvet. I touched her body with tenderness. When the long-acting surgical anesthetic would wear off, fentanyl would take effect as an analgesic.

The surgery had invaded arteries, veins, muscle, and subcutaneous tissues. Blood vessels had been ligated, and the skin had been closed using nylon sutures. I did not see the length of the wound or the "cruciate" crisscross of the nylon sutures until much later. I had brought home an e-collar in case she tried to lick the site or scratch her dressing.

Looking at Janie—cradled in her "underneath box," swaddled in gauze, and on her favorite blanket—I wondered if she had become more precious for the time and money invested in her health. I realized my feelings for Janie would never change. She was precious the day she was born, and I was glad I did not have to give her away. The fact she had become fragile made me covet her presence. I even felt a twinge of jealousy when Flyer deftly climbed into Janie's box and burrowed himself next to her, his gray body touching her shaven skin like a shield.

Flyer, the big brother, now had a defined role. He had always been Inky's shadow and Tippy's playmate. His feelings for Janie came forth in a whole new wave.

Finding Her Balance

I went to work the day after bringing Janie back home. My faith in Flyer's capacity to look after her grew from that day on. The coffee shop was only a bare scaffold around me just to support the trivia of everyday living. I was immersed in Janie, and all things faded when I stepped inside our home. Flyer got his fluids, and Janie did not. She was anemic and had received a transfusion at Sage.

I applied a cold compress to the incision site for a few days to give her comfort. I peeked beneath the bandage to look at the incision for the first time. It was an impressive length, with three inches of visible stitches running horizontally along Janie's body. She was moving around on three legs, out of her bed, to the living room and bathroom. I carried her up to the bed to have her sit at the edge and look out of the window. Her movements seemed confused, but she did not sit still.

I started taking photographs of brother and sister with a longing to make our togetherness unforgettable. Flyer and Janie lay nestled on the green fuzzy corner bed when I cleaned the wound for the first time. Warm water and gauze with gentle motions was a simple task. It was not so simple when I stumbled on an intruder in the sutures. A grain of cat litter was caught between the stitches. Janie had tried to climb the litter box when I was not looking.

Flyer still played scruff-wrestling with Janie. She was more docile on three legs. When she walked, she sometimes stopped and sat, belly to the floor. She did not trip. She forgot to "center" her right foreleg to make the tripod stride. When this happened too often, I just picked her up and took her to wherever she wanted to be.

One day I saw Janie in the bathroom, sitting on a puppy pad she used these days. She seemed nonplussed by her loss of balance. I sat with her, and many thoughts were sent to her—the first memory of her in this apartment, huddling in this bathroom with her three brothers, the grooming sessions with me sitting on the toilet seat with Janie on my lap, clipping her pale nails. Her smallness was so endearing on my lap, and she never yelled at me. Janie was a leaper, like Tippy. She loved the edge of the vanity, high as it was. The tiniest drip from the faucet would make her bend to drink. Janie's hind legs were strong. Perhaps she would have the time to try the antic again.

There was no one at home to take a photograph of Janie and me together. I stood with her, my left hand under her belly, bandages and all, and took a selfie. She gave a half smile when I said she looked like a gauze sausage. She had a sense of humor despite all her challenges.

Krista sent her words of encouragement. Sage had shared Janie's biopsy results with her. Sage's pathologist had described the mass that had been removed as densely cellular and an aggressive osteosarcoma. While talking to her, I did a second reading of the biopsy report. I looked up the meaning of neoplasm, an abnormal mass that could be benign or malignant. No one can pinpoint the exact cause of a neoplasm, and we certainly could not find the cause of Janie's. The relief came from the knowledge that Janie's lungs were clear.

Six days later, Janie shook up the little world in which we lived. I came home to my precious twosome. Although Flyer had a hearty appetite, Janie showed no interest in dinner. Her temperature was normal.

Beneath her bandage, I saw a redness that concerned me. I thought it might be the beginnings of a seroma, a bubble of clear fluid that could cause an infection in the wound.

I lay Janie on her fuzzy green bed, with Flyer climbing in to keep us company. I had Gerber's baby food in the kitchen just in case normal eating was disrupted by the painkillers.

I had never seen Janie ignore her meal. I used a feeding syringe to fill her little mouth, and I wiped spills of orange puree from her chin. I managed to feed her a four-ounce tub and removed the spattered bib. I felt as if I were feeding a human child. A while later, Janie walked to her "underneath" box bed and stretched out to sleep.

The Jitters

When Flyer said "meow," it was mellow. When Janie said "meow," it was loud. A loud meow had me to the bedroom to check up on her.

Janie lay on her side, her full length stretched out. Little tremors ran through her body, visually like soft hiccups, but I saw no stress in her breathing.

I did not wait for a speculative diagnosis on the phone. I headed straight to Sage emergency with Janie. My hug to Flyer on the way out was a very grateful one. This boy of mine had steely courage. He was going to be alone with no resentment.

Janie was listless, unaware of what was happening. In the waiting area at Sage, I checked her in and paced ferociously like a caged lion. I tried to catch a glimpse of Janie through the glass panel of the emergency room door. There were two critical cases ahead of her, both dogs.

Dr. Bell met me after a half-hour wait. The verdict was hypocalcemia, severe in proportion. Calcium in the blood comes from the bones, and too little calcium absorption in the blood had caused Janie's muscle cramps.

"Her calcium levels were normal at the time of surgery. I do not know how this could happen."

"Will she die?" I blurted out the question.

"She would have died if you had not brought her in." Dr. Bell did not mince words.

My next sight of Janie was in the ICU kennel. She was wearing an e-collar, strapped in electrodes measuring her vitals. She was playfully rolling around, protesting her confinement, and, at the same time, responding to my presence. I felt love and a determination to make every instrument of veterinary care work for her.

I looked at Dr. Bell, who was standing next to me. "She is a feral, you know. She was born in my home."

"Not anymore," Dr. Bell bantered. No feral cat has received this level of veterinary care.

Sage's pharmacy did not have calcitriol, a synthetic vitamin D3, on the shelf. The human-grade calcitriol was an expensive medication, enabling calcium to be absorbed into the bloodstream directly from the stomach. Janie needed calcitriol. A veterinary tech in ICU, getting off duty, rushed to the local CVS pharmacy with the prescription.

I was allowed a few more minutes with Janie. Her eyes were bright, her little body playful as long as I stood by her. Two veterinary techs exchanged reassurances with me. One of them, I recognized from a local congregation.

Sleep did not come to me. Flyer slept like a baby, happy to have me home by his side.

I do not remember how the day at work went. I functioned mechanically and with a semblance of precision. I even smiled at my customers. My mind was on a kennel in Sage, and there was someone very precious in a kennel waiting for me.

Body and Mind

My cat family imparted a profound lesson. The mind rules the body. Beyond instinct, my cats had the will to live. I had seen their fight to overcome illness.

I had also learned the serene acceptance of death. Both Inky and Tippy knew when their bodies were relenting to a phase in which there would be no further restoration. It was I who could not face the demise of the body.

I had pulled Janie to the edges of veterinary science. She was with me as a fragile child who was still practicing walking on three legs.

On December 28, I met Dr. Bell for a recheck. I met a grim veterinarian. Dr. Bell explained that Janie's seroma looked inflamed, and there was the possibility of an infection. Dr. Bell wanted a culture of fluid accumulation. She ran an ultrasound and radiograph on Janie. She flushed Janie's sutures and rebandaged her.

"Janie is not healing fast enough. We might have to bring her back to surgery to re-suture her."

The edges of science had a cost. Re-suturing had a price tag of as high as a surgery. There were other complications. Janie had signs of pancreatitis. However, her radiograph showed clear lungs. There was no trace of cancer in her.

"You might wish to euthanize her," Dr. Bell said quietly.

"No." My response was instant.

I brought Janie home. Flyer wore same expression, berating me for taking her to the hospital again.

I placed Inky's king-sized bed next to me, brought Janie to lie on it, and placed my arm on her body. She was sleepy. I touched her face, so beautiful, with green eyes alert. The face seemed thinner. Flyer perched himself on the pillow next to mine.

Together, we drifted off to sleep. I was dozing when I felt a disturbance in Janie. A strange quiver was shaking her, nothing like the tremors of hypocalcemia. She made no sound. I jackknifed into a sitting position.

Janie was still swathed in a heavy bandage. She turned on her back in the sway of the quiver and changed her position, facing away from me. I watched her anxiously, trying not to panic.

One more turn, and Janie was facing me again. There was a convulsion that was triggering her movements. I picked up my cell phone and called Sage emergency.

"Where is she?" the emergency receptionist asked.

"On my bed."

"Bring her to floor level. Can you show us her movements? Take a video, email us."

I took a twenty-second video on my iPhone. Before I could end the video, Janie made three sharp turns to the edge of the bed. She was on the carpet in a flash. She did not leap off. She had fallen. On the carpet, she was sitting, belly flat, entirely alert.

Flyer was at his perch, looking over his sister. Of course, at a time like this, I could not send the video to Sage. It kept bouncing.

I threw my iPhone down. I pulled on my jeans, threw on a jacket, and got Janie's carrier out. I was not waiting for phone instructions anymore. Before I picked Janie up to place her in the carrier, I brought her to face Flyer.

"Say bye for now."

I brought their faces together. Flyer did not move from the pillow. Their noses touched.

There was no resistance from Janie. She normally meowed in protest at being placed in her carrier. She was not convulsing. She was breathing normally. Her body was soft outside the margins of the bandage. My hands had a nervous tingle.

I called a cab at 1:00 a.m. I waited with Janie's carrier at the curb of my apartment driveway, and the Lyft driver pulled in. Fourteen minutes is a very long time. For me, with Janie by my side, a milestone happened.

My hand stayed on Janie's back, seeking the fur outside the bandage. The zippered opening in the carrier stayed open. The vehicle sped through the lights with no traffic impeding us. Janie was quiet. For a few brief moments, I moved my hands to my lap. Then I reached for her again. There was a stillness.

"Turn on the light," I said urgently to the driver.

He complied. I grasped Janie in the carrier, bringing her out with one hand on her rear, the other on the back of her neck. She made no movement.

Her face was close to mine. Opening her mouth with my fingers, I rendered mouth to mouth. I was attempting resuscitation in a moving vehicle. Again, I breathed into her. There was no response. Once again, Janie stayed limp. Had she left me?

The light inside the vehicle turned off. We pulled into Sage, and I rang the after-hours bell. The veterinary tech took Janie from me.

"Resuscitation," I said. My instructions were imperative. "You may have a DOA."

Time, perhaps ten minutes—I do not know how long I waited in a blackout of emotion.

The emergency veterinarian stepped out to meet me. "Unfortunately, we could not revive Janie."

A cardiac defibrillator renders an electric shock to the heart in an attempt to restore the heart to normal rhythm. The emergency procedure could not bring Janie back to me.

I sat in a room alone. There was a chair and a steel examination table. There were two doors. The details stayed with me. I stood up and paced and then sat down again. One door opened. Janie was in a soft cat bed, her bandages off, lying quietly on her side. They handed the bed to me and left me in silence.

I held Janie on my lap. My voice broke in a tearless sob. "Janie, how shall I live without you?"

Home, With or Without Janie

It was morning. I could not leave Janie at Sage. I brought her home the way I had taken her to emergency. My hand on her back, I talked to her.

"There is a half-moon out in the sky. We are going home, Janie. Flyer is waiting."

I slept in the early hours, Flyer at my side. Janie was on the bed, swathed in the blankets she loved. I caressed her face, stroked her body, and lay with my head against her side. I fell asleep, holding her right paw in my hand.

Sage sent white roses in condolence. I cremated Janie with a white rose on her body. Grief is an ache. Some part of the mind drowns in it. All of the heart goes numb.

Camino Real Pet Clinic made a memorial donation in Janie's name to the University of California's Department of Companion Animal Health. The School of Veterinary Science is at the Davis Campus. Inky and Tipper had received the same honor from their family veterinarian. The funds support research in companion animal diseases like diabetes, kidney disease, and cancer.

Flyer Becomes My One and Only

Flyer became my rock. Once a frolicking rover, he donned the role of warm and earnest companion, seldom leaving my side. On his own, he could handle being a solitary after living in the company of three siblings all his life.

He had sat by Janie with his front paws on her body, licking her face, knowing she had left us. He did this for several minutes, and it was not a gesture of parting. I watched. I understood. We both shared a deep grief.

Flyer returned to sit by his sister and spent an afternoon alone with her. Janie's face was serene. My heart was in turmoil, but I was silent like stone. Flyer was unabashed in showing his emotions. I doubted I would have ever healed from parting with Janie had it not been for Flyer flooding me with his affection.

The new year of 2020 blew in and brought a year of the coronavirus. While the world reeled from the pandemic and the upsurge of deaths, our lives stayed contained within a masked community and a diminishing social life.

Responding to a "shelter-in-place order," Starbucks closed its doors for a month with full pay to all staff. I needed the time to be home with Flyer, and I promised myself we would not be gloomy together. I do not believe in fate. Fate chisels our lifespans as it pleases. Medicine enhances the time we have together. Flyer and I were together for a reason I could not explain. The ebb of family members from illness had had a deep impact. He had shared the departures of Inky, Tippy, and Janie and quietly adapted to a different life. I had to respect this boy of mine.

On some evenings at home, missing Janie's vibrant energy around the home, I would call Flyer "brother." I folded the gray couch to a compact loveseat with Flyer's gray wool blanket and his favorite cushion. I would lie close to him on the carpet, holding his paw. He half-closed his eyes and ignored the television screen while I watched the news. If we had been given after-dinner beers, the picture would have made a human family.

Flyer continued his kidney diet for dry food. He could not be convinced to give up Fancy Feast. I cooked simple meals for myself. I had cravings for vanilla ice cream, but whenever I faced the ice cream array in a grocery store, I remembered our last night with Janie. I had eaten a bowlful sitting by her side. She had licked some from my fingers. It was a vivid recollection.

I had become an expert with subQ fluids, and Flyer was his compliant self with the routine every alternate day. On the fridge door was a chart recording fluid days for Janie and Flyer. Flyer's column carried on to the present.

Whenever I had a window of time during the day, I made entries in my journal. My journal in which I made entries had grown to several hundred pages. The journal started with my solemn word to Tippy that our story would cross bridges of our time on earth to his life beyond. Tippy, very aware of his failing health, had said to Hilary, my animal communicator friend, that he wished he could live with me forever.

The journal contains letters to my cat family. There is a letter every day. I had moved my laptop to the pine dining table. My glasstopped desk had memories of Inky on my lap and Janie at my feet. I needed to keep the desk a temple of their presence for a little while.

Sentiment aside, the pine table had better lighting. I usually worked without my bifocals.

Unusual Gifts

Mark visited me in late spring. The blue jays were still around, and the jade plant and clepia vine were blooming. I was home, filling my days with Flyer's company and occasionally pampering my neighbor's midnight-black cat, Banguela, who liked to saunter in. Mark's allergy to cats had not abated. Flyer ignored all health alerts and plopped himself on the living room carpet as Mark and I talked.

Neither of us were given to nostalgia, but vignettes from our lives came up through recollections of ups and downs in California. We had lost friends in Canada and made new acquaintances in our own neighborhoods. No longer married, we had no checklist of things to do or arguments to dispel.

Mark had brought a sketchpad—one hundred blank pages of ordinary grade paper, a fifty-pound caliper for pencil sketches. I had not sketched in years. I had coloring books for relaxation. Mark did not think very much of lending color to prefabricated outlines. He wanted me to resurrect my drawing hobby. He had discovered his own talent in art in his forties. Living in San Francisco, he sketched street scenes every day, picking up human subjects in the Mission District.

I started by sketching a tree in my front driveway. It had a bifurcated trunk and sprawling branches. I had often stood in front of it and had smoked many a cigarette but never learned its botanical name. I found out long after the drawing was complete that the tree had stopped blooming. I would not be seeing its little white flowers again.

I drew cats—lots and lots of cats. All the cats I knew came alive again with graphite pencils: Sam, the large orange tabby who sat on my back fence in my home on West Santa Inez; Charlie, the rover; Tortie and Tiger, the Seven Oaks ferals. I sketched from memory and from photographs.

Inky came back to me as a kitten. Tippy's full portrait made him imposing. I drew Janie with her mother, Toby. I practiced cat faces from photographs of Flyer and Janie. Sometimes I added color with pencils. Most of the sketches were stark line drawings with shading.

Aussie, the dog I had walked when my cat family was young, made an appearance in my artistic efforts. He was an austere sketch from an old photograph. Despite all efforts, I could not recapture his husky–cattle dog magnificence.

I drew Janie again. I saw Janie everywhere in my mind's eye, even next to Flyer when he sat alone. I acknowledged all the cards that came in sympathy from her veterinarians and sent pictures of Janie from my collection. Krista, the Scout's House physical therapist, called to say she had placed Janie on her clinic wall. Janie was one of her best-loved patients.

"I am glad you sent me photos with both front legs."

Janie's favorite nooks under my bed and her box bed hideout remained untouched.

I drew Toby, my wild girl and mother to my cat family. I made her look domesticated with a pink collar. Her sketch was done with a decade of memories circling me, and my hands moved to recreate her face effortlessly. I had not seen Toby in twelve years. Perhaps she was still prowling the San Mateo hills or had turned into an intrepid cat spirit in the cat cosmos.

When Toby's kittens were tiny creatures nestling in their birthing box, Mark had brought me an easy-to-use camera as a surprise gift. An odd fancy to take black-and-white photographs fell through when the gray tabby colors made no startling contrast. I played cat paparazzi with color film and filled three photo albums with Toby and the growing kittens.

The photo albums had Janie from the day she opened her eyes. I had even captured Toby carrying Inky in her mouth by his scruff, suckling the kittens and grooming them after mother cat play. Mother cats have no favorites, but I suspected Flyer was her favorite son. Flyer was as wild spirited as Toby had been.

My journal entries now included Janie alongside Tippy and Inky. My hardy laptop, another gift from Mark, was showing signs of age, but I was not exerting it farther than my missives to my three cats. The home front was the home they had shared with me. I wished for a peek into the great cat cosmos where they now dwelt. On earth, COVID-19 or coronavirus abbreviated raged on.

By March 2020, over twelve thousand deaths had been reported in the United States. The numbers jumped to 15,000 by April; 197,000 confirmed cases of COVID-19 had been reported. The television news reflected a worldwide gloom and human interest stories of victims in headlines. By May 2020, the worldwide daily death toll was five thousand lives. Abandoning the statistics of U.S. sources, I tracked reports of the World Health Organization.

The immunologist Dr. Anthony Fauci's face became as familiar as a television anchor. He was chief medical advisor to Pres. Donald Trump and director of the National Institute of Allergies and Infectious Diseases.

The Centers for Disease Control imposed a mask mandate, which was prophesied to become the "new normal" face gear. Pres. Donald Trump remained pugnacious about staying unmasked in public until July 2020, when he visited the Walter Reed Military Medical Center in Bethesda, Maryland.

If Flyer had an opinion on a funny piece of fabric covering my face, he did not have a voice for a snarky comment. He looked at me with a slitted slant to his eyes.

"A fashion thing?" he possibly meant to ask.

I took a selfie of myself with Flyer wearing a mask with cats on it. A Starbucks colleague had sewn it for me, knowing my passion for cats. It became an important keepsake.

The Health Watch

Flyer seemed like a complacent, jolly fellow to anyone who met him. He sat in the living room with the occasional visitor with a genuine ear to human voices. His sunshine spot at the far end of my third-floor hallway got a daily visit. The glass door to the fire escape brought in warmth and a view of trees. Flyer stretched himself out in the sun, his musings unknown to me.

I saw the same Buddha-like stance when he found his favorite spot on the back stairwell. He did not have to say a word. I just knew that he was comfortable being a loner.

Occasionally, I sat on the stairs with him, talking of Tippy and Inky's prowls in that exact spot. Janie had never ventured up the stairs, so this had been a strictly boys' hangout.

Any neighbor coming up the lower stairs to the landing would stop and ask, "How are your cats?"

The twinge in my heart was more like a stab. "This is my only boy now."

Flyer sat on the step above me solemnly. If he felt grief for the absence of his siblings, he did not whine and fuss.

Flyer now got subQ fluids every alternate day. His blood work from March 2020 indicated a marked difference in creatine and blood urea nitrogen. His chronic kidney disease had reached Stage 3. Half of his food was now prescription "K/D" with reduced protein, phosphorus, and sodium supplemented by omega-3 from fish oil. The food was dry kibble, which Flyer liked. I watched his water intake like a hawk.

Flyer had a soft spot for Dr. Aki, who had also treated Tippy. He was a "sweet fella" with the veterinarians, even with Dr. Gyulassy, who was critical of his heavyweight self. I never thought Flyer was obese, while Dr. G did. There would come a time where Flyer's weight retention would be vital in his recuperation.

Every three months, Flyer had his blood work done. The numbers came under scrutiny, and any decrease in creatinine and BUN brought a sense of achievement. Camino Real Pet Clinic was prepared for COVID-19, setting up pet-only exam protocols where a pet parent waited outside the premises. Pets were checked in at the curbside or porch. When I checked Flyer in through a link on my iPhone, a veterinary tech appeared, heaved his space-age carrier onto her shoulder, and vanished into the interior. This was not time for sentiment or protest. I conceded to "pets only" for all our safety.

At Starbucks, another regimen of health and safety was put into practice. We responded to mobile orders, delivering products through pick-up windows. All in-store traffic came to a halt. Sidewalk orders were taken with minimum contact, and customer lines diminished. Six feet apart and masked, some people still came for their morning dose of caffeine. Credit cards were preferred over cash. We meticulously washed our hands between cash transactions. An undercurrent of tension penetrated each business day as we kept in place "stay safe" measures against the dreaded virus.

After a workday, Flyer wiped away the tension of the hours gone by. I fed him, sat around idly, prepped my dinner at my own pace, and then gave him the subQ fluids. Then we retired to the couch— with Flyer on his favorite blanket, paws on a favorite cushion—and watched CNN news. I tried never to think of work while at home.

With Flyer, it was okay to talk about Janie and how much I missed her. He understood and felt her absence, perhaps more for having to spend more time in their shared space. I had a spontaneous habit of bringing Inky and Tippy into my exchanges with Flyer. He never lost track of his brothers' names, and the family circle felt like an enormous loop from an urban home front to a reachable cat cosmos.

I liked this feeling of oneness. I kept the ashes of Inky, Tippy, and Janie on the top tier of the cat tree in the bedroom. Not even Janie had leaped on this tier. Next to Janie's urn was her favorite toy bird that warbled when squeezed. It looked like an oversized sparrow, and the bird call had always made her ears do a half circle.

Flyer liked live birds. The sparrows on the balcony occasionally lingered. The flying crow at the bedroom window, too fleeting for me to catch, got Flyer leaping across the bed to the cat tree. His favorite perch was the middle tier, with a full view of the treetops and sky. I left the blinds open all the time for him.

If emotional health mattered, Flyer and I had turned bereavement into a lyrical acceptance of life after. I remembered the words of Ken White, who was then president of the Peninsula Humane Society in San Mateo: "Life is a continuum." Ken's cat had died. He was writing his animal column in the San Francisco Examiner during his bereavement. Ken had a long tenure with this transformed no-kill animal shelter.

May 25, 2020 – A Day When America Changed

A man named George Floyd died as a result of police brutality on May 25 in Minneapolis, Minnesota. He was a forty-six-year-old African American who allegedly bought cigarettes at a corner store with a counterfeit $20 bill. A 911 call from a store employee brought the police to the site.

The video recording of his death in the hands of police made the nation rise in protest. This was the second wave of a civil rights movement in the United States under the banner of "Black Lives Matter."

Humans discriminate against other humans by race—a simple matter of more melanin or less melanin under the skin. Animals do not indulge in racism, being of varied colors and markings and an array of breeds; race has no place in an animal's perceptual dictionary. Of course, I could not discuss the news headlines of "Black Lives Matter" with Flyer. He would have found the phenomenon beyond understanding.

His most frequent visitor, my neighbor's cat Banguela, was as sleek and black as a miniature panther. Humans perceive black cats to be witches' familiars. To cats, a black cat is just another cat. At two years of age, Banguela was feisty and unafraid of age and gender. She visited, spatted, and snarled, ate his kibble, rug-wrestled with Flyer, and sniffed his catnip.

On June 1, I made a journal entry in the form of a letter to my cat family:

June 1, 2020

Tippy-O, Inky, Sweet Janie

A new month has started. I am at the pine table after warming bean soup. Flyer is at the doorstep, looking at the wrong end of the world for excitement. The right of the Flyer hangout used to be a Tippy lookout. The doorstep is still a busy place.

Doing laundry this evening. It has been laundry, laundry, laundry since after the half hour I stepped in.

9:41 p.m.

Banguela is visiting. The best part of the evening was napping, hugging Flyums like Janie and I used to sleep. Like spoons, lying about with nothing on our minds but each other. I danced too but did not sing. I drew some and ate bean soup. Today was a good day, and I prayed on the balcony with the Creator and you all in my mind.

The night is middle-aged. I do not want anything to end, but I shall remember the last hours as a signature of our lives together. What you have made me to be is exactly what I am. Still full of love for you, taking joy in little things and little pleasures. The music playing comes from the old, old country. The one that is too far for you to visit, and I can only imagine what the cats there are doing. My dad had cats in the backyard, and they were the lucky ones.

The TV might come alive tomorrow. I have a new program box, and the blipping and flopping will not frustrate me anymore.

The country is an unhappy place, so I did not turn on the radio. A riot is a violent mob lashing at authority—the police, the government, the businesses that make up downtown—and people are protesting the death of a man with black skin. There is a name for this riot. It is called a "civil rights protest." America has seen such happenings forty years ago, when I was a young girl, far away from this place.

Hug Mommy Toby if you see her. Many hugs and kisses to all of you.

Outside our den, the safe home front, San Mateo's streets turned precarious. "Black Lives Matter" was a movement penetrating churches and secular community activists. The county called for curfews after 8:30 p.m. through 5:00 a.m., snuffing out restaurants, bars, and social life. I rarely went out on errands late in the evening. Flyer and I huddled in front of the television like two friends in a storm while demonstrators raised their voices downtown and vandalized local businesses. Starbucks did not barricade its glasspaneled windows. Other businesses resorted to cardboard and duct tape to protect merchandise. The mood was dismal.

When Banguela, our neighbor's cat, strode in through our open door, Flyer was excited. This was a rare emotion, and he got off the couch. A wrestling match followed, almost as if Banguela had it planned. She decided to stay the evening, frisking around and eating some pâté I served. Her human parents were watching the scale and eating at the neighbor's skewed daily calories. Nonetheless, a guest has to eat with the host. Our hospitality was impeccable.

Flyer's birthday—June 10, 2020—was celebrated with tuna cake made with Fancy Feast. I lit four candles to commemorate the presence of Inky, Tippy, and Janie in spirit. I took pictures with the three-layer cake. Flyer made a princely sight in candlelight. He nibbled at the cake. I expected him to eat voraciously.

My singing voice was not wobbly for lack of practice. I sang "Happy Birthday, Flyer" with all the wind in my lungs. He was now fifteen years old.

Banguela, the Guest

In mid-June, Banguela came to stay with us for a week when her human parents were on vacation. Flyer was pompous with her at first but gave in to Banguela's sibling-like attention seeking. A spunky, muscled female, two-and-a-half years old, Banguela had no deference for Flyer. She stepped into his territory as if she belonged and sprung on his back in mock wrestles. They spatted with sheathed claws. While Flyer was spared scratches, I was not. My forearms looked battle worn from trying to break up the two warriors.

Flyer would not admit, but he did enjoy the sojourn. Banguela did not resemble Janie. Flyer had never interacted with a female cat who was not a sibling. They made an interesting pair. I forgot that I was cat-sitting and sat back to watch them. Occasionally, they shared the couch in the living room. At night, both slept on the bed together, flanking me on the left and right.

Strangely, having a visitor did not take away the ache in my heart for Janie. I missed her even more.

My journal entry—made to Inky, Tippy, and Janie—now included Banguela. Flyer and Banguela were asleep together on the bed while I sat at my laptop.

June 14, 2020
3:31 p.m.
Tippy, Inky, Sweet Janie,

I have the lights on. Trying not to disturb Flyer and neighbor Banguela while I write this to you. I had a pleasant day at home, and I wonder how many Saturdays I shall have to myself. I cleaned the home front, fed the belly, and washed hair. I drew some. Thought of you. Found the mystery behind my cigarettes. The only way I shall stop smoking is by not having any cigarettes at all. I smoke because I do not feel or taste the smoke anymore. My breathing has returned to normal, and my cough has gone.

I shall break away for a moment and take my asthma medicine. I shall come back to the pine table in a jiffy.

Flyer is sitting by, half-grooming himself. He is in a good mood and has spent a large part of the day "underneath" for a bit in the Janie basket. You are not here in your furry selves, but your presence is strong wherever we look. Of course, the couch is always Inky's couch, sunshine or shade. Flyer is working on his toes. Back to snoozing again.

Banguela is here for two more days. Her folks are traveling for a pleasure trip. I do not believe she misses home much. She might have even got fond of me, but it is hard to compete with Mommy Dene.

I have another hour of waking to do, and I wish this evening would not end. I never wish an evening to end because each day at home is precious. I feel alive with Flyer, with the sparrows that come under the Thinking Tree, and the sounds of the passing traffic remind me that standing still is a noble thing to do. Life is not passing me by. I am passing by the invisible and trivial pages that are not worth reading . . . and here, I compare life to a book.

I crave to know what you all are doing, although all the finer points do not reach me, just the broad sweeps. The reason I do not worry is because worrying gets me nowhere. I believe you are free to roam and discover the unknown. Not my turn yet, but maybe you will teach me someday.

This was a month with two full moons. When I look at the moon, I think of cats, particularly of the black Minnaloushe of W. B. Yeats' "The Cat and the Moon."

> The cat went here and there,
> And the moon spun round like a top,
> And the nearest kin of the moon,
> The creeping cat looked up.
> Minnaloushe creeps through the grass
> From moonlit place to place.
> The sacred moon overhead
> Has taken a new phase.
> Does Minnaloushe know that his pupils
> Will pass from change to change
> And that from round to crescent,
> From crescent to round, they range?
> Minnaloushe creeps through the grass
> Alone, important and wise,
> And lifts to the changing moon
> His changing eyes.

I read this poem out to Flyer, who had been out prowling only once on a moonlit night. His sight of the moon was from our balcony. Flyer had piercing pupils that often turned into slits. Banguela was not within earshot. Even if she had been, she would not have resonated with the English language. She was used to Portuguese conversation at home.

Summer got hotter. I saw the butterflies, new birds, and bees on the balcony and counted them for Flyer. He was happy to stare into the sunshine from his perch on the couch. I had placed his kitty grass next to the water bowl on the coffee table. He rose when he needed his nibble and sip.

Dr. Aki, now a regular veterinarian with Flyer, had called asking for a follow-up with my boy. She wanted to do an ultrasound because Flyer had vocalized some discomfort during the exam. Dr. Aki had palpitated his kidneys.

Flyer's renal ultrasound revealed nothing remarkable about his kidneys or bladder. However, I could not ignore the fact that he was in Stage 3 of kidney disease. His subQ fluids were essential to his lifeline. He came home with a shaven belly, which ruffled my sense of cat aesthetics. Flyer barely noticed.

The uphills of health care aside, Flyer was happy. He sat on the pine table, stretched out beside my laptop as I plodded through an online course. I seldom do well on tests, and he was my moral support. I aced the certificate program for teaching English as a second language. I faltered in the online hiring test and harvested an unimpressive score. I had always harbored a phobia for tests since adolescence and have never outgrown it. I needed Flyer to comfort me. He thought I was a wonderful person despite the test score. Family is a good thing to have.

When Banguela came to visit, he forgot his human to lock horns with her over a catnip-smeared scratch board. He sometimes returned the visit by barreling over to Banguela's door across the hallway. Their relationship was more than neighborly. Flyer had grown fond of her and her IAMS kibble. He flouted his kidney diet each time he visited her.

My conversations with Flyer were exactly as if we were two humans who were kin. I did not need him to articulate a human language to understand his responses. After fifteen years together, I had a pulse on his emotions and he on mine. We talked of his siblings, who were no longer with us, and speculated on their life beyond the earthly realm. My belief that animals have souls made our existence on earth lyrical. We talked about the trivia of the workplace. I had rough days and merry ones. He had become familiar with the aroma of coffee and sweat.

I sketched Banguela. I did a live model sketch of Flyer sitting in front of me. On a whim, I drew a raven and a mountain lion and a Cubist rabbit. I was developing my animal repertoire. I tried human faces from memory. My mother's face looked too stern for my own liking. Don, my old friend and mentor in feral rescue, came out too lean in my rendering. I went back to drawing cats.

Not Quite Anti-Cat

We had a houseguest in July who had never lived with cats. It was not a matter of cat allergies. Jiya did not resonate with "domestic animals." To be fair, she'd had a dog in her youth, but that was a long time ago.

Flyer would not have been pleased if he heard himself being called a domestic anything. Companion, soulmate, nonhuman sibling, friend—everything but "domestic."

This was an impromptu visit. Polite as he was, Flyer did not hiss at the houseguest. He gave up his couch and his coffee table perch. He restrained his habit of jumping on the pine table where we actually ate. Had I asked him to knock on the bathroom door when he needed to use the litter box, he would have. He just let my guest use the shower without interruption. He pooped on the carpet instead.

Human voices interested him. He would sit on the living room carpet, wide-eyed, face upturned, listening to two humans talk. When the conversation switched from English to another language— and we were bilingual at times—Flyer just walked away. He found his peaceful nook on a fleece blanket under the bed where he used to sit with Janie. He did not emerge until bedtime. He never gave up the habit of sleeping next to me.

I gave my houseguest accolades for effort. As I brushed Flyer one morning, she mustered the will to stroke Flyer. Flyer accepted the gesture. He was as chivalrous as he was patient. He did not realize that this was a small victory.

I have known and liked people who have no animal affinity. Some of them have lacked an exposure to animals and are unable to relate to them as household kin. Others harbor prejudice or fear. I am always shocked by some people's indifference to animals, but I have yet to meet an animal-hating sociopath face-to-face. If I ever do, I would understand the root of speciesism.

Whether or not humans are really a superior species and designated to be on top of the food chain is debatable. The ultimate irony in this scenario lies in the fact that those who are indifferent to animals have no hesitation eating them for food. Biblically speaking, man was given "dominion" over animals. I perceive this to be a guardianship, not subjugation.

Camping Indoors

There were nights when Flyer and I camped out on the living room floor in the glow of the television. He descended from his couch to play with the fringes on the edge of my blanket and fell asleep by my side. This happened when I did not have to work early in the morning. I served him breakfast, changed the water in his bowls, and sat down to cereal and coffee. I had given up dairy and adapted to almond milk. The balcony brightened in the morning, and the back hills resonated with the chirps of birds and squirrels.

A poignant feeling would come over me on such days. Inky, Tippy, and Janie had special nesting places around the apartment. After a wakeup call, they would find their favorite spots to laze about. Their most favorite were the cat tree in the bedroom, the double glass doors at the balcony, and the kitchen counter next to the radio.

My memories were vivid, but I had no time to linger. Flyer brought me back to reality by throwing up his breakfast. He tended to have acid reflux. Pepcid aside, he got his vitamin B12 dose once a week. A cat's stomach is highly acidic, with a pH range of 1–2.5, and hyperacidity is a common condition. He tolerated the injections but hated the taste of Pepcid AC, which I pounded in a mortar and pestle and gave to him dissolved in water. As soon as the feeding syringe spurted the liquid into his mouth, I would see a grimace. If I did not tilt his head back, he would let the liquid dribble out.

Days rolled by languidly. Neither Flyer nor I were looking for excitement. Banguela stopped by for the occasional wrestling match. Flyer took his usual walk down the hallway, snooping at apartment doors. When he chose a corner to sit, I sat by him and softly talked. There was a long bench by the elevators parallel to a wall of glass bricks. The reflecting light attracted Flyer. This was a place to tell him the day's happenings and share my workday.

When the Chewy box arrived with his food and treats, I let him know. I got stung by a bee, and I looked for sympathy from Flyer. I rescued a fledgling who had fallen from its nest. I told Flyer the story. When I missed Janie and her prowling brothers, I let my emotions spill. We then walked back to the apartment.

August brought rain. The wind and downpour made music outside the window while Flyer and I sat on the bed, watching a movie on my laptop. He usually faced the screen, his forelegs crossed in front of him. His fascination for moving pictures kept him riveted until thirst got him off the bed to his water bowl.

Between us, we did not discuss Northern California's climate change and the still-raging COVID-19 pandemic. We kept our little world to ourselves until a heat wave hit us. Flyer looked spent from the rising temperatures, and I left the ceiling fan spinning for him all day. Banguela's home across the hallway was hotter than our home front. She came by with the same fatigued look and stretched out on the carpet under the fan. She had no energy for a spat, and ignoring the food bowl, she fell asleep. Her feisty self was absent.

By nightfall, the moon looked bright orange. The Mendocino National Forest was ablaze. One of the largest wildfires in the area was burning, and we could smell the smoke in San Mateo. Sparked by lightning strikes, several such fires destroyed two and a half million acres in California by September 2020.

COVID-19 deaths had declined. California was looking more upbeat. There were 107,154 reported cases of the coronavirus and 2,879 deaths by September end. This was almost a 50 percent decline of cases from August. We were still waiting for a vaccine. Moderna was getting ahead with its first clinical trial.

Flowers, Laundry, and a Surprise

I had not attended Sunday church in a year. I kept in touch with my favorite pastor, Rev. Penny Nixon, and listened to her streamed sermons. I missed seeing the beautiful sanctuary and the warmth of the congregation.

I was surprised when Kay, a church member, showed up at my door with a posey of flowers from her garden. Masked as we both were, we exchanged news from our everydays. Kay had five cats, one of them named Beethoven, who was deaf. The cat bond was instantaneous, but a long time would pass before I would see Kay again. She did come to visit on the next occasion with apricot crumble.

I busied myself with an unusual after-work project. Banguela's human parents were both mobile pet groomers. With their heavy schedule, terry cloth towels piled so high that I pitched in with a load or two every evening. While I washed and dried wet heaps of towels, I remembered my volunteer days at San Mateo's SPCA, where I had often been placed on "laundry duty." Towels from kennels of dogs and cats were washed each day, a job that paid staff dreaded. Although the laundry did not resemble the Ritz, I enjoyed the hours in front of the giant machines and even considered mentioning the experience in my résumé.

Neighbor Banguela spent more and more time with Flyer. She was growing fond of her playmate and now had to be coaxed to go home. As solemn and self-contained as he was, Flyer did lend himself to Banguela.

I began stalking the two for photographs as they sat head-to-head on the scratch board, sniffing catnip or sharing the pine tabletop as I worked on my own dinner. Banguela's toys began entering our home, and Flyer came out of his toy boycott and began to play. His particular favorite was a "ball tree" with battable fuzzy balls that he swatted when walking by. Mostly, he liked sitting at the base, watching the suspended spheres.

My neighbors started Christmas preparations early. I had taken half a pumpkin pie to their home, which was my way of observing Thanksgiving. I did not eat meat, and I deluded myself that I had saved a turkey. It was November, and red and green hues could be seen in my neighbors' living room. Ardene and Johnny had a Brazilian fervor for Christmas. They were also planning to adopt a dog.

"We were thinking of giving Banguela to you," Ardene said.

My heart skipped a beat. No one had offered me a cat before. I would be taking a young cat into a home full of mellow and poignant memories shared by Flyer and me. The ache for Janie was still with me. I had slowly healed with Flyer's presence. Would I be able to embrace Banguela with the commitment she deserved? How would Flyer react to a full-time companion? I bit back all doubts.

"I shall be happy to have her," I said, and my own voice sounded awkward to me.

Banguela appeared in the hallway and meandered into the living area. She saw me seated with her human parents and decided to wrap herself around my legs.

"I always said Banguela is your cat," Johnny said candidly.

Banguela had been a rescue kitten adopted from Redwood City's Pets in Need when she was six weeks old. Her first home was with a family known to Ardene. They moved out of state after having Banguela for two years, giving Ardene custody.

The name "Banguela" translates to "toothless" in Portuguese. All her teeth were intact. She was as nippy as she was restless. Some investigation revealed that Toothless is the name of a little black dragon in the animated series *How to Train Your Dragon*. The black cat with round green eyes looked like the animated character.

I would have taken Banguela back to my apartment the same day, but I had to talk to Flyer. We always had family discussions. Through our days with Inky, Tippy, and Janie around, we called them family conferences.

"I shall come get her soon." I went home, leaving my gift cat behind.

I was going to break a Christmas surprise to Flyer. If he were pleased with the news, I would pick him up and dance with him the way I danced with Janie in my arms. If he was annoyed, I would have him go over and see for himself what Banguela was doing in her home. Banguela was eating a second dinner, ignoring Johnny, and getting ready to curl up on Ardene's side of the bed. She was being a brat!

I had made one other good friend in the neighborhood: Eric, a man who owned a snake he had rescued from a trip to Yosemite. He was a heavy smoker and went through a pack a day. Compared to him, I was a cosmetic puffer. Through eight years, we had smoked under the same tree, rescued a bird, rehomed cats, and shared many stories of our lives. He was a carpenter. He assembled my new shelves and cooked me dinner. I cooked his favorite shrimp and made his good coffee.

Once, standing under our favorite tree, Eric said, "A person needs three things in life to be happy. Someone to love. Something to do. Something to look forward to."

I hoped to make Flyer happy, even if he and Banguela made an odd couple.

On November 25, I had an emotional conversation with Flyer. I was sitting by his side on the bed, attending to a small bump on his skin on his right flank. I put aside the Neosporin and gauze and held him to me.

"I cannot live without you," I said, with my face against his fur. His back felt like refuge.

The pathos of cat care can best be described in the silent emotions that emerge during simple acts of love. Flyer soaked up my feelings in typical silence. When he was young, he needed me. Today he had become my sustenance.

"If Banguela came to live with us, would you mind?" I asked him to break the intensity of the moment.

I hoped he would give me an impertinent answer. What did I expect him to say?

"If I said yes, would you send her back?" These were not Flyer's words.

In truth, Flyer could do without a companion. He had become entirely self-contained. If I wanted another cat in the family, I would have to decide. I wanted the decision to be ours, not merely mine.

I knew, even in the absence of words of consent, Flyer would welcome Banguela. The same evening, I opened the door for Banguela and let her in. She had crossed the hallway into her new home and went straight for the bowl of kibbles. When done with her snack, she sighted Flyer a few feet away and pounced on his back in mock attack. In a split second, they were wrestling. Flyer had the upper hand.

My boy had Banguela down with two gentle swats of his paw. I wished I had Inky, Tippy and Janie as audience in the feline wrestling championship.

Cat Scratches and a Vet's Visit

My forearms had scratches in streaks of red. Not even my feral mother cat Toby had scratched me so fiercely. Banguela had a temper. If she were annoyed with me, she would reach out and scratch. She was nippy too. I could sit too close or pick her up when she did not wish to move. The protest was instantaneous. Flyer and I exchanged knowing looks. The girl was a brat but a lovable one.

I made a vet's appointment, neither for myself nor Banguela. Flyer had developed a nagging cough. He also needed a biopsy of his bump for the cytologist. Dr. Frank was at the clinic. I needed to update her on Flyer's prescriptions and his mobility. I was giving him injections of Adequan for mild arthritis.

The vet surmised that Flyer might have tracheitis, an upper respiratory illness in cats—quite the contrary. There was no sign of an infection. Dr. Gyulassy probed further with an X-ray and a radiology consultation. The results that came at the end of December and the observations were serious. Flyer had an enlarged heart. On a humorous note, the radiologist said the heart may look enlarged because of a layer of fat. Flyer was chunky. There was also a nodule in the lungs that had the potential of a tumor.

Where there is speculation, there are more diagnostic tests. Before I planned another visit to specialists in Sage, I took Flyer for another ultrasound, this time of his abdomen.

Christmas was a private celebration. I listened to Christmas carols with Flyer by my side. This boy of mine, my emotional rock, was getting physically fragile. I drowned the separation anxiety rising within with old melodies and thoughts of the Christ child in the hay. I did not tune in to the streamed Christmas service. Streaming and Zoom were the "new normal." COVID-19 had kept us away from the sanctuary for a year.

Ardene, Banguela's other "mother," came by with gifts. I binged on chocolates and coffee and tried to coax Flyer to eat. His gait had slowed, and his appetite was less than hearty. Banguela still wolfed her food with relish. Janie had left us exactly a year ago. Every hair and whisker on her, I remembered and ached.

The new year of 2021 came without a bang. At home, the most memorable event was Flyer having his tail bitten by Banguela as she sat on the carpet below him. Flyer let his tail fall over the edge of the couch as he half-snoozed. Banguela, with her passion for teasing and dangling objects, nipped his tail.

No storm broke loose, but I did see Flyer's expression change from sublime to irate. This was a rare moment.

A Hairpin Bend

Flyer was diagnosed with cardiopulmonary disease. It was a déjà vu of Tippy's crisis from three years ago. The follow-up blood screen and urinalysis revealed that Flyer was in Stage 4 of renal failure.

The weeks that followed had me sitting by Flyer's favorite basket by my bed, watching, hearing him breathe. I logged his breathing per minute every few hours. At night, the rapid, shallow breaths and wheeze tore into me. This was my happy-go-lucky Flyer, now being hand-fed.

On the night of January 8, I observed an extreme lethargy in Flyer. He had lost orientation to the litter box and had not moved out of his basket for hours. Food remained untouched. I could not depend on my skills at home care or the effect of medications on hand. I took him to the North Peninsula Veterinary Emergency for a diagnosis because I could not depend on my skills at home care.

Flyer had pyelonephritis, kidney infection that starts in the urethra and progresses to both kidneys. There was no hematuria, although I had suspected blood in his urine. He was placed on antibiotics and continuous fluids overnight. I spent a night with sparse sleep. Banguela, frisky and curious as she was, was suddenly my solemn companion.

I brought Flyer home with a prescription of Veraflox. He was eating normally and passing urine. My vigil on him intensified. Each day, I jotted notes on his progress and the emerging symptoms of complex issues.

On January 27, I took Flyer to see Dr. Gyulassy at Camino Real Pet Clinic. Flyer's breathing was audible and heavy. Dr. Gyulassy anticipated fluid accumulation in his chest cavity. With no time to linger, he took Flyer into his surgery and drained the fluid. After the emergency procedure, Dr. Gyulassy stepped out to talk to me as I stood alone outside the clinic, and a sense of sadness filled me.

This veterinarian never minced words. I was glad for it. "He is on the decline. Keep him comfortable. He has time with you . . . a week, maybe a month."

I had serious questions to ponder. Should I take time off to be home? Did Flyer need a caregiver for the hours I spent at work? I followed instinct, without expecting answers on the chalkboard. I continued to work. Flyer got a skilled pet sitter in the evenings. Banguela, with her sprightly camaraderie, kept him company. Flyer was not alone.

On February 1, at my desk on a late evening shift at work, I picked up my sketchbook and did a pencil drawing of Flyer from memory. The text message from his pet sitter said Flyer was on his feet, not interested in food, and headed to his fleece thermal blanket under the bed—a favorite hideout, once crowded by a furry family.

On my return three hours later, I opened the front door with a sense of angst. Looking for Flyer, I rushed to the bedroom. He was on the fleece blanket, lying on his side. I knelt and brought him close. He was still breathing in a whisper. I attempted to clear his airway with mouth-to-mouth and then mouth-to-nose.

Perceiving no change, I carried Flyer to the bed, laying him on the comforter. I sat dry-eyed beside him until his breath ceased.

In the unlit room that night, I slept with my arm around Flyer, just the way we spent the peaceful hours of our lives together for so long. Banguela climbed onto the bed and stretched out by my feet. She did not move from our side until the light of the morning. I felt gratitude.

I cremated Flyer a week after his passing. The seven days without Flyer at home were acutely painful. Without Banguela's warmth, I would have gone to tiny pieces.

My neighbor Ardene and her spouse stayed close to me in my grief. When the time came to do Flyer's last rites, there was calm within me. There was a feeling of completion, a strange peace in being able to touch his body again. I witnessed the cremation. Even when his well-loved self was no more, the peace seemed indestructible.

On the balcony at home, the kitty grass Flyer loved so much continued to grow. Watching the sprouting seeds in moist soil, I remembered the "Desiderata." Love is as perennial as the grass.

The Scarf

Banguela stood alone, claiming the home turf as her own. She slept and awakened with me.

Banguela liked the feel of the metal comb on her fur. She was sleekly short-haired, unlike my feral family whose brushings yielded a comb full of gray-brown hair. The undercoat had been a light beige. For seven years, I collected the brushings in a box.

Today the mound of cat hair felt beautiful to the touch, like a living memory of our daily ritual. I started winnowing the fur, hoping to weave it into a keepsake.

Theresa entered my life as a yarn-maker. Her name came to me by chance. I had surfed websites for many weeks, searching for spinning wheels and wooleries. Nine Lives Twine was a faraway place in Pittsburgh, Pennsylvania. Theresa specialized in pet yarn, which she knit into custom memorabilia.

I shipped seven years of devotion to Theresa. If she were nearer, I would have delivered the box of hair by hand. The spinner wrote back:

Hello Indrani,

I received your package, so lovingly put together.

Your collection of brushings is wonderful and will make a very nice yarn. The amount you have is spot on for a traditional scarf of average size.

I have booked your project for May, and if that

moves up, you will hear from me sooner.

Theresa

In June 2021, just after the family birthday, the scarf arrived. Five feet of woven cat yarn became a fringed wearable scarf that I held to my chest, and I heard my heart beat faster.

The color was gray-brown. Janie's white fur had been submerged in the colors of her brothers. Inky's brown and Flyer and Tippy's gray had eclipsed her calico shades, yet they were all there. The texture was prickly, the feeling warm for cold weather.

With the scarf came a small plastic bag containing a few whiskers. The note from Theresa said, "I thought you might like to have these back."

My mother feral Toby's hair was not in the scarf. I had immortalized four of her children.

Where was Toby? She did not prowl the neighborhood anymore. She had reached her own nook of the cat cosmos, having finished her purpose in life. *Toby had sustained a human.* The human was me.

October 25, 2021—I brushed Banguela in the morning. Fall weather has set in, and yesterday's windstorm has passed.

In a little red box, I save Banguela's silky black fur. My own gray hair fascinates the cat. She rumples my scalp with her paws when I lie next to her. Banguela wakes me for her own breakfast before the sun is fully out. I am giving in to her ways. I think she loves me.

I tell her stories she has never heard before about the family that came before her. She likes the connection of two worlds. She is a strong female. She is family.

Index

Gallery of Images

Toby
Catwings

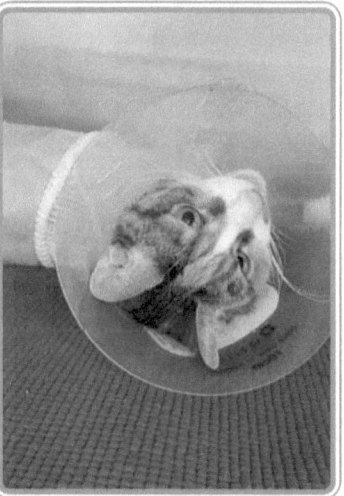

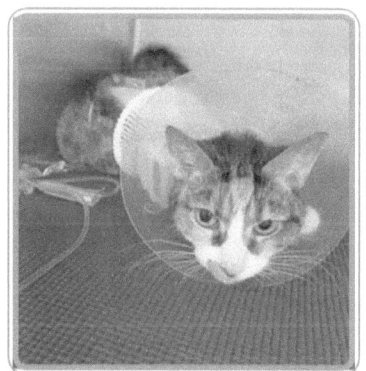

294

307

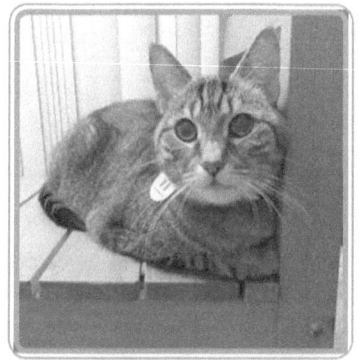

www.ingramcontent.com/pod-product-compliance
Lightning Source LLC
Chambersburg PA
CBHW021609120626
46545CB00001B/142